# COMPETENT READER, DISABLED READER:

*Research and Application*

# COMPETENT READER, DISABLED READER:
## Research and Application

*Edited by*
**Martin H. Singer**
*Bell Laboratories*

**LEA**

LAWRENCE ERLBAUM ASSOCIATES, PUBLISHERS

1982     Hillsdale, New Jersey                    London

Lawrence Erlbaum Associates, Inc., Publishers
365 Broadway
Hillsdale, New Jersey 07642

**Library of Congress Cataloging in Publication Data**
Main entry under title:

Competent reader, disabled reader.

   Bibliography: p
   1. Reading Addresses, essays, lectures. 2. Reading
disability Addresses, essays, lectures. I. Singer,
Martin H.
LB1050.R419   428.4   81-12639
ISBN 0-89859-196-1   AACR2

Printed in the United States of America

*For Andrea*

# Contents

# Preface

Reading research irritates the reading teacher. The experimental literature cloaks conclusions in forbidding language and investigates tasks that seem only marginally related to reading. Issues that motivate experiments (e.g., the order of visual and phonetic operations in identifying words) connect poorly with the pragmatic concerns of the classroom teacher. Studies contrasting the skills of good and poor readers also relay a confusing array of information, failing to isolate definite predictors of reading failure or to suggest remediation strategies. The motivated teacher who tackles the experimental journals will leave unsatisfied, unable to make sense of the evidence.

Frustration with experimental reports has caused educators to dismiss the entire reading research enterprise. Consequently, a publishing company's advertising skill dictates a school system's choice of reading programs, rather than experimental results. Researchers are largely responsible for this situation. They address only a scientific audience and their conclusions often pertain to esoteric disputes in the literature. Rarely do technical reports specify applications of research. This journalistic style cultivates the teacher's perspective that reading research and reading instruction share little common ground.

Despite this perspective, psychological and educational researchers have amassed information useful to reading teachers. Experimental investigations of competent reading have isolated factors and strategies that facilitate the analysis of written language. At the same time, research on poor reading has suggested that particular perceptual–cognitive deficits may prevent the disabled reader from acquiring certain sources of information or adaptive strategies. This evidence relates directly to selecting intervention or reading curricula materials. These studies indicate: (1) the knowledge and strategies that competent readers learn and subsequently exploit; and (2) deficits that poor readers must overcome in order to acquire reading strategies. Instructional materials, it would seem, should be evaluated with regard to this information.

This book attempts to abstract those experimental results relevant to developing effective reading programs. The book concentrates on the more mechanical aspects of reading skill such as visual discrimination ability, visual and auditory memory, visual-to-phonetic translation skills, and attentional strategies. These skills, it is argued, account for the major proportion of variance in reading ability. The research on both competent and incompetent reading indicates the special importance of such skills to reading. Higher-order abilities (e.g., comprehension) pertain to general intellectual function and not, in particular, to reading. These cognitive skills certainly explain differences between excellent and mediocre readers, but not the disabled reader's stumbling over three-letter words. Nonetheless, the book does include a chapter on a technique for improving children's ability to comprehend text (Chapter 8, Bransford, Stein, & Vye).

The book also stresses the heterogeneity of the reading-disabled population. This perspective helps interpret the evidence on poor reading, particularly those results that appear contradictory. If competent reading were uncomplicated, one might expect that a single factor accounted for reading disability. Competent reading, though, includes several skilled operations; inadequate execution of any of these operations might produce reading failure. Remembering that an isolated research project examines only a fragment of the reading process, we should expect that competing research projects uncover competing reasons for reading failure. This does not mean that all experimental information on reading is equally good; we must always evaluate the quality of the research. The argument is that disputes in the experimental literature may implicitly suggest the complexity of competent reading and the variety of reading disabilities rather than conflicting hypotheses about reading failure.

The book contains three sections. Section I reviews the experimental evidence on competent reading. The review highlights consistent threads of evidence and provides a description of the competent reader's strategies for analyzing text. Section II reviews research on poor reading. This section evaluates the concept of dyslexia and stresses, as already mentioned, that reading problems are not uniform. Section II reviews the evidence that relates reading disability to: (1) a context-use deficit; (2) sequential ordering problems; and (3) decoding difficulties (Chapter 5, Stanovich). This section also discusses neurological correlates to reading failure and provides an introduction to the interesting area of acquired reading disability (Chapter 6, Staller).

The reviews in Sections I and II lead directly to applications of reading research. Section III maintains that the information about competent reading strategies and the impediments to acquiring those strategies should guide educators in evaluating instructional materials and facilitate the diagnosis of reading failure. Evidence on what facilitates reading provides a basis for discriminating reading curricula; knowledge of what prevents acquisition of reading strategies suggests that reading programs incorporate particular skill-building components.

This section refrains from endorsing a specific reading program and, instead, imparts a technique for developing and evaluating reading programs. In particular, Carr (Chapter 7) discusses the application of reading models to evaluation and diagnosis. Singer (Chapter 9) and Bransford, Stein, and Vye (Chapter 8) review specific techniques for improving certain deficit areas (discrimination skills and comprehension).

Throughout the first two sections, unfamiliar terms are listed and defined in chapter glossaries. Also, Sections I and II are not meant as exhaustive surveys. Only recurrent themes, factors underlying competent and incompetent reading that enjoy experimental investigation, receive detailed treatment. Finally, the book is not meant as an anthology of readings on reading; instead the chapters are cross-referenced, and later chapters assume that the reader has examined earlier material in the volume.

## ACKNOWLEDGMENTS

I have studied reading disability since 1971, while an undergraduate at the University of Michigan. My youngest brother had experienced great difficulty learning to read and, because of that difficulty, suffered failure and frustration in school. He was tutored throughout elementary school but in high school, the staff psychologist concluded that he was "dyslexic" and, therefore, beyond remediation. The diagnosis crushed my parents and stripped my brother of any remaining academic ambition. At that time my brother read at a fourth grade level; he was in the eleventh grade.

The psychologist's prognosis motivated me to investigate "dyslexia". First, I located a clinical psychologist who reported success in teaching "dyslexics" how to read. My brother's remedial program focused on component reading skills and employed some of the materials discussed in Chapter 9 of this volume. The clinical psychologist and the tutor who worked with my brother, deserve much credit. By the end of the twelfth grade, my brother had achieved an average reading ability; he now reads fluently. During this same period I approached the literature on dyslexia. The divergence of experimental results and the emptiness of clinical labels (e.g., dyslexia) impressed me then. The inadequacy of the research, however, made its impression more slowly.

This book summarizes what I have learned about reading since the school psychologist's diagnosis of my brother's reading failure. I acknowledge the psychologist's incompetence as one source of motivation for this book. My brother and my parents, though, provided the most meaningful motivation. They represent all those families who have struggled with the consequences of a child who cannot read. It is distressing to imagine their anxiety and frustration multiplied thousands of times. Better information should be available to the professionals who advise such families and to the teachers entrusted with reading instruction. Our book attempts to provide that information and remove the mystery that shrouds reading failure.

I also want to acknowledge other contributions to the evolution and completion of this book. First, there are those whose thoughts have affected mine. Joe Lappin has influenced my thinking on many problems, including reading. Jim Crouse helped me articulate my dissatisfaction with traditional approaches to research on cognitive processes and, although I have never met him, Donald Doehring has influenced my thinking about reading disability. His work has always stressed the heterogeneity of poor readers, a point that is crucial in approaching the research. I also want to mention Bob Pachella and Judy Reitman who guided me during my initial approaches to reading research.

Others helped to produce the book. The contributors, in addition to producing excellent chapters, made a serious attempt to develop the book into a text. Secondly, I am indebted to Larry Erlbaum for his support of the project throughout its transformation from a single-author volume to a multi-author text. Also, I want to thank the Department of Educational Studies at the University of Delaware for providing an environment in which I could write. Finally, but most importantly, I want to acknowledge the support of my wife, Andrea. Her confidence in the project throughout the last three years has made its completion possible.

**Martin H. Singer**

# COMPETENT READER, DISABLED READER:
*Research and Application*

# COMPETENT READING:
# Introduction

Martin H. Singer

This section provides a context for the discussions in following chapters. Competent reading depends on a variety of skills; Chapter 1 attempts to identify those skills and those experimental procedures that have been important in examining the reading process.

The reading teacher or diagnostician should approach this discussion of competent reading strategies with two important questions. First, what type of reading curricula would ensure the acquisition of the skills and strategies exploited by competent readers? Carr, in Section III, pursues this question in some depth. Second, one might question whether the malfunctioning of any of the component reading skills discussed in Chapter 1 could lead to reading failure. The reviews in Section II examine this question by evaluating the various correlates to reading failure.

Chapter 1 also emphasizes relationships between apparently independent skills. In particular, Chapter 1 reviews some evidence that suggests a hierarchical model of successful reading. This evidence indicates that higher-level skills, such as context-use skills and comprehension strategies, might be ineffective if the reader has failed to master lower-level skills such as decoding and visual discrimination. This concept of successful reading is discussed throughout the volume and, again, Chapter 1 attempts to provide a background for those discussions.

# 1 Competent Reading: A Laboratory Description

Martin H. Singer
*Bell Laboratories*

Adequate descriptions require several perspectives. Literature abounds with examples. Durrell's *Alexandria Quartet* recounts identical events through the lives of different characters. Hugo (1862) drags his readers through the sewers of Paris and across Napoleon's battlefields in his description of prerevolutionary France. Perhaps the same struggle for perspective motivated Picasso to shatter conventional proportion and attempt his multifaceted portrayal of the human form.

Complex psychological issues also require several perspectives. Complicated behaviors, such as reading, demand that we examine components of the entire process and variations of the process with circumstance. It would be insufficient, for example, to examine how people scan sports scores and then base a model of reading on that investigation. A variety of perspectives—information about reading under different conditions—permits a more adequate description. Obtaining these perspectives, though, forces reading researchers to work in an arena foreign to most teachers, namely, the laboratory. Only the laboratory, though, allows researchers to manipulate reading tasks and gauge the importance of various information sources to competent reading. As discussed later, this type of information can help direct a teacher's attention to possible reasons for reading failure.

The psychological laboratory assumes sundry forms. Researchers can assault *subjects* (i.e., participants in a study) with rapidly flashed words and letter strings, or ask them questions about leisurely read passages. Different experimental approaches constitute distinct **paradigms**: different structures for investigating a problem. This chapter discusses several paradigms, and the paradigms, just as much as the research results, require evaluation. The paradigms attempt to focus on issues pertaining to reading; the critical reader must assess the sharpness of their focus.

A summary of studies on single-word recognition and analysis precedes the discussion of research with connected text. The summary, in lieu of a complete review, introduces strategies and types of knowledge exploited by competent readers. These types of knowledge—orthographic, sound-to-letter correspondences, semantic—apply to normal reading situations as well as to simple laboratory tasks. Thus the subsequent discussions of other reading research, including disability and curricula, build upon this summary.

# WORD RECOGNITION

## The Visual Perspective

One often encounters the claim that competent readers recognize words as "wholes", without any analysis of individual letters. Motorists may, in fact, carry around in their heads well-learned templates (i.e., little pictures) of STOP signs. Perhaps, they recognize "STOP" in some global fashion and never pay attention to component letters. A template model of word recognition may also explain the extraordinary reading rates of workers in news-clip agencies who can scan newspapers for names of customers at rates of 1000 words a minute (Neisser, 1964). This process might involve the matching of memorized templates with written words.

Beyond these special reading environments, however, competent readers rely on another system for recognizing words. If readers depended on whole word templates, it would be difficult to explain THEir FaCIlity IN ReaDINg OdDly PResenTEd teXt or their recognition of the mutilated words in Fig. 1.1. Also, competent readers do not experience an **all-or-none** recognition of words. A template-matching model of recognition would predict that competent readers either succeed or fail at matching a whole-word template with a written word; if they had insufficient time to match a template with a word, they would report seeing nothing at all. This does not happen. When required to recognize briefly presented words, competent readers *guess on the basis of* **partial information**. Thus, if CAB were presented, the reader might report CAP. The visual similarity of the reader's false report suggests that word recognition includes some analysis of a word's component letters, not just the matching of a memorized template for an entire word. Not surprisingly, adult readers also confuse similar letters with each other. These results suggest that a **feature detection** mechanism precedes letter and word identification: Competent readers, despite their extensive experience with letters and words, still attend to the component parts (e.g., features) of written words (Massaro, 1975, 1979).

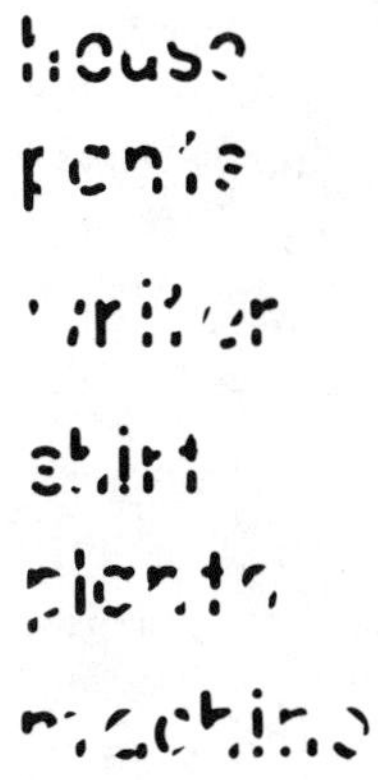

FIG. 1.1.  Competent readers will be able to read most, if not all of these mutilated words. This demonstrates their ability to recognize words on the basis of partial information.

## Redundancy

The analysis and recognition of written words, however, involves much more than feature detection. In English, letters occur in certain sequences or in particular positions of a word (Mason, 1975; Venezky & Massaro, 1980). For example, a *Q* perfectly predicts the occurrence of *U* and we never see tri*pppp*le geminates (e.g., *ggg, xxx*). Positional constraints dictate that certain letters (e.g., *y*) usually occur at the final position of a word; others (e.g., *j, c, g, & v*) rarely occur in the final position. Sequential and positional constraints often interact to restrict further the possible arrangements of letters within words. The sequence *TS*, for instance, occurs at the final, but not at the initial position in English words. Structural rules such as these influence letter orderings in other languages. In Hebrew, the letters *gimel* and *tet* combine to spell the word GET, which means *divorce*. That combination of letters never occurs in any other Hebrew word (Posner, 1980). Hebrew also designates certain letters as final letters and they can occur only at the ends of words.

Competent readers use this knowledge about letter order. Massaro (1975) describes a situation in which a reader obtains enough information from a two-letter word to reduce the possibilities to an *A* or *E* for the first letter and a *T* or *F* for the second letter. This partial information allows the reader to deduce that the word is *AT*, as all other combinations spell nonwords.

Massaro's example indicates the benefit derived from spelling constraints. Rules of combination create a *redundant stimulus complex*. **Redundancy** refers to situations in which different types of information occur together. If someone teaches a kindergartner to distinguish between red circles and blue squares, a glimpse of blue will allow the child to guess that the form is a square; the correlation of shape and color (two distinct stimulus dimensions) permits guessing. Similarly, the correlation of different letters with each other (e.g., *Q* and

*U*) or with certain positions (e.g., *Y*'s with final positions) allows competent readers to guess. If competent readers abstract skimpy visual information (letter features), they can intelligently combine those features by exploiting knowledge about spelling patterns. *Redundancy, in the form of sequential and spatial constraints, permits readers to construct words on the basis of partial information.*

## Orthographic Information

Researchers refer to the redundancy created by sequential and positional letter constraints as **orthographic structure**. Experimental evidence has demonstrated the utility of orthographic structure in the analysis and recognition of words. Late in the 19th century, Cattell (1886) reported that adults remembered more letters from briefly presented words than from random letter strings. Later, Miller, Bruner, and Postman (1954) demonstrated that adults could search more rapidly for a target letter through columns of regularly spelled nonwords (e.g., **pseudowords** such as VERNALIT) than through columns of random letter strings. Reicher (1969) and Wheeler (1970) reported a compatible result from letter **recognition** experiments. They required subjects to determine which of two letters (e.g., *D* or *K*) had appeared in a previously presented display. Figure 1.2 schematically describes this paradigm. They found that subjects performed more accurately when letters were embedded in a word (e.g., WORK) than when embedded in a nonword (WKRO) or when presented in isolation. Reicher first explained the advantage for letters embedded in words (the *Word Superiority Effect*) as a function of the word's meaningfulness. In fact, this result had nothing to do with the semantic value of the letter strings that spelled words. Baron and Thurston (1973) reported the same recognition advantage for letters embedded in pseudowords (e.g., NERK) versus nonpronounceable nonwords (e.g., NRKE). Because neither of these letter strings conveys meaning, information related to spelling patterns must explain the difference in letter recognition between pseudowords and random letter strings.

Critics of this research claim that recognition paradigms measure only how well subjects *remember* displays. According to this argument, competent readers in the Baron and Thurston study remembered all the letters in pseudowords because they could pronounce them. The pronunciation served a mnemonic function, helping subjects to remember a display and its component letters. This competing explanation of the Word Superiority Effect is reasonable. Other researchers, however, have shown that orthographic structure influences how rapidly competent readers *perceive* letter strings. In a **detection task**, where subjects search displays (e.g., words, nonsense strings, and single letters) for a predetermined target letter, orthographic structure facilitated target detection even when subjects memorized the various displays prior to the experiment (Carr, Lehmkuhle, Kottas, Astor-Stetson, & Arnold, 1976). In that study, subjects memorized both the words and random letter strings to remove any special mnemonic advantage for the word displays. In the subsequent detection task, subjects still were more accurate in detecting letters embedded in words than

WORD                (FIRST PRESENTATION)                WDRO


$$$$                (ERASE THE SCREEN)                  $$$$


D   K               (PRESENTATION OF TWO                D   K
                    LETTERS; THE SUBJECT
                    MUST DETERMINE WHICH
                    ONE OCCURED IN THE
                    FIRST PRESENTATION)


●   ●               (RESPONSE BUTTONS; THE              ●   ●
                    SUBJECT PRESSES THE
                    LEFT BUTTON FOR A d;
                    THE RIGHT FOR A k)

FIG. 1.2.  A schematic representation of the recognition paradigm used to explore the Word Superiority Effect.

those embedded in random letter strings. The persistence of the Word Superiority Effect, even when memory is eliminated as a factor, emphasizes the role of orthography in the perception of words.

One might still argue that pronounceability, and not the visual quality of words and nonwords accounts for the Word Superiority Effect. According to Spoehr and Smith (1975), competent readers group letters into pronounceable units prior to the recognition of individual letters (See Massaro, 1975 for a criticism of the Spoehr and Smith study). An experiment with artificial letters, though, separately contrasted the value of visually based orthographic information and phonetic information. Singer (1980) required graduate students to memorize sets of targets, where four unfamiliar (e.g., artificial) letters composed each target. In two conditions, these targets were artificial representations of pronounceable non-words in English (the Reading and Orthographic Conditions); if one substituted the Latinic letters (the letters we use in English) for the Artificial letters according to a code, one could pronounce these targets. Figure 1.3 displays this code. In two other conditions (Arbitrary Targets and Paired–Associated) the targets were artificial translations of nonsense letter strings. In the Orthographic and Arbitrary Targets Conditions, the graduate students *never learned any phonetic information*; they simply memorized their eight four-letter targets on the basis of their visual form. In the Reading Condition, subjects learned the translation code and could actually read their targets. In the Paired–Associated Condition, subjects were taught paired–associated verbal labels for each target.

The experimental task required subjects to discriminate their eight targets from foil items. In *all* conditions, foil items were artificial translations of nonsense strings. If one applied the code in Fig. 1.3, the foil items would have been nonpronounceable letter strings in English. Thus, targets and foils were quite similar for subjects in the Arbitrary Targets and Paired–Associated Conditions:

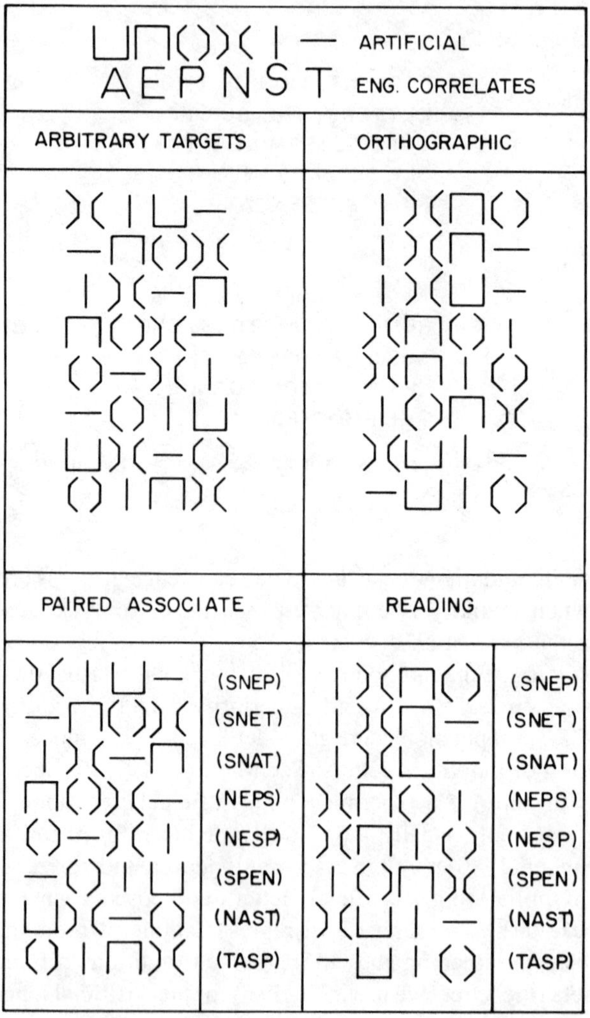

FIG. 1.3.   Targets in the paired-associate and arbitrary targets conditions were translations of nonpronounceable letter strings in English. Targets in the reading and orthographic conditions were translations of pseudowords. English-to-Artificial translations were made according to the code listed at the top of the figure. The verbal labels in the paired-associate condition and the translations in the reading condition are enclosed in parentheses (Singer, 1980). Reprinted with permission from the Psychonomic Society, Inc.

In both conditions, targets *and* foils were artificial translations of nonpronounce-able letter strings in English. In the Orthographic and Reading Conditions, however, targets and foils were structurally dissimilar, as targets were artificial translations of pronounceable pseudowords.

In this task, the graduate subjects in the Orthographic and Reading Conditions enjoyed a great advantage over students in the other conditions. Apparently, this advantage reflected the visually based, structural distinction between targets and foils in the Reading and Orthographic Conditions (or, alternatively, the lack of any such distinction in the other two conditions). Phonetic information contrib-uted no additional advantage to these rapid discriminations, as the students in the Orthographic Condition (who never learned phonetic information) performed just as well as those in the Reading Condition (who could actually read the artificial letter strings). Also, students in the Orthographic Condition performed more accurately than those in the Arbitrary Targets Condition. This advantage must have reflected the difference in the visual distinctions between targets and foils across the two conditions, as *neither group learned phonetic information.* An experiment with deaf subjects corroborates this strong role for visually based, orthographic information. In that study (Gibson, Shurliff, & Yonas, 1970), deaf subjects enjoyed an advantage for recognizing pseudowords over nonsense strings.

## Other Types of Visual Information

Visual information other than orthographic structure adds to the redundancy of written words; word shape and length also contribute to a competent reader's ability to guess at the identity of words. Neisser (1967) notes that a reader, confronted with P★★★★★★★★★★★★, will more likely report PHILADELPHIA than PEORIA simply on the basis of length. Moreover, Neisser mentions that words printed in uppercase letters are more confusable with each other than words printed in lowercase letters. Words printed in lowercase letters provide more information about word shape to the reader than do those in uppercase letters (compare HEAD and HEAP with head and heap).

Experiments with a clever task invented by Stroop (1935) also demonstrate the importance of word shape in recognizing words. The original **Stroop test** required subjects to ignore words that named specific colors. Words such as RED, GREEN, and BROWN were written in different inks so that RED was printed in brown ink, GREEN in red ink, and BROWN in green ink. Subjects had to name the color of the ink and ignore the printed word. This task proved extremely difficult: You can demonstrate the difficulty by coloring the printed words in Fig. 1.4.

This task can also provide useful information about reading. For example, one can gauge the importance of an information source in printed words by measuring a competent reader's difficulty in ignoring that information. As an example, experienced teachers might guess that competent readers guess at a word on the

1. COLOR THIS YELLOW

2. COLOR THIS BLUE

3. COLOR THIS BROWN

4. COLOR THIS GREEN

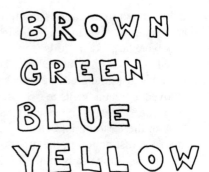

5. NOW, TRY TO NAME THE COLOR INSIDE THE LETTERS AND IGNORE THE WORDS.

FIG. 1.4. The above exercise should suggest how experimental psychologists easily obtain a Stroop effect.

basis of the initial letters. That is, the initial letters provide more important information to readers than other letters. Singer, Lappin, and Moore (1975) demonstrated the validity of this intuition with the Stroop test. Color words, such as GREEN were presented to readers as GRBNW (initial two letters plus three random letters), BNEEW (middle two letters and random letters), or BNWEN (final letters with random letters). Competent readers could not ignore GRBNW and quickly name the color ink in which the letters were written. They easily ignored, however, BNEEW or BNWEN and named the color of the ink. According to the logic of the experiment, the initial letters provided more compelling information than other letters because competent readers encountered difficulty only in ignoring the initial letters.

Posnansky and Rayner (1977) and Rayner and Posnansky (1978) employed a variation of the Stroop task to examine directly the value of word shape information. In those studies, subjects were presented with words and letter strings printed across pictures. For example, a line drawing of an apple could have had printed across it: (1) apple; (2) aqqte; (3) azzme; (4) oqqtc; (5) kzzmf; or (6) house. The nonwords that preserved the shape and final letters of the picture label (e.g., aqqte printed across a line drawing of an apple) caused less interference than nonwords that altered this visual information. Posnansky and Rayner (1977) obtained these results with third-graders and sixth-graders, whereas Rayner and Posnansky (1978) obtained their results with adult readers. Both experiments implied that readers sample visual features when extracting the meaning from printed words. A template-matching model of word recognition could not account for these results.

## Redundancy and Guessing

A number of other studies suggest the importance of visual information in word recognition and analysis, but the essential point from these experiments is already clear: Orthographic rules and word shape allow competent readers to guess a word's identity on the basis of partial information. One need not rely on a memory-consuming, template-matching process to explain the competent reader's facility in recognizing words. Indeed, the average high school student's reading vocabulary of 50,000 words would cause brains to burst at their seams with little templates. Instead, one can suppose that readers sample features from written words and impose their stored knowledge about words (i.e., orthographic knowledge, word shape knowledge) on a retinal mosaic of partial information. The abbreviated model in Fig. 1.5 outlines the mechanisms necessary for this effective guessing strategy. The competent reader, according to this model, stores orthographic and word shape knowledge in long-term memory and imposes this knowledge on a rapidly decaying retinal record of visual features (See Massaro & Taylor, 1979, for a more complete description of this model). The use of this stored information allows the competent reader to reduce uncertainty about printed words. A similar process has been suggested to explain how chess masters succeed in remembering accurately the positions of all the chess pieces on a briefly displayed chess board. The chess masters, much like competent readers, impose a well-learned structure (e.g., probable relations between pieces, common openings, and middle-game positions) on the partial information they can extract from the brief presentation (Simon, 1969). The chess masters do not employ templates of board configurations; rather, they embellish impoverished information with their knowledge of chess.

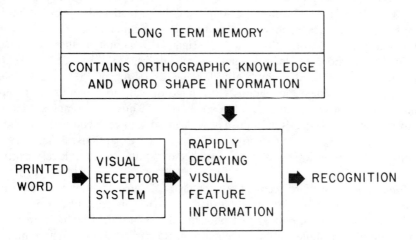

FIG. 1.5.   The above model of word recognition posits a Long-Term Memory that contains information about the relationship of letters to each other. This knowledge allows competent readers to recognize words on the basis of partial information.

## A Caveat

Some reading researchers (Goodman, 1973; Smith, 1973) have made strong claims about reading curricula based on experimental results with adult readers. The competent reader's effective use of visually based, orthographic information caused them to argue against the teaching of phonics. They reasoned that because competent readers rely on visual information to recognize words, reading curricula ought to de-emphasize phonics or decoding training. One must note, however, the great danger in leaping from experimental results on *competent reading* to *reading instruction*. Even if competent readers relied exclusively on visual information to recognize words, beginning readers might rely on phonics to acquire orthographic knowledge. For example, beginning readers probably do not memorize specific visual sequences such as *QU, ST*, and others. Instead, phonics training might allow beginning readers to make a connection between visual symbols and their spoken language; the sound of a letter cluster could then facilitate the rehearsal and remembering of these sequences. Moreover, the following sections on the phonetic and semantic perspectives indicate that the relative importance of visual and phonetic information to competent reading varies as a function of the specific reading task.

## The Phonetic Perspective

English presents readers with a perplexing set of rules for translating visual strings into their phonetic counterparts. Venezky (1970) concluded that: "English has the most complex relationship between spelling and sound of any major modern language." Despite this complexity, Venezky cautions that the spelling-to-sound relationship is not "the primeval chaos portrayed by spelling reformers [p. 70]." Knowledge of spelling-to-sound rules helps readers decipher unfamiliar words (names in Russian novels) and permits them to generate and read thousands of regularly spelled words. Rozin and Gleitman (1977) point out that the average English high school student reads and understands 50,000 words. Chinese scholars, on the other hand, know only 4000 words of the 50,000 in a Chinese dictionary. In Chinese, ideograms correspond directly to a word and its pronunciation; each word must be rotely memorized. Thus, the complex relations between letters and sounds in English provide an advantage to competent readers, despite the initial struggle to learn the rules and their exceptions. Brooks (1977) claims that spelling-to-sound correspondence constitutes another level of orthographic structure.

Some models of word recognition emphasize the use of letter-to-sound rules to retrieve a word's meaning (i.e., *lexical access*). This complicates the model outlined earlier and stipulates that phonetic information, in addition to visual information, contributes to word recognition. Researchers refer to these models as *phonetically mediated* models of word recognition (Fig. 1.6). Alternatively, one could suggest a **direct access** model of word recognition. Direct access models propose that competent readers rely only on visual features to retrieve a word's meaning.

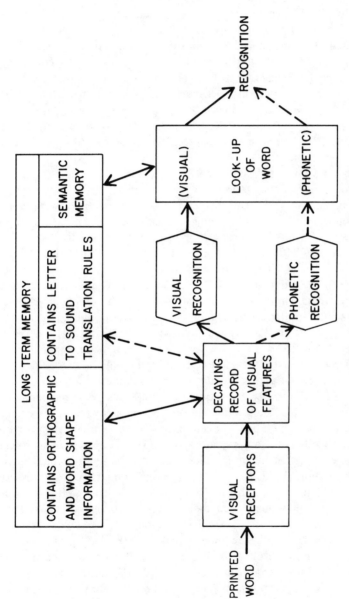

FIG. 1.6. This model schematically describes word recognition with (broken lines) and without the contribution of phonetic information. In the phonetically mediated model, a competent reader imposes letter-to-sound translation rules decaying visual features. This leads to visual and phonetic recognition. A match of the phonetic representation of the word with semantic memory leads to word recognition.

Proponents of phonetically mediated models often cite experiments with **lexical decision tasks**. A lexical decision task requires subjects to determine whether a letter string is a word or a nonword. Subjects respond "YES" to words and "NO" to nonwords. An experimenter can manipulate several aspects of the task. He or she can vary the similarity of the nonwords to words, the number of letter strings presented at a time, and the relationship of word items to each other. Although this task only remotely resembles reading, the results concern the organization of *semantic memory* and the necessity of a phonetic operation to word recognition. For instance, an experimenter might present BRIBE and follow it with TRIBE or COUCH. If subjects more quickly recognized the second member of a rhyming pair (e.g., BRIBE–TRIBE) than of a nonrhyming pair (e.g., BRIBE–COUCH), one might conclude that phonetic information influences word recognition.

Meyer, Schvaneveldt, and Ruddy (1974) used the lexical decision task to explore the role of phonetic information in reading. In that study, subjects determined whether two simultaneously presented letter strings were words. Subjects responded "YES" if both letter strings were words; "NO" if either one or both were nonwords. Subjects saw phonetically and visually similar letter strings (e.g., BRIBE–TRIBE) and phonetically dissimilar but visually similar pairs (e.g., COUCH–TOUCH). Not surprisingly, subjects' fastest responses were to the confusing pairs such as COUCH–TOUCH. The facilitation caused by phonetic and visual similarity and the confusion caused by phonetically dissimilar but visually similar pairs, suggest that a phonetic operation mediated lexical access. Rubenstein, Lewis, and Rubenstein (1971) support this conclusion. They found that "NO" responses to nonword homophones (e.g., RANE) took longer than other "NO" responses. Rubenstein et al. concluded that phonetic mediation of lexical access accounted for this delay.

This conclusion, however, warrants qualification. The letter string pairs in the Meyer et al. study probably encouraged a phonetic strategy. Subjects engaged this strategy because, sometimes, phonetic information facilitated word recognition. Davelaar, Coltheart, Besner, and Jonasson (1978) explored this criticism. They also reported that phonetic information sometimes biased subsequent lexical decisions. For example SALE facilitated the recognition of SAIL. When, however, the distractor items (i.e., the nonwords) also sounded like English words (e.g., BRANE), subjects abandoned their phonetic strategy to avoid errors. Under these circumstances, phonetic similarity no longer biased lexical decisions.

Another recent experiment (Stanovich & Bauer, 1978) qualifies the Meyer et al. and Rubenstein et al. results in a different way. The lexical decisions (for single words) in the Meyer et al. study required 600 to 700 msec (milliseconds). These are relatively long response latencies for a simple word recognition task. The recognition response times in the Singer (1980) study, for example, ranged from 225 msec to 375 msec. Long response latencies may encourage a contribution from phonetic sources of information. Stanovich and Bauer, in fact, reported that phonetic information *only* contributed to lexical decisions at longer latencies. In that study, subjects attempted to recognize regularly (WON) and irregularly (ONE) spelled words. Stanovich and Bauer reasoned that if lexical decisions involve a phonetic decoding stage, responses to words with irregular letter-to-sound correspondences (ONE) should require more time. This delay, however, occurred only at longer response latencies (550 msec). When subjects were required to make their decisions within shorter time periods (350 msec), the delay due to irregular letter-to-sound correspondence disappeared.

None of these qualifications denies the contribution of phonetic information to word recognition under certain conditions. Aside from lexical decision tasks that encourage a phonetic strategy, situations that require articulation of words will yield phonetic effects. For example, Bradshaw (1974) required subjects to pronounce an ambiguous word, such as BOW, where the letter string permits two pronunciations. He found that peripherally presented words, far enough outside of central vision that subjects reported not seeing them, biased the pronunciation. That is, the presentation of LOW in the periphery caused subjects to say BOW (as in OH!) rather than BOW (as in OUCH!); COW caused them to say BOW (as in OUCH). Generally, anytime a competent reader is uncertain about a word, phonetic information will help the reader reduce uncertainty. The use of phonetic information, however, will consume more time than a visual analysis. Posner and Mitchell (1967) demonstrated this time difference with a simple task: Subjects take longer to determine that "Aa" are the same (a phonetic judgment) than that "AA" are the same (a visual judgment). Similarly, Singer (1980, Experiment III) reported that subjects took longer to determine that NXRS–NXRS sounded the same than to determine that they looked the same. Again, phonetic information contributes to recognition but *phonetic judgments require more time.*

## The Semantic Perspective

Word meaning (**semantics**) also influences word recognition. The paradigms already discussed—The Stroop and lexical decision tasks—demonstrate the semantic contribution to word recognition. In a lexical decision task, for example, the presentation of NURSE prior to DOCTOR speeds the recognition of DOCTOR (Meyer et al., 1974). Also, competent readers recognize nominal compounds (e.g., STUMBLING BLOCK) more rapidly than ordinary noun phrases (COPPER BLOCK) and faster than the sum of the recognition times for the two words that compose the nominal compound (e.g., STUMBLING and BLOCK). Osgood and Hoosain (1974) concluded from these results that competent readers recognize meaningful units rather than individual letters or words. Furthermore, in the Stroop task, words from similar categories interfere with each other more than words from dissimilar categories (Golinkoff & Rosinski, 1976). Thus, if an experimenter printed the word GREEN in blue ink, a competent reader will find it difficult to say "blue"; the printed word TABLE, however, will cause less interference. In the previously mentioned Posnansky and Rayner studies, any word printed across an incompatible picture (e.g., HOUSE printed across a picture of a horse) interfered with naming the picture more than nonsense letter strings.

Perfetti, Goldman, and Hogoboam (1979) reported a connected text example of semantic influences on word recognition. In their study, subjects pronounced: (1) words that appeared in isolation; (2) words embedded within columns of words; and (3) words that followed a congruent or incongruent passage. As teachers familiar with *cloze* tasks might expect, competent readers more rapidly named words that followed a congruent passage than words in any other conditions: A context consistent with the meaning of word facilitates a reader's recognition of that word. It should be mentioned here (and is discussed in the chapter on context-use and reading disability) that context reduced the **vocalization latencies** (i.e., speed of pronunciation) for both good and poor readers.

## More Models

How does semantic context contribute to word recognition? Probably in some way similar to the contribution of orthographic information to word recognition. In both cases, knowledge stored in long-term memory *constrains a reader's guesses about a word's identity*. In the lexical decision task, for example, the presentation of NURSE directs the subject's attention to a network of information (Rips, Shoben, & Smith, 1973). The word NURSE might direct a reader's attention to words related to NURSE (e.g., hospitals, syringes, doctors, and so on); subsequent presentations of related words will benefit from this predirected attention. Instead of developing hypotheses about the word's identity solely on the basis of visual information, the reader can confine his or her hypotheses to those words related to NURSE. This strategy works only when context, or prior semantic information, actually relates to the word; presenting NURSE will not facilitate the recognition of MORTAR. In reading connected text, competent readers have good reason to believe that the words relate to each other; authors rarely attempt to present random thoughts to their readers. Figure 1.7 outlines a model of reading that allows for the contribution of semantic information to word recognition.

## BEYOND SINGLE WORDS

Word recognition provides only limited insights into reading. True, the types of information (e.g., orthographic) that contribute to word recognition also contribute to reading paragraphs, but reading paragraphs goes well beyond the demands of single-word recognition and involves almost every aspect of human cognition. Competent readers sample visual information from text while comprehending previously read information. Thus, questions pertaining to attention and its allocation apply to the reading process. Competent readers explore the

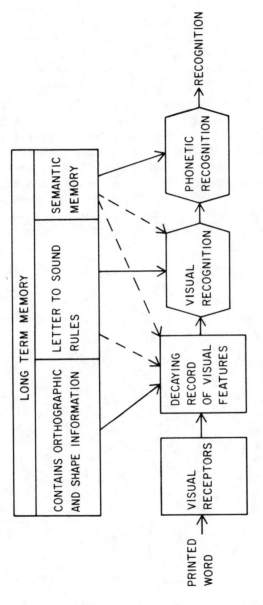

FIG. 1.7.   This model allows the contribution of semantic knowledge at all levels or processing. Context, for example, would allow a competent reader to guess on the basis of partial visual or phonetic information.

printed page and utilize impoverished **peripheral information**; consequently, eye movement data and perceptual models relate to reading. Furthermore, competent readers must integrate sentences and words with previously read material, and, thus, characteristics of memory and reasoning bear upon these operations. Perhaps this complexity caused Elkind (1981) to lament that reading "is a very large problem." Despite this complexity, however, average college students read about 250 words a minute—an impressive, but very common accomplishment.

Several factors contribute to competent reading. Figure 1.8, by analogy, illustrates the task confronting reading researchers. Reading researchers agree that practice, intelligence, attentional mechanisms, and others *all* explain successful reading. They disagree, though, on the relative importance of the various components and which factors explain differences (i.e., *variance*) in reading ability. As a result, the reading research literature contains disputes about what mechanisms *really* underlie reading. These disputes closely resemble the arguments between the proverbial blind men about what *really* is an elephant. One blind man, who chances upon the elephant's tail, describes the beast as long and skinny. Another, who pats the elephant's side, describes it as hard and wrinkled. A third blind man cannot believe the inanity of these descriptions and informs

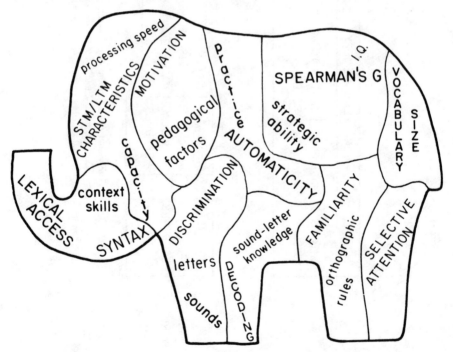

FIG. 1.8. One might think of the elephant as containing factors that contribute to reading skill. Different researchers could easily examine different aspects of the elephant and subsequently argue about which skill explains differences between good and poor readers.

his colleagues that elephants are tall, round, and heavy; he has tried to lift the elephant's leg. In much the same way, reading researchers offer varying definitions of the reading process that reflect the peculiar characteristics of their experiments. The summary of the research on word recognition makes it clear that different task demands and materials examine different aspects of the reading process and we should *expect* different researchers to offer competing descriptions.

The present account attempts to avoid these disputes and discusses a few of the major issues in competent reading, among them attention and automaticity, the role of phonetic information, and semantic and syntactic context. The discussion intends only to outline strategies and sources of information that contribute to competent reading; it does not describe the entire elephant.

## Automaticity, Attention, and Context Use

As already mentioned, competent readers simultaneously do various things. In this way, reading is similar to all complicated behaviors. As Laberge and Samuels (1974) pointed out, skilled basketball players learn to dribble and run at the same time; as political comedians quip, everyone but Gerald Ford learns to chew gum and walk at the same time. Human beings, however, have difficulty *attending* to more than one source of information at the same time (Broadbent, 1962). According to this perspective, competent readers could have difficulty attending to the visual analysis of words while appreciating the meaning of the text. Yet, competent readers handle simultaneous operations. How is this done? They circumvent limitations on attention by performing some operations without conscious effort, or **automatically**.

Bryan and Harter (1897/1973) provide a colorful account of the development of automaticity—the ability to perform certain tasks without the allocation of attention. Harter, before enrolling in the graduate psychology program at Indiana University, had worked as a railroad telegrapher. He and Bryan collaborated on an investigation of how telegraphers acquired skill in rapidly transmitting and receiving Morse Code. The acquisition of expert telegraphic skill requires approximately 2½ years; Bryan and Harter (1897/1973) skeptically dismissed anecdotal accounts of prodigies with these words: "A story is told of an Indiana operator, who, after three months' practice, was able to receive Garfield's Inaugural Address. Stories of this sort must be taken with a grain of salt. The more of telegraphy you know, the more salt it takes [p. 29]."

Their skepticism has some foundation. Telegraphers must learn to distinguish the fine distinction between dots and dashes (e.g., the brush of an armature against a screw) and the exact sequence of signals for each letter. Furthermore, Bryan and Harter reported that expert operators made up to 429 impacts within a minute; they received messages at even faster rates. Telegraphic operators develop from "plodders," who attend to details of individual signals, to "explorers," who actively construct incoming messages and exploit their knowledge of syntax and semantic context (The "plodder/explorer" terminology is from Rozin & Gleitman, 1977). According to Bryan and Harter (1897/1973): the "beginner must copy each letter as it comes" but the "expert ceases to recognize . . . consciously" letters and the spaces between letters; "expert operators read words . . . later, the sentence becomes the conscious unit, much as in the reading of printed matter [p. 28]." Eventually, "expert operators 'copy behind' three or four words; sometimes ten or twenty words; that is, the receiving operator allows the sender to write a number of words before he begins to copy [p. 32]." This last characteristic of telegraphers bears directly on the development of automaticity.

Copying behind a message permits an operator to use context. Previous words allow the operator to structure subsequent signals, restricting hypotheses about a word's identity. The application of context to incoming signals implicates the allocation of attention to semantic information; conversely, little or no attention is devoted to the recognition of individual signals. Even when receiving messages at 85 words a minute a skilled operator: "is able at will to think about the significance of the dispatches [sic] or to think of anything else he chooses. An Associated Press man, who . . . worked for years in one of our large cities, said . . . : 'I am in danger of allowing errors made by the sender to get into my copy, if I let my mind wander; but the truth is that in the last weeks, while taking press, my mind has been most of the time at home with a sick child' [p. 352–53, Bryan & Harter, 1899/1973]."

How do operators develop automaticity for incoming signals so that they can exploit context? In much the same way that one gets to Carnegie Hall: *Practice.* Although the speed and accuracy of the expert operators reflect their use of language structure (e.g., syntax and context), Bryan and Harter (1899/1973) want the beginner to know that: "it is not possible to gain freedom in using the higher language units until the lower have been so mastered that *the attention is not diverted by them: . . . . There is no freedom except through automatism* [p. 368]."

The role of automaticity in exploiting context also applies to reading. Although expert telegraphy represents a listening skill, competent readers might follow an acquisition pattern similar to telegraphic operators (see Carr's Chapter 7, Section I, on skill acquisition; also Stanovich's discussion on developmental differences in the use of phonological recoding). Initially, beginning readers might have to attend to individual letters just as beginning operators must copy each incoming letter. Practice, however, permits readers to explore the text surrounding individual letters. Much like the expert operator who reads behind incoming messages, competent readers read ahead of words in central vision; experiments on the eye–voice span demonstrate this characteristic of competent reading.

## Eye–Voice Span

The **eye-voice span** (EVS) paradigm requires subjects to read text through a lighted window; the experimenter records how many words the subject can read after the light has been turned off. This paradigm assumes that the number of words read in the dark indicates the distance between the word being read aloud and the words being read outside of central vision, or in the periphery (Buswell, 1920). Beginning readers have an extremely small eye–voice span; they cannot read aloud any words after the light has been turned off. Competent readers enjoy a larger eye–voice span, its size increasing with age and experience (Buswell, 1920; Levin & Turner, 1968). These experiments suggest that beginning readers rivet their eyes and attention on single words and letters. One interpretation is that their decoding is not yet well automatized, so they cannot attend to peripheral information. Competent readers, who enjoy automatized decoding operations, can freely sample peripheral information and, thus, have an opportunity to make use of context.

## Braille Readers

This facility in using peripheral information parallels not only experienced telegraphic operators but, also, readers of Braille. Bryan and Harter (1899) discuss an experienced teacher's observations about children learning to read Braille at the Indiana Institute for the Blind. She reported that:

> In a First Reader class . . . everyone kept his finger on the letters, spelling each word out loud or to himself . . . In the Fourth Reader class . . . the larger number gave attention to the words. . . . In the highest grades the attention was upon the thought. . . . [pp. 354–355].

As far as a "finger–voice span," she reports that finger and voice coincide in the First and Second Reader classes; this continues into the Third and Fourth Reader classes but:

> In the highest reading classes . . . several read three or four words ahead. One pupil, a very bright boy, keeps a line ahead, eight or ten words. He reads the end of one line with the finger of his right hand and at the same time reads the beginning of the next line with his left hand . . . [Generally] . . . pupils who study each day . . . are able to read smoothly, rapidly, and several words ahead of the voice [p. 355].

This description of Braille reading adds to the generality of the conclusions drawn from reading and telegraphy: Skilled readers rely on context but the use of context presupposes a mastery or automatization of lower-level skills. Telegraphers cannot copy behind without intense practice at recognizing individual signals; skilled readers use context (as evidenced by an expanding eye–voice span) as their experience with written text increases; finally, the readers of Braille who read ahead with their fingers are those "who study each day." These conclusions relate to reading curricula, especially those that recommend that children learn about the linguistic structure of text, prior to the mastery of component, decoding skills. Bryan and Harter (1897/1973, 1899) would argue that the ability to exploit context depends directly on the automatization of decoding skills, not blurry instruction as to what comprises linguistic structure.

## More on Automaticity

Contemporary accounts of automaticity pale beside Bryan and Harter's investigation of telegraphers. Clever experimental procedures, though, describe some of the characteristics of an automatic process.

Laberge (1973) and Laberge and Samuels (1974) developed a task that manipulated a subject's expectations about visual presentations of letters. In this task, a subject determines if two letters match. For instance, the letter *a* is presented; if the following letter is also an *a*, he or she presses a button. This procedure directs the subject's attention to the visual characteristics of the first letter, or the cue (i.e., the *a*). If the two letters match, regardless of the cue, the subject still responds ''same'' by pressing a button. This procedure is outlined in Fig. 1.9. The unexpected change (e.g., being presented with two letters rather than a single letter) requires the subject to *switch* attention from the visual features of the cue (.e.g., the *a*) to the visual features of the letter pair (e.g., *b b*). The switching time, according to Laberge and Samuels, measures the automatization

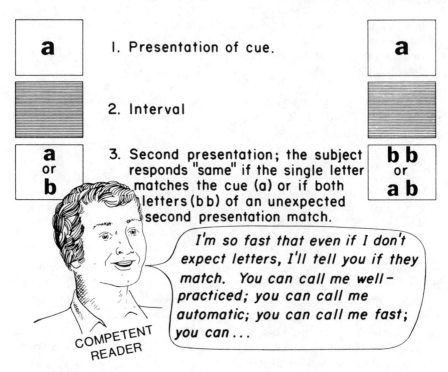

FIG. 1.9. A schematic representation of the Laberge and Samuels (1974) paradigm.

of the letter recognition process: If subjects take no longer to respond "same" to an unexpected letter pair (e.g., *b b*) than to an expected letter (e.g., *a*), then the recognition for the letter pair must be automatic. Stated in another way, an automatic process is not affected by expectations or predirected attention, nor should it be, as an automatic process, *by definition*, requires no devotion of conscious attention.

Laberge and Samuels (1974), in fact, demonstrated the automatization of letter recognition using this paradigm. Predirected attention did not help or hinder letter recognition, there was no *switching* time. Their experiment clarifies an important point for reading researchers. Automaticity implies more than great speed in executing some skill; automaticity denotes the absence of conscious attention and the resistance of that skill to expectations.

## More on Context

Automaticity allows competent readers and telegraphers to use "higher language structures" or context. What type of information, however, represents context in reading? Competent readers, it turns out, rely heavily on syntax (e.g., grammatical structure) and *semantics* (e.g., meaning) to construct a message relayed to text. Kolers (1970) demonstrated the competent reader's use of syntax and semantics in an experiment with transformed text (Fig. 1.10). The task required subjects to read sentences in English that had been visually altered; some had been written right to left; others were written left to right, but each word had been written backwards; in others, individual letters were rotated. Subjects made many errors in the oral reading of such sentences; rarely, however, did they commit an error that violated the semantic sense or the syntactic structure of a sentence. For example, in the analysis of the reading errors, Kolers reported that subjects often substituted a word or guessed at one of the words within a sentence but that these guesses and substitutions preserved the meaning of the sentence almost all the time. Also, they substituted verbs for other verbs, nouns for nouns, and so on. Syntactically, their substitutions were correct 75% of the time. Kolers (1975) reported related results in a memory task that required subjects to detect changes in previously learned, transformed sentences. Competent and incompetent readers almost always detected semantic or syntactic changes. Furthermore, in an analysis of first-graders' oral reading errors, Weber (1970, 1976) rarely found semantic or syntactic errors; even first-graders exploited context in guessing at a word's identity.

## Eye Movement and Context Use

The eye–voice span studies cited earlier suggest that readers use context from the periphery, the text that lies outside central vision. Although beginning readers may struggle to sample context in the periphery, competent readers *cannot avoid* using context (just as they cannot avoid the meaning of printed words in the

Stroop test). Willows and MacKinnon (1973) developed a reading task that demonstrated this unavoidable use of context. The task required subjects to read selectively a series of sentences printed in black ink. Between these sentences were others, printed in red. Subjects were instructed to ignore the "red" sentences and answer questions about the content of the selectively read "black" sentences. Competent readers could not ignore the "red" sentences; they literally read between the lines and their answers to questions about the passage reflected the *intrusion* of the unattended lines.

Recent work by Rayner and McConkie (1977) ingeniously used the laboratory computer to explore the use of peripheral information in reading. In their studies, a computer generated sentences that were displayed on a television-like screen. The computer not only manipulated characteristics of the display but also monitored the subject's eye movements. Rayner and McConkie used this procedure to examine where competent readers looked for information and what they extracted from the periphery. They reported that competent readers directed their fixations to certain parts of a sentence. For instance, they spent little time looking at the final letters of a sentence. When they did fixate this region, the fixations were relatively short. Rayner and McConkie suggested that the eye movement patterns indicated that competent readers use peripheral information to guide subsequent fixations. Rayner and McConkie explored this possibility in the following way: They presented information in the periphery and then changed that information once those letters occurred in central vision. Rayner and McConkie reasoned that if competent readers exploit peripheral information, any changes should disrupt fluent reading.

Competent readers did notice visual changes 8 to 12 letters outside of central (**foveal**) vision. Changes within this region disrupted fluent reading; other changes produced little effect. The major disruption in reading pertained to speed rather than comprehension and Rayner and McConkie emphasized that even with severely restricted peripheral information, their subjects could comprehend the text. One must note that the Rayner and McConkie procedure tested the effect of peripheral information along the horizontal axis. As Fig. 1.11 illustrates, even the use of information 8 to 12 letters in the periphery could allow the competent reader to extract information from preceding and subsequent lines. Again if, as Rayner and McConkie suggest, the competent reader directs his eye movements, this limited peripheral information can serve as a **heuristic**, providing a game plan for attacking the text.

It should be pointed out that recent work reported by McConkie and Zola (1981) suggests that the competent reader may *not* exploit peripheral information (e.g., context) as successfully as portrayed in the present discussion. For example, in an eye-tracking experiment, Zola reported that competent readers fixated highly constrained words (words that could be predicted from their context) almost as long as unpredictable words. McConkie and Zola concluded that: "there seemed to be no tendency for skilled readers to skip over a highly predictable word as they were reading [p. 166]." This, and the finding that

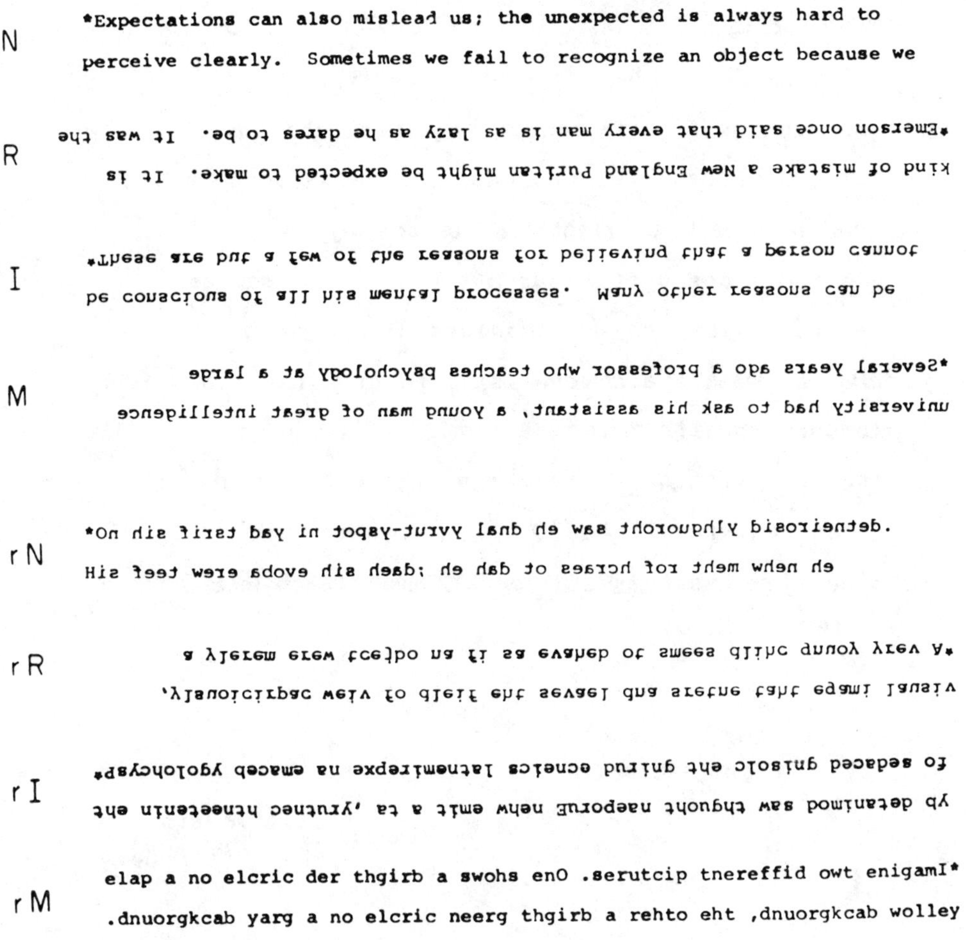

N

*Expectations can also mislead us; the unexpected is always hard to
perceive clearly. Sometimes we fail to recognize an object because we

R

*Emerson once said that every man is as lazy as he dares to be. It was the
kind of mistake a New England Puritan might be expected to make. It is

I

*These are but a few of the reasons for believing that a person cannot
be conscious of all his mental processes. Many other reasons can be

M

*Several years ago a professor who teaches psychology at a large
university had to ask his assistant, a young man of great intelligence

r N

*On his first day in grad school he was thoroughly disoriented.
His feet were above his head; he had to reach for them when he

r R

*A very young child sees most of behave as it an object were every
visual image that answers the label that reveal and relate that nearby

r I

*The determined saw thought, at a nineteenth century, when purjng the
to sedaed closing an experimental science na emacde psychology*

r M

*Imagine two different pictures. One shows a bright red circle on a pale
blue background, the other a bright green circle on a gray background.

FIG. 1.10.   These are some of the transformed texts that Kolers (1970) presented
to subjects. Reprinted with permission of Basic Books.

competent readers detected minor visual changes, can be interpreted as straining
the hypothesis that peripheral information influences eye movements and allows
the competent reader to skip over information.

## The Phonetic Mediation Issue

The experiments on single-word tasks indicated that competent readers can identify words without phonetically translating groups of letters. Baron (1973) extended this result to the reading of phrases. He asked subjects to determine if
groups of words represented meaningful sentences. In some cases they did (e.g.,
*Tie the knot*), but not in others (e.g., *Tie the not; Ill him*). Baron reasoned that
if a phonetic process mediated competent reading then it should have taken

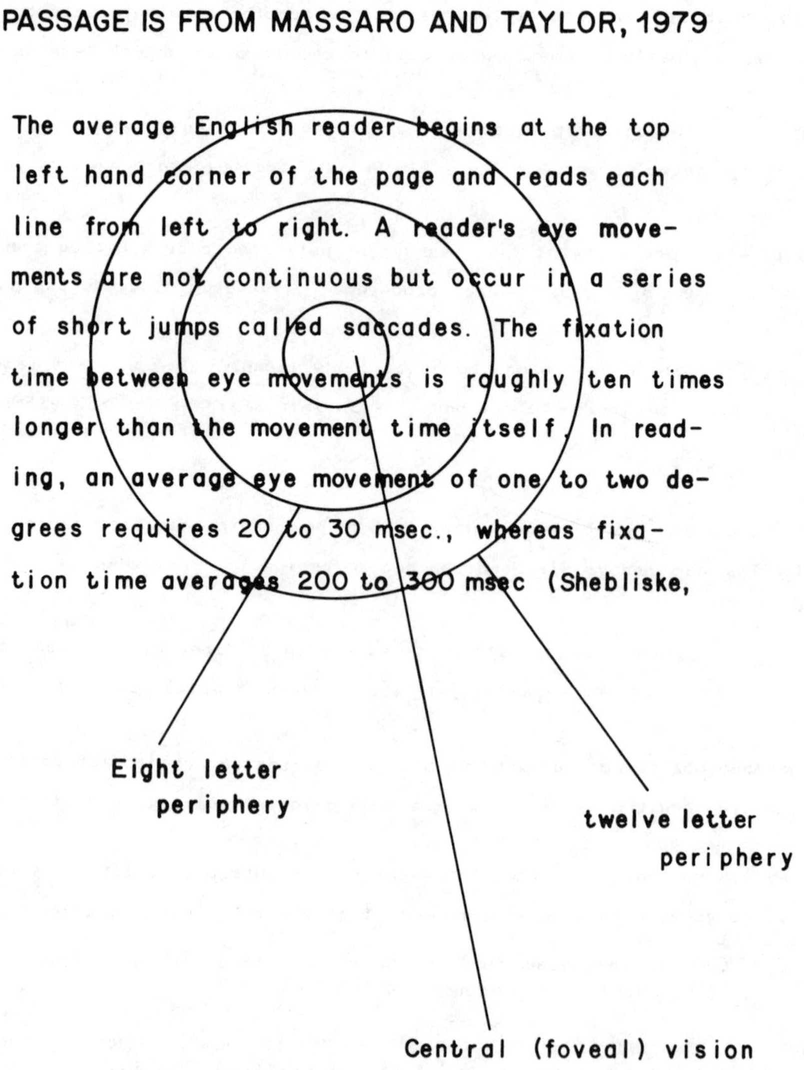

## PASSAGE IS FROM MASSARO AND TAYLOR, 1979

The average English reader begins at the top
left hand corner of the page and reads each
line from left to right. A reader's eye movements are not continuous but occur in a series
of short jumps called saccades. The fixation
time between eye movements is roughly ten times
longer than the movement time itself. In reading, an average eye movement of one to two degrees requires 20 to 30 msec., whereas fixation time averages 200 to 300 msec (Shebliske,

Eight letter
periphery

twelve letter
periphery

Central (foveal) vision

FIG. 1.11. A competent reader would clearly see and attend to letters within
central or foveal vision while sampling information (letters, context) from an 8-
to-12 letter periphery.

subjects more time to determine that "Tie the not" was nonsense (visually
incorrect but phonetically correct) than to decide "Ill him" was nonsense (visually and phonetically incorrect). Subjects, however, took no longer to determine
the illegality of the two types of nonsense strings.

Baron (1973) properly entitled his report "Phonemic stage *not necessary* for
reading" (emphasis added). His task encouraged subjects to employ a visual
strategy because a phonetically mediated strategy would have led to errors (In

fact, his subjects did err more often with sentences such as *Tie the not*). Another task, which encouraged a phonetic strategy, might have implicated a phonemic stage. Proofreading, for example, encourages readers to read slowly, possibly sounding out each letter, or letter cluster, to catch errors. Corcoran (1966) reported that when proofreaders must cancel *e*'s, they most often miss the silent *e*'s. Later, Corcoran (1967) demonstrated that this effect could not be attributed to the position of most silent *e*'s; that is, that they occur at the ends of words. Proofreaders also fail to note the absence of an initial, but silent *k* in words such as *knot* and *know* more often than other *k*'s.

It should be noted also that a recent study (Doctor & Coltheart, 1980) disputes Baron's report. Young readers had great difficulty with sentences such as "I no him." That is, they frequently reported that the sentence made sense. Doctor & Coltheart (1980) report that, whereas older readers rely on visual features in evaluating the meaning of a sentence, younger readers engage in phonological recoding when reading for meaning.

Again, as with the experiments with single words, the presence of a phonemic stage in reading depends on the specific task demands and the characteristics of the subjects. The disparate results reported by Baron (1973) and Corcoran (1966, 1967) simply indicate the flexibility of competent reading; competent readers maintain a system that permits the phonetic translation of written words; they are selective, though, in deploying that system.

## Summary

The laboratory description of competent reading should confirm most of the suspicions of an experienced classroom teacher. Teachers know that practice and familiarity lead to increased skill and speed; they may not have dubbed this increased facility with a word such as *automaticity* or thought about the role of *conscious attention* in competent reading. Similarly, teachers know that good readers learn spelling patterns; they may not, however, have called this *orthographic knowledge* and thought about how such *redundant* knowledge helps to resolve *partial information*. In the same way, teachers know that *context* assists readers in deciphering words; they may not have though about *peripheral information* guiding eye movements or allowing a competent reader to *restrict hypotheses* about a word's identity. Finally, teachers realize that visual cues allow readers to recognize words; they may not have thought about the flexibility of competent reading and the competent reader's ability to bypass any phonemic stages in certain situations.

The description of the knowledge and strategies used in competent reading should suggest certain possibilities about incompetent reading: For example, if competent readers rely on orthographic information, could the poor reader's difficulty pertain to a failure to utilize orthographic information? Alternatively, one could ask if poor readers fail to exploit context or letter-to-sound relations, other sources of information important to the competent reader. The following section explores some of these possibilities in reviewing the evidence on why certain people fail to learn how to read.

# GLOSSARY

**"All or None".**   A possible description of perception; the notion that we attempt to match a letter with a memorized template for that letter. If one succeeds in making the match then one recognizes the letter. Otherwise, recognition fails.

**Automaticity.**   A description of a process that requires no devotion of conscious attention.

**Detection Task.**   An experimental procedure in which a subject searches for a predesignated target.

**Direct Access.**   Describes a model of reading in which the reader apprehends the meaning of a word without engaging a visual-to-phonetic decoding operation or any phonetically mediated process.

**Eye–Voice Span.**   The measured distance between where a reader is looking (ahead) and the word that is being read.

**Feature Detection.**   In contrast to an "all-or-none" recognition process, a feature detection model of perception allows for the recognition of the components of a letter.

**Foveal Vision.**   The highly accurate vision that is associated with the retinal fovea; an area that subtends a visual angle of two degrees and that allows fine discriminations.

**Heuristic.**   Literally, this means to help discover or learn. In this chapter, it refers to the competent readers' use of peripheral information; they use peripheral information to guide their search for information helping them to construct or learn about the text.

**Lexical Decision Task.**   An experimental procedure that requires subjects to determine if a letter string represents a word.

**Orthographic Structure.**   The system of rules that governs the order and position in which letters may occur.

**Paradigm.**   A system; a perspective; a method of operation. In the present context it denotes an experimental procedure or method for examining an issue.

**Partial Information.**   Competent readers abstract only fragments of information from text. This information (partial), however, is adequate for sophisticated guesses about the text.

**Peripheral Information.**   In reading, anything that lies outside foveal or central vision.

**Pseudowords.**   Letter strings that visually or phonetically resemble words.

**Recognition Task.**   An experimental procedure that requires the subject to determine if something (e.g., a letter) occurred in a previous display.

**Redundancy.** Technically, the correlation of two distinct stimulus dimensions. More broadly, redundancy describes any situation in which two or more types of information usually occur together. In reading, we can take advantage of redundancy in text: Orthographic structure dictates that certain letters occur together, syntax regulates word order, and semantic context increases the likelihood of certain words. Competent readers use this knowledge to guess.

**Semantics.** As used here, any information pertaining to the meaning of a passage.

**Stroop Test.** An experimental procedure that requires subjects to name the color in which a string of letters are printed. This can become difficult when the letter string spells a color word different from the color of the ink.

**Vocalization Latency.** The time it takes to say something. As used in this chapter, the time taken to name a visually presented word.

## REFERENCES

Baron, J. Phonemic stage not necessary for reading. *Quarterly Journal of Experimental Psychology*, 1973, *25*, 241–246.

Baron J. & Thurston, I. An analysis of the word-superiority effect. *Cognitive Psychology*, 1973, *4*, 207–228.

Bradshaw, J. L. Short reports. Peripherally presented and unreported words may bias the perceived meaning of a centrally fixated homograph. *Journal of Educational Psychology*, 1974, *103*(6), 1200–1202.

Broadbent, D. E. Attention and the perception of speech. *Scientific American*, April 1962.

Brooks, L. Visual pattern in fluent word identification. In A. S. Reber & D. L. Scarborough (Eds.), *Toward a psychology of reading: The proceedings of the CUNY conferences.* Hillsdale, N.J.: Lawrence Erlbaum Associates, 1977.

Bryan, W., & Harter, N. Studies in the physiology and psychology of the telegraphic language. New York, 1897. (Reprinted in H. Gardner & J. K. Gardner (Eds.), *The psychology of skill.* New York: Arno Press, 1973.)

Bryan, W. L., & Harter, N. Studies on the acquisition of a hierarchy of habits. *Psychological Review*, 1899, *6*(4), 345–375.

Buswell, G. T. An experimental study of the eye–voice span in reading. *Supplementary Educational Monographs*, No. 17. Chicago: University of Chicago, Department of Education, 1920.

Carr, T. H., Lehmkuhle, S. W., Kottas, B., Astor-Stetson, E. C., & Arnold, D. Target position and practice in the identification of letters in varying contexts: A word superiority effect. *Perception & Psychophysics*, 1976, *19*, 412–416.

Cattell, J. M. The time it takes to see and name objects. *Mind*, 1886, *11*, 63–65.

Corcoran, D. W. J. An acoustic factor in letter cancellation. *Nature*, 1966, *210*, 658.

Corcoran, D. W. J. An acoustic factor in proofreading. *Nature*, 1967, *214*, 851–852.

Davelaar, E., Coltheart, M., Besner, D., & Jonasson, J. T. Phonological recording and lexical access. *Memory & Cognition*, 1978, *6*(4), 391–402.

Doctor, E. A. & Coltheart, M. Children's use of phonological encoding when reading for meaning. *Memory & Cognition*, 1980, *8*, 195–209.

Elkind, D. Stages in the development of reading. In I. Sigel, D. Brodzinski, & R. M. Golinkoff (Eds.), *Piagetian theory and research: Directions and applications.* Hillsdale, N.J.: Lawrence Erlbaum Associates, in preparation, 1981.

Gibson, E. J., Shurliff, A., & Yonas, A. A utilization of spelling patterns by deaf and hearing subjects. In H. Levin & J. P. Williams (Eds.), *Basic studies on reading*. New York: Basic Books, 1970.

Golinkoff, R. M., & Rosinski, R. R. Decoding, semantic processing, and reading comprehension skill. *Child Development*, 1976, *47*, 252–258.

Goodman, K. S. On the psycholinguistic method of teaching reading. In F. Smith (Ed.), *Psycholinguistics and reading*. New York: Holt, Rinehart, & Winston, 1973.

Hugo, V. *Les Miserables*. 1862. (Available through New York: Amsco School Publications, Inc.)

Kolers, P. A. Three stages or reading. In H. Levin & J. P. Williams (Eds.), *Basic studies on reading*. New York: Basic Books, 1970.

Kolers, P. A. Pattern-analyzing disability in poor readers. *Developmental Psychology*, 1975, *11*, 282–290.

LaBerge, D. Attention and the measurement of perceptual learning. *Memory & Cognition*, 1973, *1*, 268–276.

LaBerge, D., & Samuels, J. Toward a theory of automatic information processing in reading. *Cognitive Psychology*, 1974, *6*, 293–323.

Levin, H., & Turner, A. Sentence structure and the eye–voice span. In H. Levin, E. J. Gibson, & J. J. Gibson (Eds.), *The analysis of reading skill*. Final Report Project No. 5–1213, from Cornell University to US Office of Education, December 1968.

Mason, M. Reading ability and letter search time: Effects of orthographic structure defined by single-letter positional frequency. *Journal of Experimental Psychology: General*, 1975, *104*, 146–166.

Massaro, D. W. *Understanding language*. New York: Academic Press, 1975.

Massaro, D. W. Letter information and orthographic context in word perception. *Journal of Experimental Psychology: Human Perception and Performance*, 1979, *5*, 595–609.

Massaro, D., & Taylor, G. *Reading ability and the utilization of orthographic structure in reading*. Technical report No. 515., July 1979. Wisconsin Research and Development Center for Individualized Schooling.

McConkie, G., & Zola, D. Language constraints and the functional stimulus in reading. In C. Perfetti & A. Lesgold (Eds.), *Interactive processes in reading*. Hillsdale, N.J.: Lawrence Erlbaum Associates, in press, 1981.

Meyer, D. E., Schvaneveldt, R. W., & Ruddy, M. G. Functions of graphemic and phonemic codes in visual word recognition. *Memory & Cognition*, 1974, *2*, 309–321.

Miller, G. A., Bruner, J. S., & Postman, L. Familiarity of letter sequences and tachistoscopic identification. *Journal of General Psychology*, 1954, *50*, 129–139.

Neisser, U. Visual search. *Scientific American*, 1964, *210*, 94–102.

Neisser, U. *Cognitive psychology*. Englewood Cliffs, N.J.: Prentice–Hall, 1967.

Osgood, C. E., & Hoosain, R. Salience of the word as a unit in the perception of language. *Perception and Psychophysics*, 1974, *15*, 168–192.

Perfetti, C., Goldman, S. R., & Hogoboam, T. Reading skill in the identification of words in discourse context. *Memory & Cognition*, 1979, *7*(9), 273–282.

Posnansky, C., & Rayner, K. Visual-feature and response components in a picture–word interference task with beginning and skilled readers. *Journal of Experimental Child Psychology*, 1977, *24*, 440–460.

Posner, M. I., & Mitchell, R. Chronometric analysis of classification. *Psychological Review*, 1967, *74*, 392–409.

Posner, Z. Personal communication, April 1980.

Rayner, K., & McConkie, G. W. Perceptual processes in reading: The perceptual spans. In A. S. Reber & D. L. Scarborough (Eds.), *Toward a psychology of reading*. Hillsdale, N.J.: Lawrence Erlbaum Associates, 1977.

Rayner, K., & Posnansky, C. Stages of processing in word identification. *Journal of Experimental Psychology: General*, 1978, *107*, 64–80.

Reicher, G. M. Perceptual recognition as a function of the meaningfulness of the material. *Journal of Experimental Psychology*, 1969, *81*, 275–280.

Rips, L. J., Shoben, E. J., & Smith, E. E. Semantic distance and the verification of semantic relations. *Journal of Verbal Learning and Verbal Behavior*, 1973, *12*, 1–20.

Rozin, P., & Gleitman, L. R. The structure and acquisiton of reading: The reading process and the acquisition of alphabetic principle. In A. S. Reber & D. L. Scarborough (Eds.), *Toward a psychology of reading*. Hillsdale, N.J.: Lawrence Erlbaum Associates, 1977.

Rubenstein, H., Lewis, S. S., & Rubenstein, M. A. Evidence for phonemic recoding in visual word recognition. *Journal of Verbal Learning and Verbal Behavior*, 1971, *10*, 645–657.

Simon, H. A. *The sciences of the artificial*. Cambridge: MIT Press, 1969.

Singer, M. H. The primacy of visual information in the analysis of letter strings. *Perception & Psychophysics*, 1980, *27*(2), 153–162.

Singer, M. H., Lappin, J. S., & Moore, L. P. The interference of various word parts on color naming in the Stroop test. *Perception & Psychophysics*, 1975, *18*(3), 191–193.

Smith, F. *Psycholinguistics and reading*. New York: Holt, Rinehart, & Winston, 1973.

Spoehr, K. T., & Smith, E. E. The role of orthographic and phonotactic rules in perceiving letter patterns. *Journal of Experimental Psychology: Human Perception and Performance*, 1975, *104*, 21–34.

Stanovich, K. E., & Bauer, D. W. Experiments on the spelling-to-sound regularity effect in word recognition. *Memory & Cognition*, 1978, *6*(4), 410–415.

Stroop, J. R. Studies of interference in serial verbal reactions. *Journal of Experimental Psychology*, 1935, *18*, 643–662.

Venezky, R. *The structure of English orthography*. The Hague: Moriton and Co., 1970.

Venezky, R., & Massaro, D. The role of orthographic regularity in word recognition. In L. Resnick & P. Weaver (Eds.), *Theory and practice of early reading*. Hillsdale, N.J.: Lawrence Erlbaum Associates, 1980.

Weber, R. M. First graders' use of grammatical context in reading. In H. Levin & J. P. Williams (Eds.), *Basic studies on reading*. New York: Basic Books, 1970.

Weber, R. M. Reading. In R. Wardhaugh & H. D. Brown (Eds.), *A survey of applied linguistics*. Ann Arbor: The University of Michigan Press, 1976.

Wheeler, D. D. Processes in word recognition. *Cognitive Psychology*, 1970, *1*, 59–85.

Willows, D. M., & MacKinnon, G. E. Selective reading: Attention to the "unattended" lines. *Canadian Journal of Psychology*, 1973, *27*(3), 292–304.

# READING DISABILITY:
# Introduction

Martin H. Singer
and Keith E. Stanovich

The first step in *mis*understanding the research on reading disability is to take seriously the terminology. Specialists diagnose children as dyslexic and yet, a decade ago, the National Advisory Committee on Dyslexia and Related Reading Disorders "unanimously concluded that there was no prospect of arriving at a definition of dyslexia which could be accorded general acceptance [p. 9, HEW, 1969]." In making this decision, the Committee considered but dismissed definitions such as "an inability to read understandingly due to a central lesion [Dorland's Illustrated Medical Dictionary, 1957]" or a "disorder in children, who despite conventional classroom experience, fail to attain the language skills of reading . . . commensurate with their intellectual abilities [World Federation of Neurology, 1968]."

It should irritate the critical reader that despite a paucity of neurological evidence, a medical dictionary attributes reading failure to a central lesion. Given this definition, one wonders if the same source would describe an inability to compose music as the result of a central lesion. How, exactly, would this central lesion prevent reading? The explanatory net of a central lesion is seemingly large enough to include any failure. The definition provided by the World Federation of Neurology only restates in stilted language that dyslexia represents instances of reading failure for which we lack explanation. Neither definition provides precise etiological or clinical claims. Both definitions imply that if we understood the reason for a child's reading failure, the child would suffer from something else, not dyslexia. Perhaps this nonsense prompted Money (1962) to define dyslexia simply as "defective reading."

Other diagnostic labels also fail to relay useful information. Teachers often describe a child as suffering from a reading deficit. What this means remains unclear. Imagine the novice tennis player who consistently drills his or her serve into the net. He or she turns to a professional tennis instructor for help. The tennis instructor watches the novice for a while and then shakes his or her head slowly, sadly informing the poor server that he or she suffers from a serving disability. The value of this observation parallels the value of the diagnosis that a child has a reading disability. These labels thinly disguise the absence of any real understanding of reading problems. These terms also prevent communication between teachers, researchers, and the concerned community.

Popular descriptions of reading failure (Simpson 1979) add to the confusion. In her book, *Reversals: A Personal Account of Victory over Dyslexia*, Simpson "explains" that: "there was something wrong with my brain . . . I seemed to be like other children, but was not like them: I could not learn to read or spell . . . when I was 22 it was diagnosed . . . I was dyslexic [preface]." This personal account, however, fails to clarify how dyslexia differs from other reading problems. Simpson reports only that her reading failure was not *ordinary*. She recalls being told that: "It's as I suspected . . . Yours is not the functional illiteracy of night school students . . . Your errors are not *ordinary* spelling errors. Hasn't anyone told you you have dyslexia?" Predictably, Simpson responded, "Lysdexia?" only perpetuating the myth that a tendency to reverse letters somehow causes reading failure (Pp. 169–170). Later, Simpson again states (without any strong evidence) that: "It did not surprise me to learn that the seat of the disorder is in the brain. [p. 205]"

The present treatment of reading failure attempts to avoid this use of empty diagnostic labels. Instead, it is assumed that reading failure occurs for a variety of reasons and proposes that diagnostic labels reflect those reasons (e.g., an inability to distinguish visual forms; to associate sound and visual stimuli). In order to appreciate the heterogeneity of reading failures, this section reviews the different types of experimental evidence on poor reading. Chapters 3 and 4 review the relationship of context use and the ability to handle ordered information to poor reading (Singer). Chapter 5 reviews evidence that relates decoding problems to poor reading (Stanovich) and Chapter 6 discusses some of the known neurological correlates to acquired reading failure (Staller). In addition, Chapter 2 provides an introduction to the types of approaches used to investigate disabled reading and a corresponding critique of prevailing research methods in reading disability research.

## Agreement, Disagreement, and the Spirit of Science

The reader will be aided in interpreting the research literature if he or she comes to some understanding of the attitudes of the scientific community from which the research originates (for a more complete discussion, see Bronowski, 1956, 1973, 1977; Cournand, 1977; Popper, 1963, 1972). This is particularly true in the reading field where attitudes that are antithetical to the spirit of science have continually impeded progress. For example, the "phonics" versus "whole-word" debate of the 1960s had a tendency to develop along conservative/liberal political lines. This unscientific acrimony damages the field. It delays the advancement of theory and curricula ("I won't consider this; it involves phonics!") and jeopardizes the reading researcher's standing with the interested community (e.g., teachers and parents).

The scientist is engaged in a search for the truth about the natural world. It follows that the scientist admits that he or she does *not* possess the full, absolute truth. Collectively, scientists pool their resources to cross-check each other (a simple way of thinking about how science works) and eliminate some of the errors in their models of certain processes (e.g., reading). They cannot however, eliminate all errors. It is with this view that we should approach the reading literature. For example, one of the reviews in this section (Chapter 5) reflects experience in the laboratory and suggests an important role for phonological coding in reading success. The chapter represents what that researcher (K. Stanovich) considers a "best guess" as to what causes reading failure. Thus, the information presented in this section is not a final statement on what causes reading failure, but the present state of our gropings toward an understanding of the problem. Of course, we must *act* on the best knowledge currently available, however imperfect. But every act should be viewed as a tentative hypothesis that we will abandon for an alternative whenever the evidence dictates that our hypothesis is untenable.

In the foregoing discussion, science has been characterized as the pooling of resources in order to attain a more accurate description of certain processes. The *critical tradition* of science is important to this pooling. Only by criticizing the ideas emanating from each observer do scientists progress beyond the understanding attained by a single individual. It is necessary that the critical tradition be maintained for science to progress. Thus, it should be clear that the idea of an "authority," a person who interprets and/or dictates the truth to others, is completely antithetical to the critical tradition of science, where the mechanism of progress involves submitting one's idea to others for criticism. If scientists recognized an individual as the sole repository of truth, they would undermine the rationale for curiosity-driven research ("Why examine this question if authority $X$ has already concluded $Y$?").

Unfortunately, the reading field has been prone to the "authority syndrome" and has often been plagued by a lack of a critical attitude. Coltheart (1979) has documented how mistaken concepts about reading readiness have been promulgated because of uncritical acceptance of incorrect generalizations from some early studies. We are all aware of the "cults" that have grown up around certain individuals and curricula. Unfortunately, as with real cults, these schools of thought (to use a less pejorative term) often withdraw beyond a veil of beliefs that are beyond question, and the resulting absence of a critical tradition isolates them from the mainstream of science. Theoretical and empirical progress become virtually impossible under such conditions. Hopefully, our emphasis on the complexity of the issues involved in reading research will lead to skepticism regarding claims of the "one right way" to teach reading.

Objectivity is a value that is fundamental to science and simply means that we let nature "speak for itself" without imposing our wishes on it. Cournand (1977) has stated that in striving toward objectivity scientists must: "avoid the undisciplined introduction of subjective elements [and] prevent their desires and aversions from penetrating their observations of the phenomena that they study and their analyses of these observations [p. 700]." The fact that this goal is not 100% attainable should not dissuade us from holding objectivity as a value (this would be confusing what "is" the case with what "ought" to be). The sorry state of fields that have abandoned objectivity is perhaps the strongest argument for holding to it as a value. To use a convenient and well-known example, the inability of ESP researchers to screen out subjective wishes and desires from their observations has filled their field with charlatans and scandal, made progress impossible, and alienated a scientific world that was once quite supportive of the field (Hansel, 1980; Marks & Kammann, 1980).

If a student of reading has an understanding of the role that the aforementioned attitudes play in the scientific process he or she will be able to interpret the research literature more meaningfully and apply the findings to practice more accurately. In short, the student will be able to avoid a feeling of anger or frustration. For example, some students become annoyed with the research literature because it always seems that if there is a scientist arguing one side of an issue, you can find one who will argue the other side. It always seems that after reading a study arguing for Theory $X$, you can find a study that argues against Theory $X$. This view of research, quite understandably, leads to feelings of futility and cynicism. This view is, however, incorrect. It is incorrect because it fails to realize that all knowledge is to some extent imperfect. If one believes that scientific knowledge must be perfect, then when confronted with conflicting studies, one is tempted to think that truth is being fudged in one study (leading to a feeling of cynicism), or that the issue is undecidable (leading to a feeling of futility). In science, though, there are very few "crucial" experiments: experiments that completely decide a given issue. Each experiment is to some extent "fuzzy" in its implications. Issues are decided only after many such studies, each somewhat flawed in its own way, point in a similar direction and display a pattern that is largely consistent with a particular theory. This process of sifting through results and constructing an explanation from "fuzzy" experiments requires tolerance. This tolerance comes in two forms. One is the tolerance for divergent opinion, obviously necessary if any sort of critical tradition is to be sustained. The second aspect of tolerance involves an appreciation for prior work. Science is a cumulative endeavor. Our understanding of reading will not improve by wiping the slate clean. Instead, our understanding improves as we make theoretical adjustments and empirical additions to an existing data base.

In summary, teachers should not succumb to the appeal of curricula that claim to teach all children to read or a research result that "explains" reading failure. Instead, one should "hold out" for a theory that can withstand *objective* and *critical* analysis that receives support from a variety of sources. When data from a variety of paradigms (laboratory, training, remediation) *converge* to support the same model of reading, it increases the likelihood that the theory accurately describes reading. Still, even with this converging evidence, critical scientists will batter away at this model and attempt to improve this description, not "destroying" the model but building upon it. These modifications must, however, be constrained by the data (objectivity, again). Differences in methodology will sometimes yield conflicting results, but ultimately these different perspectives will result in a new convergence and our next best guess about how people read and what causes reading failure.

## REFERENCES

Bronowski, J. *Science and human values*. New York: Harper & Row, 1956.

Bronowski, J. *The ascent of man*. London: British Broadcasting Company, 1973.

Bronowski, J. *A sense of the future*. Cambridge, Mass.: MIT Press, 1977.

Coltheart, M. When can children learn to read—and when should they be taught? In T. G. Waller and G. E. MacKinnon (Eds.), *Reading Research: Advances in theory and practice* (Vol 1), New York: Academic Press, 1979.

Cournand, A. The code of the scientist and its relationship to ethics. *Science*, 1977, *198*, 699–705.

*Dorland's Illustrated Medical Dictionary*. Philadelphia: W. B. Saunders, 1957.

Hansel, C. E. M. *ESP and parapsychology: A critical re-evaluation*. Buffalo, N.Y.: Prometheus Books, 1980.

Health, Education, and Welfare (HEW). *Reading disorders in the United States: On dyslexia and related reading disorders*. Reprinted by Developmental Learning Materials, Chicago, 1969.

Marks, D., & Kammann, R. *The psychology of the psychic*. Buffalo, N.Y.: Prometheus Books, 1980.

Money, J. *Reading disability*. Baltimore: Johns Hopkins Press, 1962.

Popper, K. R. *Conjectures and refutations*. New York: Basic Books, 1963.

Popper, K. R. *Objective knowledge*. Oxford: Oxford University Press, 1972.

Simpson, E. *Reversals: A personal account of victory over dyslexia*. Boston: Houghton–Mifflin, 1979.

*World Federation of Neurology*. Research group on developmental dyslexia and world illiteracy. April 3–5 1968.

# 2 Reading Disability Research: A Misguided Search for Differences

Martin H. Singer
*Bell Laboratories*

Reading disability researchers assault us with claims about *differences*. Indeed, the literature is reminiscent of the prologue to *A Tale of Two Cities*. We learn that good and poor readers differ in decoding ability and that they do not; that their use of context differs and that it is similar; that pedagogical factors succeed in explaining reading ability differences and that they fail; that visual processing differences explain differences in reading ability and that they explain nothing. A paucity of agreement fitfully coexists with this surplus of differences and what Neisser (1967) wrote more than a decade ago about reading applies to reading disability research today:

> Reading . . . has been a source of continuous controversy since the nineteenth century. Yet despite its liveliness, an author who approaches this subject has some reason to fear that his readers may find it tiresome or even painful. In the last 20 years, psychologists have made tall mountains out of several molehills . . . with discouraging results [p. 105].

Some attribute the discouraging research results to the complexity of the reading process and the variety of reasons for which a child may fail to acquire reading skill. Although one cannot deny the complexity of reading or the variety of reading disabilities, the "painfulness" of the reading and the variety of disabilities make the literature interesting rather than "tiresome." Reading disability research suffers instead from the application of an inappropriate experimental design, an improper approach to the problem.

The following sections discuss the inadequate response of traditional experimental procedures to problems plaguing reading disability research. These problems concern: (1) the **heterogeneity** of poor readers; (2) the absence of **task equivalence** in comparisons of various abilities; and (3) the **abundance of differences** between good and poor readers. The discussion of these issues supports the claim that experimental approaches to the complexity of reading disability, rather than the complexity itself, explain the controversy and corresponding "pain" of disability research. The discussion is intended to provide guidelines for evaluating the literature on disabled reading (presented in subsequent chapters) and to supply a context in which to handle conflicting research results. The discussion also suggests an alternative experimental approach to reading disability. This approach recognizes the heterogeneity of reading disability and estimates the relative importance of various skills in explaining reading ability and reading failure. Recognizing that several factors contribute to reading disability can also help in avoiding a competitive search for one factor that explains reading disability and will result in securing a prestigious prize. Such competitive searches (a **Nobel Prize Syndrome**) impede the development of a comprehensive model of disabled reading.

## Walking on the Bad Side of Heterogeneity

The prevailing approach to disability research contrasts groups that differ in their reading ability. These experimental designs define good and poor readers according to some criterion and subsequently compare the performance of these readers on tasks that relate to reading. Thus, children reading below grade level might be compared to children above their grade level on a series of visual and auditory discrimination tasks. Researchers reason that dissimilarity between the groups' performance on any of the tasks will suggest which skills predict poor reading.

Researchers *sometimes* recognize that members within each reading group vary from each other. In other words, some researchers recognize that all poor readers are not alike and that good readers may also read well for different reasons. Moreover, extremely poor readers differ from moderately poor readers as do exceptional readers from mediocre ones. This variability (**heterogeneity**) tends to obscure all comparisons between groups of good and poor readers. Whereas one poor reader may manifest some difficulty on a task designed to measure memory capacity another poor reader might suffer from a subtle hearing deficit but possess an unimpaired memory (Singer & Crouse, 1981).

Researchers sometimes circumvent such problems by comparing extremely different groups: Instead of comparing below average readers with above average readers within some population, researchers contrast the performance of the best 10% with the worst 10% of readers. This strategy increases the *power* of the comparison (or the likelihood that the two groups will differ on some task). According to this experimental logic, extreme groups attenuate the obscuring effects of heterogeneity in two ways. First, removing the moderately poor and mediocre readers from the comparisons also removes a substantial source of variability: Extremely poor readers are more similar to each other than to all of those individuals who read below their grade level. Second, researchers hope that differences between such extreme groups would be great enough to overcome the obscuring effects due to heterogeneity.

Experimentalists also attempt to increase the strength of these comparisons by removing confounding variables. As an example, intelligence correlates with reading ability. Stated in another way, knowing someone's IQ score permits some prediction about his or her reading ability. This correlation suggests that groups varying in their reading ability may also vary on intelligence measures. Differences between the groups on task performance may therefore reflect intelligence differences rather than varying reading ability. To eliminate this competing possibility researchers usually *control* for IQ, ensuring similar IQ averages for both groups. Comparable attempts are made to eliminate factors pertaining to socioeconomic status.

Vellutino, Harding, Phillips, and Steger (1975) provide an example of this approach to reading disability research. In a study testing the ability of poor and normal readers to associate verbal and visual information, Vellutino et al. described their experimental subjects as children:

> from . . . middle to upper-middle socioeconomic areas. . . . Differentiation of the poor and normal readers was based upon two measures of reading achievement. . . . Only those children scoring two or more years below grade level were chosen for the poor reader sample. Conversely, candidates for the normal reading group were to have scores at or above grade level . . . there [were] the poor and normal readers in . . . Performance and Full Scale IQ [p. 6].

Vellutino et al. stress that they intended to study "specific reading disability" or reading problems: "not . . . attributable to subnormal intelligence . . . inadequate home or school environment, or other extrinsic factors [p. 3]." Thus, Vellutino et al. implemented the standard research paradigm as well as those strategies designed to increase the power of their comparisons.

These traditional responses to heterogeneity among poor readers *only appear* reasonable. If differences exist between good and poor readers, the experimental design exploited by Vellutino et al. should capture those differences, but one must question the relevance of differences obtained by contrasting extreme, narrowly defined reading groups. For one thing, intelligence, socioeconomic status, and family and school environment explain much of the variation in reading ability (Jencks, 1979). These factors usually predict individuals reading ability. Investigations of variation in reading ability that control for these factors *necessarily examine a small proportion of the variation in reading ability*. Figure 2.1 illustrates the variation in reading examined by the Vellutino et al. study.

Suppose that this type of design yields a "significant" difference between

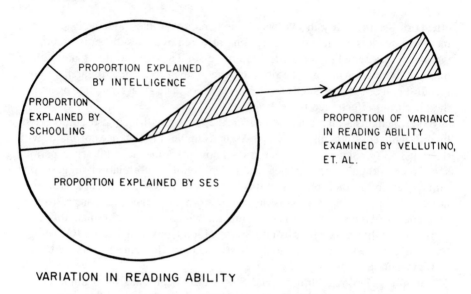

PROPORTION EXPLAINED BY INTELLIGENCE

PROPORTION EXPLAINED BY SCHOOLING

PROPORTION EXPLAINED BY SES

PROPORTION OF VARIANCE IN READING ABILITY EXAMINED BY VELLUTINO, ET. AL.

VARIATION IN READING ABILITY

FIG. 2.1.   If the "pie" represents variation in reading ability and factors such as IQ and income explain a substantial portion of this variation, an experimental design that eliminates these factors examines only a small piece of the pie.

good and poor readers on some task. For example, Vellutino et al. reported that good and poor readers differed on a visual–verbal integration task (a task that required children to remember associations between visual forms and verbal labels). This information can explain only the variation in reading ability not explained by intelligence and environmental factors (Fig. 2.1). Furthermore, even within extremely disabled groups, a variety of deficits exist. The paradigm employed by Vellutino et al. provides no information on the relative importance of *their particular* difference in explaining the reading ability of these extreme groups (a clue to the potential importance, though, is that group factors account for only 25% of the variance in task performance). Thus, Vellutino et al., implementing the traditional approach to disability research, have systematically reduced the potential importance of their study. Their attempt to circumvent issues pertaining to heterogeneity produces results with extremely limited application.[1]

This experimental approach also accounts for much of the controversy in

---

[1]Traditional experimental approaches to heterogeneity encounter another serious problem. As already stated, IQ usually correlates with reading ability. The standard procedure employed by Vellutino et al. examines a group of poor readers for whom this normal correlation disappears. The absence of this correlation may actually reflect the interesting characteristic of the poor reading group: that they read poorly despite normal intelligence. Alternatively, the absence of a normally present correlation might suggest that measurement error mars the validity of either the reading ability or IQ test. The group may represent a statistical quirk. This possibility attenuates further the importance of differences between good readers and narrowly defined groups of poor readers.

disability research. Researchers who use the approach outlined previously will still obtain a variety of differences between good and poor readers (despite their attempts to compare extreme groups). If they invest too much in the parochial focus of their study, these researchers might argue much like the blind men who stumble upon different parts of an elephant (cf. Chapter 1). For example, researchers often report that good and poor readers differ on difficult perceptual discrimination tasks (Bakker, 1970). Some might interpret this data as conflicting with the Vellutino et al. study because Vellutino et al. only reported differences on a visual–verbal integration task but not on the perceptual tasks. One must remember, though, that different researchers can glimpse only that aspect of reading disability that lies within the focus of their investigative tools. (i.e., the specific tasks in their study). The variety of reading disabilities, the variety of experimental tasks, and the complexity of the reading process all predict that researchers will find many differences between good and poor readers. Unfortunately as the focus of experiments narrows, the number of "significant differences" between good and poor readers will increase. In the same way, an increase in the number of blind men touching different parts of an elephant will increase the number of different descriptions. The literature on reading disability overflows with disputes among researchers that reflect only the confidence of blind men in their points of view.[2]

## Problems with Task Equivalence

As already described, traditional research on disabled reading examines the performance of good and poor readers across various tasks. Typically, researchers attempt to find some task on which the two groups perform similarly. They then adjust the task in some way that causes the groups to perform disparately. Often the two (or more) tasks attempt to measure different underlying skills. Thus, one task might measure visual skills and the other verbal skills. A researcher might reason that if the two groups perform similarly on the visual task but differently on the verbal task, then verbal abilities account for **variance** in reading ability.

Again, this approach *appears* reasonable. Consider, though, an extreme example. Suppose a researcher believes that verbal skills but not visual skills explain variation in reading ability. To prove this, he or she compares groups of poor and good readers on their ability to locate an $x$ in a letter string (the visual task). He or she then contrasts their ability to read and explain a sentence

---

[2]Researchers satisfied with the explanatory power of *their* obtained difference bemoan attempts to isolate other factors. Reading researchers sometime bring to mind the characters in Raskolnikov's dream who suffered from a "horrible, unprecedented and unparalleled plague . . . the men who had been infected . . . immediately became possessed and went mad. But never, never had men considered themselves so wise and implacably right as these infected men . . . Each one thought that he and he alone was the sole repository of truth, and suffered torments looking at the others, weeping and wringing his hands as he did so [Crime and Punishment, p. 570]."

from the Tax Law Code (the verbal task). Not surprisingly, he or she demonstrates his point. Both groups easily find the $x$ but only good readers have any success with the tax law. The researcher concludes that verbal skills discriminate good from poor readers.

The experimental design clearly biases the outcome of the study. The two tasks *vary* in their difficulty. The absence of **task equivalence** prevents any conclusions about cognitive differences between the two groups. If we compare the two groups on tasks that tap different abilities but those tasks vary in their difficulty we cannot conclude anything about ability differences between the groups. If good and poor readers both succeeded in finding $x$'s in a printed line but only good readers could explain a sentence from the Tax Law Code, we could not conclude that good and poor readers differed in verbal skill but not visual discrimination. We could only observe the similarity of good and poor readers on easy tasks but their dissimilarity on difficult tasks. Furthermore, as the difficulty of a task increases, it begins to measure less easily defined skills. Clearly, we cannot claim that explaining tax law involves only "verbal ability." The task measures aspects of intelligence as well as reading skill.

Most experimentalists will avoid constructing tasks that are as distinctly difficult as these. Yet, the absence of task equivalence appears in more subtle forms, confounding the interpretation of many reading disability studies. A recent study by DiVesta, Hayward, and Orlando (1979) provides an example of how

### SUBSEQUENT TEXT CONDITION
(SHEEP) was probably the second (ANIMAL) to be used for (CLOTHING). One reason is because (SHEEP) have been (RAISED) in many parts of the world. We do not know where people first thought of cutting off the sheep's wool and spinning it into yarn. However, we do know that very early in history people from all parts of the world were weaving wool clothes.

### RUNNING TEXT CONDITION
Modern skating really came of age with the successful development of artificial ice. It is true that natural ice gives better spring to the skater, but it is practically impossible to control the wind that ripples water as it freezes naturally. Artificial (ICE) is easily (FROZEN) to provide a glasslike (SURFACE/ICE). Man-made (ICE) now permits us to (SKATE) all year.

FIG. 2.2. An example of materials used by DiVesta et al. (1979).

the absence of task equivalence obscures the interpretation of experimental results. DiVesta et al. examined poor and good readers' use of context. They required children to fill in blanks that occurred within short paragraphs (a cloze task). In one condition (Running Text), information from previous sentences allowed the children to fill in the blanks. In a second condition (Subsequent Text), only information from succeeding sentences provided information that helped children fill the blanks. Figure 2.2 illustrates the two conditions. DiVesta et al. reported that both reading groups performed well on the Running Text Condition but the two groups differed on the Subsequent Text Condition. DiVesta et al. concluded that good readers are those who develop: "the expectation that information is located 'in the text' rather than just at the point of fixation . . . [and] that instruction which unduly emphasizes accuracy in word recognition may be incompatible with developing the expectation that information occurs in Subsequent Text. . . . The less skilled reader has not acquired a full appreciation of [the subsequent text's] value [p. 104]." They argue, in effect, that the use of subsequent text discriminates poor from good readers.

DiVesta, Hayward, and Orlando (1979) expressed interest in satisfying criticisms related to the equivalence of the Running Text and Subsequent Text conditions. They stated that:

> Obviously, the desired objective was to obtain separate measures of the two strategies [use of Running Text and Subsequent Text] and not to make one measure more difficult than the other. . . . In order to minimize the possibility that an alternative explanation of the data (e.g., difficulty) was more tenable than the hypothesized explanation (i.e., use of Running Text and Subsequent Text strategies) . . . the paragraphs for both measures [were] from similar sources [p. 99].

Despite DiVesta et al.'s effort to use similarly difficult paragraphs in both tasks, the two tasks vary in difficulty. The tasks vary in the degree to which they strain memory, rely on intelligence, reflect strategic skill, and demand search skills.

In the Running Text Condition children could perform the task without consulting their memories for integrated information about the text. The immediate text supplied the solution to the cloze task. The Subsequent Text Condition required that children retain information from the text and integrate that information prior to solving the cloze. Furthermore, the Subsequent Text Condition placed greater demands on inferential or logical skills—the types of abilities we normally associate with intelligence. Also, the Subsequent Text Condition required that children adopt an unusual strategy. Although research suggests that competent readers exploit information up to 12 letters outside central vision (Rayner & McConkie, 1977), no one has seriously suggested that competent readers sample information three to four sentences ahead of their fixation. Thus, children who performed well in the Subsequent Text Condition successfully adopted a *novel* strategy. This may have reflected a strategic sophistication that poor readers lacked. Finally, the Subsequent Text Condition required children to engage in a directed visual search. They had to conjure up a vague impression of the critical information and then search for that information.

These differences allow one to suggest that the Running and Subsequent Text Conditions *vary in difficulty* (that *both* groups performed worse on the Subsequent Text Condition corroborates this suggestion). Children who performed well on the Subsequent Text Condition may have possessed better memories or enjoyed superior intelligence. Such factors correlate with reading skill. Thus, differences in memory or intelligence might predict: (1) who reads well; and (2) who performs well in a Subsequent Text Condition. That is, if we first consider the extent to which intelligence or memory predicts reading ability, performance on the Subsequent Text Condition provides little additional predictive power. Thus, the suggested relationship between performance on the Subsequent Task and reading ability is **spurious** (Kenny, 1979; Singer & Crouse, 1981; Suppes, 1970). As Fig. 2.3 illustrates, the relationship can be explained by a third factor (memory, intelligence). Also, because the tasks vary in difficulty one could conclude that good and poor readers perform similarly on easy tasks (e.g., Running Text) but dissimilarly on difficult tasks (e.g., Subsequent Text). One cannot conclude with DiVesta et al. (1979) that the use of Subsequent Text predicts differences in reading ability. The absence of task equivalence allows a competing interpretation of the results.

## Differences, Differences Everywhere

The **abundance of differences** between good and poor readers relates to the previously discussed issue of heterogeneity. The complexity of reading predicts that children will fail to read for various reasons. In addition, the dependence of reading on intelligence, language, and perceptual skill implies that poor readers will compare unfavorably to good readers on a variety of tasks.

Recently, Jackson and McClelland (1979) reported that poor readers performed worse than good readers on *several* tasks (*all* the reaction time tasks) examined in their study. These tasks measured speed of letter naming, word naming, and paragraph reading as well as aspects of comprehension and intelligence. The abundance of differences complements the experimental procedures outlined previously. Almost *any* task implemented by a researcher should succeed in obtaining a "significant difference" between poor and good readers. Balance beam skill, handwriting, and finger tapping may discriminate good from poor readers. Jackson and McClelland, in discussing their data, state that: "Any conclusion we might have drawn from *differences on just one of these tasks* spanning the range of task would have been highly misleading [p. 55]." Un-

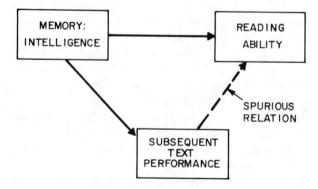

FIG. 2.3.   An illustration of the suggestion that a third factor (e.g., intelligence) explains the difference between good and poor readers on the Subsequent Text Condition in the DiVesta et al. study.

fortunately, experimentalists have been content to report such differences without an estimate of their relative importance in reading ability. There are, of course, a few exceptions (Doehring, 1976; Jackson & McClelland, 1979; Shankweiler & Liberman, 1972). Generally, though, researchers have bitten off less than they can chew, ferreting out easily found differences but neglecting to explain how these differences predict reading ability.

Jackson and McClelland's (1979) report that poor and good readers differ on several tasks supports Doehring's (1976) criticism of the unitary hypothesis approach to reading disability. A unitary hypothesis approach to reading disability assumes that a single factor accounts for variation in reading ability. This approach contradicts intuition because a breakdown in any of several mechanisms could disrupt fluent reading (cf. the elephant in Chapter 1). Doehring argued that researchers might consider the disabled reading population as containing several subgroups. Members of a subgroup would share similar deficits but the subgroups would vary from each other.

If researchers adopted Doehring's approach, disability research might avoid senseless claims about a single factor accounting for all reading disorders. Instead, researchers would recognize that conflicting results can reflect different samples (e.g., subgroups) of poor readers or that poor and good readers differ in a variety of areas. Varying subgroups and the narrow investigative tools described earlier can account for much of the disagreement in the disability literature. A rational approach to the area, however, will probably not prevail.

Smith's (1973) argument that poor reading results from an insensitivity to the "psycholinguistic" nature of reading represents an instance of exclusive focus on a single factor. He and Goodman (1965, 1973) have argued that a failure to realize that text conveys meaning explains reading disability. Their claim lacks solid empirical support (cf. Chapter 3), but more distressing is their corresponding attack on all other explanations of reading failure. Smith (1973) denies the contribution of other skills (e.g., phonics, word identification) to competent reading. He insists, for example, that knowledge of letter-to-sound correspondences *interferes* with successful reading. One of Smith's "Twelve easy ways to make reading difficult" is to teach phonics. According to him:

Reading is not accomplished by decoding and . . . phonics is conspicuously unreliable and cumbersome . . . [it is] remarkable that anyone should expect children ever to try to learn . . . an arbitrary . . . system. Even if a child were gifted and gullible enough to learn such a system, there is absolutely no evidence that he could ever actually use it [phonics] in the process of reading [and] it is easy to show that any attempt to read by [the] integration of phonic rules could result only in catastrophic overloading of short-term memory. Besides, the use of spelling-to-sound rules to identify words is as absurd as clipping a lawn with nail scissors [p. 186].

The evidence presented in Chapter 1 directly contradicts Smith's attack on the importance of decoding skills: The use of orthographic structure and rapid letter-to-sound translation is part of a competent reading strategy. Also, a recent study (Doctor & Coltheart, 1980) indicates that very young readers obtain meaning through phonological recoding.

In addition to Smith's lack of empirical support, it should be clear that a competent reader's use of higher-level information (e.g., syntax, semantics) does not eliminate the importance of other sources of information (e.g., phonics) in successful reading or in learning to read. Goodman (1965, 1973) shares Smith's sentiments concerning the importance of context in reading and also claims that decoding skills are unimportant to successful reading. He reported that children exploit context in correcting their oral reading errors. He concluded from this *unsurprising* finding that:

> Shotgun teaching of so-called phonic skills to whole classes or groups . . . seems highly questionable. . . . In fact, it is most likely that . . . many children are suffering from difficulties caused by overusing particular learning strategies [e.g., phonics]. . . . I believe we must abandon our concentration on words in teaching reading and develop a . . . methodology which puts the focus . . . on language . . . [p. 643].

Again, neither Goodman nor Smith demonstrated that phonic skills were unimportant in competent reading or useless in explaining disabled reading or unnecessary in teaching reading. They found only that readers were sensitive to context. Their attack on the importance of decoding to competent reading reflects their inability to accept the heterogeneity of reading disability and the variety of factors implicated in competent reading.

## An Alternative Approach

The experimental design criticized in the foregoing attempts to uncover differences between good and poor readers on a variety of tasks. These experiments rarely contribute information on the *relative* importance of particular differences and the obtained differences reflect only the performance of narrowly defined groups on narrowly defined tasks. Figure 2.4 provides a schematic representation of the information obtained through this type of experiment.

An alternative approach restructures investigations so that they conform to the *fiat* of reading research: explaining variation in reading ability. Rather than asking "Do two extreme reading groups, A and B, perform differently on tasks C, D, . . . , and n?" This alternative approach asks "How do skills X, Y, Z . . . , and n combine to cause or explain variation in reading ability?" Figure 2.5 represents this alternative approach, using only a few of the known component reading skills.

This restructured approach attempts to develop a *causal model* of reading ability. A causal model approach avoids many of the problems associated with an atheoretical search for differences between good and poor readers. First, a

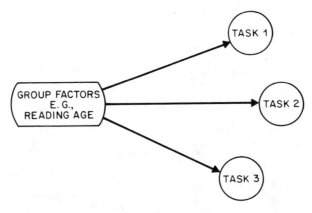

FIG. 2.4.   Examining the performance of different groups on various tasks only suggests how differences in group type predict differences in task performance, not how differences in skills predict differences in reading ability.

causal model design examines all types of readers: *The approach recognizes that readers vary along a continuum* (e.g., bad to good) and that reading ability varies for several reasons. It responds to this heterogeneity by weighing the importance of the various factors. This differs from the traditional response to heterogeneity in reading ability. The experiments outlined earlier eliminate certain factors (e.g., IQ) so that one factor (e.g., verbal ability) might be observed. Traditional designs also examine extreme groups to eliminate obscuring effects due to heterogeneity. As described earlier, both of these procedures limit the applicability of results, failing to explain variation in reading ability. An attempt to construct a causal model, on the other hand, would result in a matrix of data (Table 2.1) that described the contribution of several factors to reading ability.

How does one construct a model of the ways in which various factors predict reading ability? Singer and Crouse (1981) described a simple technique. In that study, Singer and Crouse attempted to explain differences in Reading Comprehension, as measured by a standard reading test. They reasoned that intelligence would affect performance on any type of task, particularly on one involving reasoning. To ensure that their intelligence (IQ) test was different in content from the Reading Comprehension test, they used a measure of Nonverbal IQ (the Ravens) rather than an IQ test with vocabulary and general knowledge subtests. The arrow connecting Nonverbal IQ and Reading Comprehension in Fig. 2.5 indicates Singer and Crouse's assumption that Nonverbal IQ predicts Reading Comprehension. Similarly, Singer and Crouse's model assumes that Nonverbal IQ predicts (or explains *some* of the **variance** in) Letter Discrimination skill, Decoding skill, Vocabulary, and Context-Use skill.

This type of model also makes strong claims about the *independence*, or *relative importance* of component reading skills. For example, the arrow between Context Use and Reading Comprehension in Fig. 2.5 suggests that context use influences reading comprehension. The reader must note, however, that the

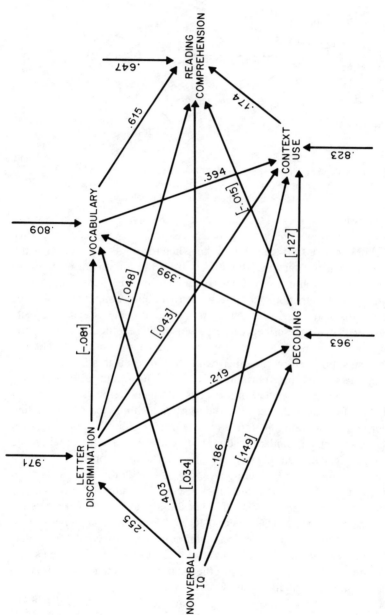

FIG. 2.5. The methodology schematically described above would suggest how differences in certain component reading skills predict variation in reading ability. This model reflects data reported by Singer and Crouse (1981). (Reprinted with permission from the Society for Research on Child Development).

This data matrix indicates the relationship between various reading skills and reading comprehension. The matrix also indicates the relationship of component skills to each other. Adapted from Singer and

TABLE 2.1
Correlations Among Selected Text Scores for Sixth-Graders[a]

|  | 1 | 2 | 3 | 4 | 5 | 6 |
|---|---|---|---|---|---|---|
| 1. IQ (Ravens) | 1.000 | | | | | |
| 2. Letter Discrimination | .255 | 1.000 | | | | |
| 3. Decoding | .205 | .257 | 1.000 | | | |
| 4. Vocabulary | .464 | .124 | .461 | 1.000 | | |
| 5. Context Use (Cloze) | .406 | .172 | .358 | .544 | 1.000 | |
| 6. Reading Comprehension | .413 | .162 | .364 | .755 | .542 | 1.000 |
| Mean | 100.000 | 27.79 | 26.73 | 7.70 | 37.46 | 8.09 |
| Standard Deviation | 15.00 | 8.59 | 10.07 | 1.96 | 12.15 | 2.74 |

[a]$N = 127$ sixth-graders with data on all variables in the table.

model assumes that Nonverbal IQ, Vocabulary, Letter Discrimination skill, and Decoding skill influence Context Use. In other words, Singer and Crouse argued that a good reader may have good context-use skills but this skill depends on their Vocabulary and Nonverbal IQ and their ability to automatically decode and discriminate letters.

Importantly, such models—and the assumptions that are embedded in these models—can be put to the test. If Context Use fails to affect Reading Comprehension after one first considers the influence of Nonverbal IQ, Vocabulary, Letter Discrimination, and Decoding, then one can argue that the model is supported. Also, if two factors (e.g., Letter Discrimination and Nonverbal IQ) correlate to Reading Comprehension but not to each other (i.e., Letter Discrimination and Nonverbal IQ are uncorrelated) one might argue that both explain *independent* portions of the variance in Reading Comprehension; both predict reading skill for different and separate reasons.

This approach addresses other problems associated with task equivalence. For example, tasks measuring specific skills might be too easy or too difficult. Variation in these tasks will be limited (e.g., all subjects will perform similarly well or poorly) making it impossible to claim *anything* about the skills measured by those tasks and their relation to reading ability. Traditional approaches to disability research, however, base their interpretations on the *absence* of differences. Vellutino, Steger, DeSetto, and Phillips (1975) administered a novel letter-recognition task to good and poor readers and found that all readers performed similarly. They concluded that good and poor readers shared comparable visual memories. Differences on other tasks caused Vellutino et al. to conclude that other factors predict reading ability.

This logic permits an absence of task equivalence to bias results. If someone wanted to demonstrate the unimportance of a certain factor (e.g., visual memory) and the importance of another in explaining reading ability, they could simply administer an extremely hard or easy measure of the first factor. In the alternative approach suggested here, an absence of variation would be sufficient reason to drop a measure from the matrix of correlations in Fig. 2.5.

This approach has obvious limitations: One limit is the number of different component reading skills included in the model; researchers can never be certain that *all* important skills have been examined. A second problem pertains to the test selection. The tests should be decent measures of the skill (e.g., the Decoding Test should measure decoding skill) and the simple model in Singer and Crouse (1981) fails to provide relevant information on the effectiveness of the tests. One possible solution to both problems has been pursued by Frederiksen (1978). Fredericksen has used a **factor analytic** technique that allows him to determine: (1) if various tests measure the same underlying factor; and (2) the number of independent factors predicting a particular skill or ability (e.g., Reading Comprehension). Thus, this approach allows one to include an unlimited number of tests and provides some indication of the tests' **validity** (whether the test measures the intended skill or ability) and independence.

The appeal of these approaches is *not* the superiority of one statistical method (e.g., multiple regression or factor analysis) over another (e.g., analysis of variance). Indeed, one can draw inane conclusions on the basis of a simple correlation. Instead, the appeal of a causal model approach pertains to its attempt to evaluate the contribution of several factors to reading ability. It accepts heterogeneity in reading disability and systematically examines the relation of factors to each other. An attempt to evaluate the contributions of these factors, rather than claiming complete explanatory power for a single factor, would raise the level of debate in the reading disability research literature.

## A caveat

One must always caution against careless claims regarding causality. For example, in the matrix displayed in Table 2.1, one might note a high correlation between Reading Comprehension and Vocabulary. One might suggest that this correlation proves that Vocabulary size explains variation in reading ability. Stated in another way, a researcher might claim that Vocabulary *precedes* and *predicts* reading comprehension. This suggestion, however, overlooks the influence of reading on Vocabulary. Someone who reads well probably reads more often than a poor reader. This increase in experience causes familiarity with several aspects of text, including more and varied words. Consequently, the correlation between Vocabulary and Reading Comprehension might indicate the *influence of reading comprehension vocabulary* and not vice versa. The possibility that reading ability influences the measures implemented in a study often makes difficult the interpretation of correlations. This caveat relates to the condition of *time precedence* in drawing a causal inference.

## Summary

Conflicting results permeate the reading disability literature. Often these conflicts reflect the inadequate response of traditional experimental approaches to: (1)

heterogeneity; (2) issues regarding task equivalence; and (3) the abundance of differences between good and poor readers. The response has been more than inadequate; strategies to circumvent heterogeneity restrict the importance of research results and proliferate the number of different subgroups in investigations of poor reading. An attempt to develop causal models, evaluating the relative importance of differences between good and poor readers, would better serve this research area. The issues discussed in this chapter should cause the reader some skepticism when reviewing the "evidence" in the remainder of this section.

## GLOSSARY

**Abundance of Differences.**   The complexity of reading, or the contribution of several factors to successful reading, would lead us to expect that good and poor readers would differ on a variety of tests (IQ, vocabulary, etc.), backgrounds, and skills. This expectation suggests that it would be extremely easy for a researcher to isolate a difference between good and poor readers on a particular test or skill. The abundance of differences helps explain the controversy in reading disability research.

**Factor Analysis.**   An attempt to isolate explanations (e.g., skills, aptitudes) for performance on different types of tasks. For example, this procedure might uncover a factor that explains performance on IQ, Vocabulary, and Comprehension Tests.

**Heterogeneous.**   "A mixed bag." This description applies to any group whose members are dissimilar. The population of reading-disabled children is heterogeneous because children fail to learn to read for a variety of reasons.

**Homogeneity.**   Researchers sometimes fly in the face of reason and attribute (falsely) homogeneity to the population of reading-disabled children. Homogeneity means similarity and the assumption that all poor readers are similar leads to the Nobel Prize Syndrome.

**Nobel Prize Syndrome.**   Dramatic discoveries lead to Nobel prizes. It is not particularly dramatic to point out that reading failure occurs for various reasons. Perhaps, some researchers maintain that a single factor causes reading failure, and hope that their dramatic discovery will result in a Nobel Prize.

**Spurious Relation.**   A relationship that can be explained by considering a third variable. For example, one might claim that vocabulary size predicts reading skill on the basis of a high correlation between measures of these skills. A third variable such as IQ, though, might explain this relation: Both vocabulary and reading skill tests might measure IQ, or IQ might predict who can acquire a vocabulary and read well. Thus, the relationship between vocabulary and reading skill would be spurious as it can be explained by a third variable, IQ.

**Task Equivalence.**   As used in this chapter, task equivalence refers to the level of difficulty of measures or procedures that assess different abilities.

**Validity.**   This refers to the relationship of a test or task to the attribute that the test measures. A measure is invalid if someone can demonstrate logically or empirically that it fails to test the intended attribute or skill. For example, the distance one can throw a ball is unrelated to, and therefore an invalid measure of reading comprehension.

**Variance.**   Refers to the variations in performance or skill level between two groups or within a single group (i.e., among members of a group). Statistically, variance refers to the range of a distribution of scores.

## REFERENCES

Bakker, D. J. Temporal order perception and reading retardation. In D. Bakker & P. Satz (Eds.), *Specific reading disability*. Rotterdam: Rotterdam University Press, 1970.

DiVesta, F., Hayward, K. G., & Orlando, V. P. Developmental trends in monitoring text for comprehension. *Child Development*, 1979, *50*, 97–105.

Doctor, E. A., & Coltheart, M. Children's use of phonological encoding when reading for meaning. *Memory & Cognition*, 1980, *8*, 195–209.

Doehring, D. G. Evaluation of two models of reading disability. In R. M. Knights & D. J. Bakker (Eds.), *The neuropsychology of learning discorders: Theoretical approaches*. Baltimore, Md.: University Park Press, 1976.

Dostoevsky, F. *Crime and Punishment*, New York: Washington Square Press, 1968. *Crime and Punishment* was first published serially in Russian in Russy Vestnik, St. Petersburg, 1866.

Frederiksen, J. R. *A chronometric study of component skills in reading*. Cambridge, Mass.: Bolt, Beranek, & Newman, 1978. (Report No. 3757, Technical Report No. 2, ONR Contrast N00014–76–C–0461, NR 154–386).

Goodman, K. A linguistic study of cues and miscues in reading. *Elementary English*, 1965, *42*, 639–643.

Goodman, K. S. On the psycholinguistic method of teaching reading. In F. Smith (Ed.), *Psycholinguistics and reading*. New York: Holt, Rinehart, & Winston, 1973.

Jackson, M. D., & McClelland, J. L. Processing determinants of reading speed. *Journal of Experimental Psychology: General*, 1979, *108*, 151–181.

Jencks, C. *Who gets ahead?* New York: Basic Books, 1979.

Kenny, D. A. *Correlation and causality*. New York: John Wiley and Sons, 1979.

Neisser, U. *Cognitive psychology*. Englewood Cliffs, N.J.: Prentice–Hall, 1967.

Rayner, K., & McConkie, G. W. Perceptual processes in reading: The perceptual spans. In A. S. Reber & D. L. Scarborough (Eds.), *Toward a psychology of reading*. Hillsdale, N.Y.: Lawrence Erlbaum Associates, 1977.

Shankweiler, D., & Liberman, I. Y. Misreading: A search for causes. In J. Kavanaugh & I. G. Mattingly (Eds.), *Language by ear and by eye*. Cambridge: MIT Press, 1972.

Singer, M. H., & Crouse, J. The relationship of context-use skills to reading: A case for an alternative experimental logic. *Child Development*, 1981, 52, 1325–1329.

Smith, F. *Psycholinguistics and reading*. New York: Holt, Rinehart, & Winston, 1973.

Suppes, P. *A probabilistic theory of causality*. Amsterdam: North–Holland, 1970.

Vellutino, F. R., Harding, C. J., Phillips, F., & Steger, J. A. Differential transfer in poor and normal readers. *Journal of Genetic Psychology*, 1975, *126*, 3–18.

Vellutino, F. R., Steger, J. A., DeSetto, L., & Phillips, F. Immediate and delayed recognition of visual stimuli in poor and normal readers. *Journal of Experimental Child Psychology*, 1975, *19*, 231–232.

# 3 Context Use and Reading Disability

Martin H. Singer
*Bell Laboratories*

Competent readers exploit semantic and syntactic context. As described in an earlier chapter, Kolers' (1970) experiments with **transformed text** demonstrated that competent readers avoid syntactic and semantic errors even when struggling through unusually presented text. They substitute words that conform to syntactical rules (**syntax**), making intelligent guesses that do not violate the text's meaning. Weber (1970) extended Kolers' findings, demonstrating that even first-graders rely on context in oral reading. In her analysis of first-graders' oral reading errors, Weber reported that beginners rarely violated syntactic structure or the semantic content of the text despite considerable error rates. This use of context becomes unavoidable. Willows and MacKinnon (1973) reported that competent readers failed to ignore words designated as irrelevant (and printed on different lines and in different colors). To some extent, this last finding represents a connected discourse version of the Stroop effect.

Contextual facilitation also applies to reading individual words. These studies were described earlier (Bradshaw, 1974; Meyer, Schvaneveldt, & Ruddy, 1974). Meyer et al. demonstrated that when a semantically or phonetically related word precedes another word, competent readers recognize that word more quickly than if the word were preceded by an unrelated word. Bradshaw (1974) reported a similar contextual effect exerted by peripherally presented words. Bradshaw's effect occurs even when subjects report not seeing anything in the periphery.

Competent readers' use of context (**context-use skill**) has prompted some researchers to posit a direct relationship between "contextual abilities" and reading achievement. They claim that poor readers fail to appreciate that printed text relays meaning (Goodman, 1965; Smith, 1973). Poor readers focus instead on mechanically decoding individual letters and words, neglecting contextual information that would allow them to guess. These mechanical readers plod through every letter, never advancing to the "exploring" stage described by Rozin and Gleitman (1977).[1]

Many researchers view skeptically the claim that an inability to exploit context explains much of the variance in reading ability. Shankweiler and Liberman (1972), for instance, state that:

> one often encounters the claim that there are many children who can read individual words well yet do not seem able to comprehend connected text. The existence of such children is taken to support the view that methods of instruction that stress spelling-to-sound correspondence and other aspects of decoding are insufficient and may even produce mechanical readers who are expert at decoding but fail to comprehend sentences. It may well be that such children exist; if so, they merit careful study. Our experience suggests the problem is rare and that poor reading of text with little comprehension among beginning readers is usually a consequence of reading words poorly (i.e., with many errors and/or at a slow rate [p. 294].

Shankweiler and Liberman's criticism outlines a crucial problem for context-based explanations of poor reading: It would seem difficult to isolate a deficit in a poor reader's ability to exploit context when that same reader may fail in **decoding** single words. Stated in another way, if a poor reader exhausts his or her attention discriminating individual letters or decoding letter strings (because he or she finds decoding difficult) he or she cannot easily monitor contextual information. As Bryan and Harter (1899) reported, telegraph operators effectively used their knowledge of syntax and context *only after* complete mastery of the Morse Code. Their use of context depended on great facility in recognizing individual Morse Code letters and letter parts. Bryan and Harter explained the increased use of context as a function of the operators' *automaticity* in deciphering the code (which resulted from "hard work and intense effort"). When elements of the Morse Code could be recognized without devoting conscious attention, the telegraphic operators could read "behind" an incoming message (cf. discussion in Chapter 1). Similarly, the eye–voice span in readers of English expands with development. As described earlier, increased facility in reading skills (e.g., decoding) allows the competent reader to explore ahead of the word being read aloud (Buswell, 1920; Levin & Turner, 1968). This ability to explore spatially

---

[1]Rozin and Gleitman (1977) have made it clear that they have difficulty with Goodman's emphasis on the importance of meaning in reading. Rozin and Gleitman readily agree that competent readers exploit meaning and context in rapid reading. They dispute with Goodman, however, on the importance of component skills such as decoding. They compare Goodman's suggestion for teaching reading ("Look for Meaning!") to a misguided Drivers' Education school. In this Drivers' Education school a student: "might be placed in a car on the New Jersey Turnpike, moving at 50 mph, and told to "Drive to Philadelphia! [p. 501]." This "whole-destination method" would avoid producing students: "who can turn wheels and shift gears all day long, but without having the faintest notion *where* they are going or *why* [p. 501]."

represented discourse also develops in Braille readers. As mentioned earlier, when the Braille readers' facility in recognizing individual letters increases, they "explore" the Braille text with two hands. In all of these cases—reception of telegraphic messages, Braille reading, and reading of visually presented text—the facility to exploit context depends on decoding skill.

In addition to this **automaticity confound**, skill in utilizing context may depend on general strategic ability. One can imagine a myriad of paradigms in which performance on standardized reading tests determines good and poor reading groups. Subsequently these groups differ dramatically on a context-use test. One might reasonably wonder, however, if such studies merely demonstrate that reading tests implicitly measure strategic abilities. Differences in strategic abilities most likely correlate with measures of intelligence. Thus, differences in performing the context-use task may reflect differences in intelligence. Stated in another way, the contribution of the ability to use context and performance on a standardized intelligence measure would explain the same portion of the variance in reading ability. This problem was discussed in Chapter 2.

Many researchers have ignored the interdependence of intelligence, decoding skill, and reading ability in their investigations of context use. These studies circumvent complicated questions concerning the role of automaticity or general strategic ability in using context. This review considers such issues and critically examines the claim that poor reading results from an inability to exploit context. When attentional allocation, decoding skill, and the contribution of general intelligence to reading ability are considered, the evidence reviewed here fails to support the claim that poor readers are good mechanically (e.g., decoding skills) and simply cannot appreciate the meanings supplied by either syntactic or semantic structure.

## SIMPLE CONTEXT EFFECTS AND POOR READERS

If poor readers were somehow insensitive to the relationships between words, then semantic or phonetic similarity between words should not facilitate their word recognition. One could easily test this hypothesis within the paradigm described in the Meyer et al. (1974) study. Again, that paradigm (a lexical decision task) required subjects to determine if rapidly presented letter strings were words or nonwords. When related words preceded the presentation of a second word the reaction time required to recognize the second word decreased.

In a recent study, Schvaneveldt, Ackerman, and Semlear (1977) employed the lexical decision task to determine if less skilled readers were also less sensitive to relations between words. Schvaneveldt et al. examined second- and fourth-graders. The children in both grades were divided into groups of poor and good readers and, as one might expect, poor readers took longer to recognize words. They found that reaction times decreased as reading ability test scores increased. When a word was preceded by a semantically related word, however, the performance of both reading groups improved. The presentation of a related word facilitated poor readers' recognition of a subsequent word just as it facilitated the performance of competent or adult readers. Schvaneveldt et al. concluded that poor readers did not suffer from some special inability to benefit from the relations between individual words.

In a different type of task Golinkoff and Rosinski (1976) and Pace and Golinkoff (1976) reported results that agree with the Schvanaveldt et al. study. Those studies used a variation of the Stroop task. The classic Stroop task described earlier involves the printing of color words in different colored inks. Thus, the word *green* might be printed in blue and the task would be to name the color of the ink and ignore the word. Competent readers find this task very difficult (cf. Chapter 1). Variations of the Stroop task present a picture (e.g., a horse) with a word printed across the picture (e.g., *cow*). The task requires subjects to ignore the word and name the picture. Again, readers seem unable to ignore the printed word no matter how clear the instructions to name the picture (Posnansky & Rayner, 1977). Golinkoff and Rosinski and, later, Pace and Golinkoff employed this picture–Stroop task to examine whether poor readers accessed meanings of printed words and experienced similar interference in naming pictures. If poor readers failed to access the meaning of words they should *not* experience the Stroop effect; there would be no semantic conflict between the words and the pictures if they never (or more slowly) accessed the meaning of words. In both studies, however, less skilled readers suffered a Stroop effect. The printed word interfered with their ability to name the pictured item, the interference occurring only when the printed word and picture shared the same semantic category.[2]

The results reported by Pace and Golinkoff (1976) and Golinkoff and Rosinski (1976) support the Schvaneveldt et al. (1977) study. Interestingly, both studies report that poor readers recognize or decode words more slowly than good readers. Slow decoding, though, did not attenuate their ability to access meaning from words or to profit from the relations between words. At the level of individual words, then, context similarly affects both poor and good readers.

## COMPLICATED CONTEXTUAL EFFECTS

Kolers (1975) extended his **transformed text** paradigm to investigate the differences between poor and good readers. As in his earlier study, subjects read connected, but transformed text (e.g., upside down, written right to left, or

---

[2]Pace and Golinkoff argue that if the interference *had* occurred when any word appeared with a picture, the effect might have been due to something other than the poor reader's access of meaning for the word (e.g., stimulus overload, laborious decoding). Because the effect was specific to words and pictures sharing the same category, though, it reflects interference due to semantic access for printed words.

rotated letters). In this study, Kolers examined the performance of the best and the worst readers from a seventh-grade class (average age 12½ years). On a control task (normally presented text), poor readers took almost five times as long as the good readers to read normally presented text. They took approximately three times as long to read the transformed text. The decrease in disparity between the two groups across the regular and transformed-text condition indicates that good readers had "more to lose" than poor readers. Poor readers already were reading normal text slowly; they could not go much more slowly in the transformed-text condition.

More informative was another aspect of the study. Kolers asked his subjects to read transformed sentences and in a subsequent task determine if the same sentences reoccurred. The sentences in this subsequent task were altered in some way. Either the meaning or the visual characteristics of the sentences were changed to produce a "different" sentence. If sentences were altered the subjects were to respond that the sentence was "new." Kolers reported that good readers were more sensitive to the visual changes than were poor readers. Despite this (and a generally higher error rate than good readers), *poor readers detected semantic and syntactic changes in the sentences*. The experiment suggests that poor readers are sensitive to the semantic quality of connected text. Also, Kolers reported that poor readers exploit their knowledge of context in guessing about the identity of words in transformed text. Their errors, just as competent reader errors, left intact the syntactic and semantic sense of the text.

Guthrie (1973) also supports the claim that poor readers exploit context. Guthrie required good and poor readers to determine which of three words best fit within a sentence (a **maze task**). For example, they saw sentences like "Both ——— lifted their ears. They ——— heard the forest ranger's ———." At each blank, three words were printed representing alternative words to place in the blank. The first blank had as choices: *horses, flowers, talk*; the second blank: *had, were, some*; the third: *blanket, kept, voice*. Guthrie explored effects due to different age groups, reading abilities, and passage difficulty. He reported that although disabled readers had problems with difficult passages, error types across the two groups did not differ. Poor and good readers were similarly skilled in determining the correct choice for each blank. Guthrie's paradigm explicitly requires that the subject attend to the contextual value of the sentences. The poor reader's performance implies an unimpaired ability to use context.

Although convincing in some respects, both Kolers' and Guthrie's studies suffer from the task equivalence problems discussed in Chapter 2. Both studies attempt to isolate mechanisms (use of context, visual information) implicated in poor reading but neither study controls for the difficulty of the various tasks. For example, Kolers employed an extremely simple context ask (judging if meaning had been changed) but a very difficult visual task (noting some visual discrepancy between the two sentences). The simplicity of the context task, it could be argued, allowed near-perfect performance by all readers, good or bad. The visual task, on the other hand, might have been difficult enough to measure differences between the two groups. *The absence of task equivalence* permits the competing interpretation that good and poor readers perform similarly on easy tasks but disparately on different ones. The same criticism weakens Guthrie's study. His maze task also allowed excellent performance by both good and poor readers.

Recent work by Hogaboam and Perfetti (1978) and Perfetti, Goldman, and Hogoboam (1979) attempted to overcome problems with task equivalence in their investigation of context use. Perfetti et al. required children to perform a vocalization latency task (VLT): Subjects rapidly named visually presented words. In one condition the words were presented in isolation. As one might expect, poor readers took longer than good readers to name the words. This difference agrees with models of reading disability that emphasize decoding processes (Shankweiler & Liberman, 1972). In a second condition, good and poor readers named words that were preceded and followed by lists of unrelated words (a **cloze task**). Again, poor readers had longer vocalization latencies than good readers. In a third condition, a meaningful context preceded words that were to be named. In this condition, poor readers performed comparably to good readers. This increase in the poor readers' performances occurred when the preceding context was visually or aurally presented.

The decreased time for poor readers to name words when preceded by a context strains a contextual-use deficit hypothesis of poor reading. The particular appeal of this study is that Perfetti et al. demanded the same performance from subjects in each task. That is, subjects always identified a single word. Thus, one cannot easily argue that the context condition was simply less difficult than the other conditions. It is of further interest to compare their report with the DiVesta, Hayward, and Orlando (1979) study described in Chapter 2 (cf. "Problems with **Task Equivalence**"). DiVesta et al. claimed that poor and good readers *differed* in using context. This difference was manifested in a comparison of good and poor readers' use of subsequent text. Ostensibly, the Perfetti et al. finding conflicts with the DiVesta et al. result. Such conflicts make the disability literature confusing.

This conflict, however, is more apparent than real. Figure 3.1 illustrates the *compatibility* of the two studies. The context task in the Perfetti et al. experiment required children to exploit information from previously occurring sentences. This task resembles the Running Text Condition of the DiVesta et al. study (Chapter 2). In both studies poor and good readers utilized previously occurring context. Perfetti et al. defined context-use abilities in terms of performance on this task. On the other hand, DiVesta et al. defined context-use abilities with reference to performance in a Subsequent Text Condition (a task that probably measures differences in intelligence rather than context-use skills). The conflict between the two reports reflects varying **operational definitions** of context-use skill, not different results. As Fig. 3.1 illustrates, both studies obtain identical results given the same context-use task (i.e., the Running Text Condition in DiVesta et al.; the Context Condition in Perfetti et al.).

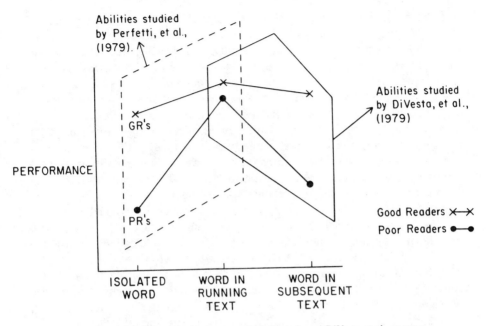

FIG. 3.1.   The disagreement between Perfetti et al. and DiVesta et al. on poor readers' ability to exploit context may reflect a difference in the *operational definition* of context use. When the two experiments used similar tasks, their results were also similar.

Other researchers (Levin, 1973; Staller, 1980) have also reported that poor readers profit from context. Levin (1973) examined the comprehension of fourth-graders with varying vocabularies. A deficited group (more than a year below grade level) performed poorly relative to normal and average groups in answering questions about short stories. When children in the deficited group were provided with a picture relevant to the story's content, however, their comprehension improved. They were apparently able to generate a context that facilitated their comprehension. In the same way, Staller (1980) reports that an adult "dyslexic" read passages with greater fluency when given prior information pertaining to the passage's content.

## EVIDENCE FOR A CONTEXT-USE DEFICIT

### A Problem With Time Precedence

Chapter 2 mentioned **time precedence** as a prerequisite for inferring causality. In order to conclude that $x$ causes $y$ one needs to demonstrate that $x$ precedes $y$. The condition of *time precedence* applies to research on context use and reading ability in the following way: Suppose someone administers reading achievement and verbal IQ tests to the children within some school district. The researcher finds that scores on the verbal IQ test predict scores on the reading ability test (i.e., they correlate). The researcher concludes that differences in verbal IQ explain variation in reading ability. This conclusion implies that the characteristic measured by a verbal IQ test *precedes* the skills measured by a reading test. Can one justify the implicit assumption of time precedence? If one reads well one will read often. The number of hours spent reading certainly affects language skills (e.g., vocabulary, general knowledge, syntactical skills). If the verbal IQ test measures vocabulary, general knowledge, or use of syntax one could claim that scores on a reading test *predict* verbal IQ scores. In other words, *reading affects IQ scores* and not vice versa. The inability of the researcher to establish the time precedence of verbal IQ allows alternative explanations of the relation between reading and intelligence.

In his analysis of the relation between context-use skills and reading ability, Vellutino (1977) argues that: "direct evidence" suggests that "poor readers may be deficient in syntactive development." In fact, these studies fail to satisfy the condition of time precedence. Vellutino cites Fry (1967) and Schulte (1967), who found that poor readers in the second grade lacked sophistication in knowledge of grammar. These studies (unpublished dissertations) focused on the use of grammatical transformations in oral language. The studies both fail, however, to establish that an insensitivity to the underlying structure of syntax *precedes* poor reading. Fry, Johnson, and Muehl (1970) claim that the insensitivity to grammar must precede reading disability, as the investigation examined second-graders. Vellutino (1977) agrees with this analysis. According to this reasoning, reading experience has not accumulated in sufficient quantity to influence syntactical knowledge.

A recent study by Guttentag and Haith (1979), though, indicates that effects due to reading experience accrue quickly. In a picture–Stroop effect study, Guttentag and Haith reported that words interfered with the naming of incompatible pictures for *first-graders*. The ability of young readers to access meaning quickly from words (even when instructed to ignore the words) suggests the early effects of reading experience. Thus, one cannot agree with Fry et al. that differences among second-graders in grammatical knowledge *necessarily precede* reading ability differences among second-graders. We should expect that reading ability will influence knowledge of syntax if children who read well read often. We might also wonder if tests of syntactical knowledge and reading ability actually test the same underlying skills (e.g., reading tests often include cloze tasks and word choice questions. Such tests measure syntactical knowledge).

The failure to demonstrate time precedence attenuates other context studies. Suppose that the Subsequent Test condition in the DiVesta et al. (1979) study satisfied the criticisms regarding task equivalence (cf. Chapter 2). In other words, suppose that DiVesta et al. demonstrated that, independent of memory and intelligence, poor readers lacked skills in exploiting subsequent context (e.g., sentences following a currently fixated word or phrase). One might conclude under these circumstances that a context-use deficit explained variation in reading ability. The failure to demonstrate time precedence, however, precludes this conclusion. Clearly, reading experience will affect reading strategies. Practice of any skill increases the flexibility and efficiency of that skill. Accordingly, good readers will acquire sophisticated reading strategies as a function of practice (and those who succeed in the first grade are likely to practice). Performance in the Subsequent Test condition is an effect, rather than a cause, of reading ability. Thus, in addition to the task equivalence issue discussed earlier (Chapter 2), DiVesta et al. demonstrated only that good readers read well, using strategies that result from practice.

## The Automaticity Confound

Willows (1974) also reported that good and poor readers differ in their ability to exploit context. Willows required subjects to read paragraphs, skipping every other line. The irrelevant lines were written in red ink, whereas the relevant lines were written in black. Good and poor readers both made errors. Good readers, however, committed more intrusion errors (i.e., they read the words written in red). Willows concluded that good readers cannot avoid using context, whereas poor readers focus on decoding words in central vision. Willows implies that a difference in context-use skills explains differences in reading ability.

The ability to exploit context, however, depends on the *automaticity* of decoding operations. If a child cannot translate letter groups to sound with *great facility*, little attention will be left to explore the context of a passage. No doubt the poor readers in the Willows' study possessed poorer decoding skills than the good readers. Decoding the passage probably exhausted their attentional energy and, consequently, the "red" words posed no difficulty; poor readers had no choice. Good readers, on the other hand, could "explore" the passage as the decoding of words occurred automatically, without the conscious use of attention. That poor readers read slower and committed more errors (nonintrusion) supports an automaticity-based analysis of the poor readers' lack of intrusion errors.

Some researchers have attempted to control for automaticity in decoding skill in their investigations of context use. In two such studies (Dahl, 1975; Samuels, Dahl, & Archwatemy, 1974) groups of poor and good readers were drilled on a set of words. The researcher ensured that all readers could recognize these words and attempted to increase the speed with which poor readers recognized the words. The children were then required to read passages composed of these words and answer questions that measured their comprehension. Good and poor readers differed in their comprehension and these reports concluded that differences in context-use skills rather than decoding skills discriminated good from poor readers.

Despite their attempt, these studies again fail to control for decoding differences between good and poor readers. Recognition is a *weak* test of an individual's facility in decoding. Good and poor readers could recognize words with comparable accuracy but differed greatly in the amount of attention necessary for accurate recognition. In both aforementioned studies the training on the word set never increased the *speed* of word recognition. Any procedure that claimed to control for decoding skill or automaticity in decoding must examine the *time required* to perform specific operations. Laberge and Samuels (1974), of course, have developed a more sensitive procedure for estimating automaticity, one that involves the manipulation of expectations (cf. Chapter 1).

## An Indirect Demonstration: An Engineering Approach

If an inability to use context causes poor reading, then manipulations that *increase* context use ought to help poor readers. This logic underlies a particular experimental approach to disability research. One proposes that a certain deficit produces reading disability and tests the theory by circumventing the deficit. For example, suppose that a child fails to discriminate letters. His or her teacher *guesses* (develops a theory!) that a "visual deficit" accounts for the failure. The teacher tests the theory by making sandpaper stencils of the letters, attempting to teach the letters haptically (by touch). The procedure succeeds (e.g., the child learns to discriminate letters) and the teacher claims to have demonstrated the theory: A visual problem prevented the acquisition of the alphabet *because* bypassing the visual system permitted the child to learn.

Actually, the teacher has only *failed to disprove* the theory. The child's success in haptically learning the alphabet is not *sufficient* to conclude that a visual problem prevented learning. Requiring a child to trace sandpaper letters with his or her fingers might focus attention on relevant visual features or increase motivation to learn. The success of the haptic technique, however, *increases the probability* that some type of visual problem caused the child's difficulty in learning letters. This information is still valuable in determining the viability of a theory. Researchers rarely succeed in proving a theory within one investigation; they successively eliminate competing explanations. Furthermore, this indirect approach appeals to the engineer: One tests the theory for failure (e.g., a visual deficit) by finding out if another procedure (e.g., haptic training) permits the child to learn. Thus, the theoretical investigation simultaneously attempts to "fix" the problem.

Cromer (1970) employed this approach to demonstrate that some poor readers fail to organize text, losing opportunities to profit from context. Cromer reasoned that if text were artificially organized, poor readers should improve. The appeal of Cromer's study goes beyond his attempt to test a specific model of poor reading. He also stated explicitly the heterogeneity of poor readers. Cromer argued that poor reading occurs for a variety of reasons and that his study examined only two broad categories: readers with general language difficulties, including reading (the Deficit group), and those with generally sound language skills but below average reading skill (the Different group). Cromer determined the Deficit and Different groups on the basis of reading achievement and performance on a vocabulary test. The deficit group was comprised of college students with low reading achievement and poor vocabularies. The Different group included students with low reading achievement but mediocre rather than poor vocabularies.[3] Cromer predicted that the Difference group, but not the Deficit group, would profit from an artificial organization of text.

The artificial organization of the text simply meant that words were meaningfully grouped, emphasizing relations between words (e.g., the words within one prepositional phrase might be close together, preceded and followed by spaces). Cromer, in fact, found that the Difference but not the Deficit group improved (i.e., had greater comprehension) under these circumstances. He failed, as explained before, to disprove his theory. It must be noted, however, that the effect is small. The distinction between the two groups accounts for only 6% of the variation in task performance. Moreover, we know little about the importance of context-use skills and "artificial organization" relative to all other skills and manipulations that might improve reading. Still, Cromer's (1970) study retains its appeal. One could expand upon his paradigm and investigate the effects of a variety of manipulations on different poor reading subgroups. This expanded version of Cromer's paradigm would permit an evaluation of alternative strategies for overcoming poor reading. Bransford, Stein, and Vye expand on this engineering approach in Chapter 8.

## SUMMARY

Research on semantic context-use skills and reading ability fails to demonstrate that an insensitivity to context predicts poor reading. First, the research has not demonstrated the *time precedence* of context-use skills. Differences between good and poor readers in their use of context could reflect differences in reading experience of the two groups. Second, the relation between context use and reading ability may be *spurious*. That is, a third factor (e.g., intelligence, vocabulary size) might predict performance on context-use tasks and reading ability measures. Consequently, the ability to use context would explain nothing about reading ability not already explained by a vocabulary or intelligence test. Third, investigations of context use inadequately control for the decoding abilities of good and poor readers. If poor readers exhaust attentional information decoding individual words they will be unable to devote any attention to context. Fourth, several research projects (Pace & Golinkoff, 1976; Kolers, 1970; Perfetti, Goldman, & Hogoboam, 1979; Schvaneveldt et al. 1977) report an unimpaired ability of poor readers to exploit context.

Cromer (1970) and Levin (1973), however, report that focusing the poor readers' attention on context (with a picture or by "phrasing" the text) facilitates

---

[3]Some might question Cromer's use of a vocabulary test as a measure of language skill. It is therefore worthwhile to mention that the vocabulary subtest of the WISC and WAIS are the single best predictors of total verbal IQ (Jensen, 1980).

their reading. This engineering approach suggests that poor readers are able to utilize text but, under normal circumstances, do not. Also, this effect applies only to particular categories of poor readers. Finally, this research does not permit an estimation of the *relative* importance of context use. Poor readers are likely to profit from a variety of strategies. Cromer's and Levin's reports do not indicate if highlighting context influences poor readers more than reducing the number of words in a sentence (memory manipulation) or increasing the discriminability of letters (visual manipulation). Thus, one must be cautious in evaluating the importance of their results.

## GLOSSARY

**Automaticity Confound.** Differences between good and poor readers on higher-level skills (e.g., context use) may be due to differences on lower-level skills (e.g., visual discrimination). According to this argument good readers can attend to contextual information because other skills have been automatized.

**Cloze Task.** A procedure that requires subjects to choose a word that will appropriately fill a blank that occurs in some passage.

**Context-Use Skill.** An ability to exploit context in deciphering words; it is a skill often measured by a cloze task.

**Decoding.** This often denotes the translation of visual symbols (e.g., letters) into their phonetic counterparts (e.g., phonemes, or more broadly, sound). Some consider decoding to include the use of stored visual information (orthographic structure) that facilitates the translations.

**Maze Task.** Although similar to a cloze task, this procedure specifies two or more words as the choices for the blank that occurs in a sentence or text.

**Operational Definition.** In an experiment, researchers do not examine directly a concept, skill, or attribute. Instead, they examine an "instance" or a special definition of the concept, skill, or attribute. Thus, performance on an IQ test is not intelligence but one possible interpretation or definition of intelligence. In studies of reading skill, experimenters use performance on certain tasks (e.g., a cloze task) as an operational definition of certain skills (e.g., context use). Disagreement between experimenters often reflects a disparity in operational definitions.

**Syntax.** The rules that dictate word order within a sentence.

**Task Equivalence.** This refers to the level of difficulty of measures or procedures that assess different abilities.

**Time Precedence.** If one claims that *A* causes *B* one must demonstrate that *A* occurs prior to *B*. Thus, time precedence refers to one of the necessary conditions for demonstrating a causal relation. As an example, we cannot claim that IQ causes reading ability differences unless we can prove that the differences in IQ precede differences in reading ability; otherwise any relation between the two might mean only that differences in reading ability cause differences in IQ.

**Transformed Text.** A procedure in which sentences, letters, or words are rotated, inverted, or written in some way to increase the difficulty of reading.

# REFERENCES

Bradshaw, J. L. Short reports: Peripherally presented and unreported words may bias the perceived meaning of a centrally fixated hemograph. *Journal of Educational Psychology*, 1974, *103*(6), 1200–1202.

Bryan, W. L., & Harter, N. Studies on the acquisition of a hierarchy of habits. *Psychological Review*, 1899, *6*(4), 345–375.

Buswell, G. T. An experimental study of the eye–voice span in reading. *Supplementary Educational Monographs* (No. 17). Chicago: University of Chicago, Department of Education, 1920.

Cromer, W. The difference model: A new explanation for some reading difficulties. *Journal of Educational Psychology*, 1970, *61*, 471–483.

Dahl, P. R. A mastery-based experimental program for teaching high-speed word recognition skills. *Reading Research Quarterly*, 1975, *2*, 203–211.

DiVesta, F., Hayward, K. G., & Orlando, V. P. Developmental trends in monitoring text for comprehension. *Child Development*, 1979, *50*, 97–105.

Fry, M. A. *A transformational analysis of the oral language structure used by two reading groups at the second-grade level.* Unpublished doctoral dissertation, University of Iowa, 1967.

Fry, M. A., Johnson, C. S., & Muehl, S. Oral language production in relation to reading achievement among select graders. In D. J. Bakker & P. Satz (Eds.), *Specific reading disability: Advances in theory and method.* Rotterdam: Rotterdam University Press, 1970.

Golinkoff, R. M., & Rosinski, R. R. Decoding, semantic processing, and reading comprehension skill. *Child Development*, 1976, *47*, 252–258.

Goodman, K. A linguistic study of cues and miscues in reading. *Elementary English*, 1965, *42*, 639–643.

Guthrie, J. T. Reading comprehension and syntactic responses in good and poor readers. *Journal of Educational Psychology*, 1973, *65*, 294–299.

Guttentag, R., & Haith, M. Developmental study of automatic word processing in a picture classification task-note. *Child Development*, 1979, 50, *3*, 894–896.

Hogaboam, T. W., & Perfetti, C. A. Reading skill and the role of verbal experience in decoding. *Journal of Educational Psychology*, 1978, *70*, 717–729.

Jensen, A. R. *Bias in mental testing.* New York: The Free Press, 1980.

Kolers, P. A. Three stages of reading. In H. Levin & J. P. Williams (Eds.), *Basic studies on reading.* New York: Basic Books, 1970.

Kolers, P. A. Pattern-analyzing disability in poor readers. *Developmental Psychology*, 1975, *11*, 282–290.

LaBerge, D., & Samuels, J. Toward a theory of automatic information processing in reading. *Cognitive Psychology*, 1974, *6*, 293–323.

Levin, J. R. Inducing comprehension in poor readers: A test of a recent model. *Journal of Educational Psychology*, 1973, *65*, 19–24.

Levin, H., & Turner, A. Sentence structure and the eye–voice span. In H. Levin, E. J. Gibson, & J. J. Gibson (Eds.), *The analysis of reading skill.* Final Report Project No. 5–1213, from Cornell University to US office of Education, December 1968.

Meyer, D. E., Schvaneveldt, R. W., & Ruddy, M. G. Functions of graphemic and phonemic codes in visual word-recognition. *Memory & Cognition*, 1974, *2*, 309–321.

Pace, A. J., & Golinkoff, R. M. Relationship between word difficulty and access of single-word meaning by skilled and less skilled readers. *Journal of Educational Psychology*, 1976, *68*(6), 760–767.

Perfetti, C., Goldman, S. R., & Hogoboam, T. Reading skill in the identification of words in discourse context. *Memory & Cognition*, 1979, *7*(9), 273–282.

Posnansky, C., & Rayner, K. Visual-feature and response components in a picture–word interference task with beginning and skilled readers. *Journal of Experimental Child Psychology*, 1977, *24*, 440–460.

Rozin, P., & Gleitman, L. R. The structure and acquisition of reading: The reading process and the acquisition of alphabetic principle. In A. S. Reber & D. L. Scarborough (Eds.), *Toward a psychology of reading*. Hillsdale, N.J.: Lawrence Erlbaum Associates, 1977.

Samuels, J., Dahl, P., & Archwatemy, T. Effect of hypothesis test training on reading skill. *Journal of Educational Psychology*, 1974, *66*, 835–844.

Schulte, C. *A study of the relationship between oral language and reading achievement in second graders*. Unpublished doctoral dissertation, University of Iowa, 1967.

Schvaneveldt, R., Ackerman, B., & Semlear, T. The effect of semantic context on children's word recognition. *Child Development*, 1977, *48*, 612–616.

Shankweiler, D., & Liberman, I. Y. Misreading: A search for causes. In J. Kavanaugh & I. G. Mattingly (Eds.), *Language by ear and by eye*. Cambridge: MIT Press, 1972.

Smith, F. *Psycholinguistics and reading*. New York: Holt, Rinehart, & Winston, 1973.

Staller, J. Personal communication, 1980.

Vellutino, F. R. Alternative conceptualizations of dyslexia: Evidence in support of a verbal-deficit hypothesis. *Harvard Educational Review*, 1977, *47*, 334–355.

Weber, R. M. First-graders' use of grammatical context in reading. In H. Levin & J. P. Williams (Eds.), *Basic studies on reading*. New York: Basic Books, 1970.

Willows, D. M. Reading between the lines: Selective attention in good and poor readers. *Child Development*, 1974, *45*, 408–415.

Willows, D. M., & MacKinnon, G. E. Selective reading: Attention to the "unattended" lines. *Canadian Journal of Psychology*, 1973, *27*(3), 292–304.

# 4 Insensitivity to Ordered Information and the Failure to Read

Martin H. Singer
*Bell Laboratories*

Chapter 1 indicated that competent readers rely on orthographic knowledge (e.g., letter order, letter position[1], and word shape) to resolve their uncertainty about words; stored information that pertains to the visual characteristics of a letter string permits competent readers to guess on the basis of partial information. It stands to reason that a failure to acquire orthographic information would eliminate an apparently effective reading strategy.

What would prevent the acquisition of orthographic information, knowledge about the order and positions in which letters occur? First, any difficulty in discriminating individual letters would interfere with a beginning reader's ability to abstract higher-level order and positional information: If simple letter discrimination exhausted a reader's attention, he or she could not devote attention to orthographic patterns. Second, it is possible that a specific disability, one that interfered with either the detection or remembering of ordered information, could prevent the acquisition of orthographic knowledge. If one could not remember the order of several items, then one would experience difficulty in learning orthographic information. The present section discusses this second possibility.

This possibility—that poor readers fail to acquire orthographic knowledge because of an insensitivity to **ordered information**—requires a complicated

---

[1]Letter position is difficult to distinguish from letter order (i.e., if a letter commonly occurs in the fourth position of five-letter words then that letter has sequential (or ordered) relationship with letters that commonly occur in the third and fifth positions). Although I will discuss experiments (Mason, 1975) that emphasize the relative importance of positional information, bear in mind that the distinction between *position* and *order* is more apparent than real.

proof. It is not enough to demonstrate that they fail to exploit orthographic information when it would be useful; we should expect that poor readers would fail to use a variety of information simply because of insufficient practice. Instead, one must show that poor readers exhibit some general problem with detecting or remembering ordered information. The following discussion presents evidence related to this last issue.

## POOR READERS' FAILURE TO EXPLOIT
## ORTHOGRAPHIC INFORMATION

Mason (1975) and Mason and Katz (1976) have reported results suggesting that poor readers fail to exploit orthographic information. In letter detection tasks, good and poor readers perform comparably when the letters are embedded in nonsense letter strings (to refresh your memory on the letter detection paradigm see Chapter 1). These nonsense strings are composed of letters that occur in improbable positions. For example, a *y* might occur in the middle of a string rather than at the end, where it usually occurs. These same groups of good and poor readers, however, perform *disparately* when the target letters are embedded in probable letter strings—ones that conform to orthographic rules. In other words, good readers are better at detecting target letters *only when the target is embedded in a letter string that conforms to normal spelling patterns*. These results suggest that good, but not poor readers can profit from orthographic structure. Guttentag (1978) reported findings that corroborate these conclusions. In a letter-recognition task, good and poor readers differed only when pseudo-words conformed to normal spelling patterns. On nonsense strings and highly familiar words (which might be rotely learned), good and poor readers performed comparably. All these findings are compatible with Schwartz and Doehring's (1977) report that poor readers lag behind good readers in their knowledge of spelling patterns.

Spelling patterns, or the orthographic information that poor readers fail to exploit, certainly reflect ordered information (again, refer to Chapter 1 for a discussion of the sequential nature of orthographic information). Still, the failure of poor readers to use orthographic information does not, in itself, suggest that poor readers have a special insensitivity to ordered relations. Lack of reading experience might easily explain the poor reader's insufficient orthographic knowledge. Reber (1967, 1976), for example, has shown that experience with sequences permits the abstraction of those rules that govern the ordering of items in those sequences (without any instruction). In order to suggest that some poor readers *lack the ability* to acquire orthographic information, one needs to demonstrate that with nonalphabetic items (things with which good and poor readers have similar experience), poor readers still display a particular difficulty with ordered information.

## A Caveat

Even if the following discussion demonstrates that a failure to detect or remember ordered information plagues the poor reader, the criticisms in Chapter 2 (''A misguided search for differences'') must qualify one's enthusiasm for this research. First, the poor reader's failure to use orthographic information must be measured against a variety of other failures: Our evaluation should include some statement about the *relative* importance of a failure to use orthographic knowledge. The aforementioned studies never supply this type of data. Secondly, if research succeeds in isolating a general insensitivity to ordered relations, one needs a statement on the generality of this deficit: How many poor readers share this problem and what proportion of the variance in reading ability can this deficit explain? Finally, it must be reemphasized that inexperience with text might explain a poor reader's failure to use orthographic information: One needs to demonstrate that poor readers experience difficulty with strings of nonalphabetic items if one wishes to claim that a failure to detect or remember ordered information hinders the poor reader.

## INSENSITIVITY TO THE ORDER OF NONALPHABETIC ITEMS

Corkin (1974) examined the ability of poor readers to *remember* ordered information. Corkin required poor and normal readers to remember the order in which six wooden cubes were tapped (Knox Cube Test). In one condition the experimenter tapped the cubes in a certain order and then immediately requested the subjects to reproduce that order (No-Delay Condition). In another condition a 6-second delay intervened between the experimenter's production of the sequence and the subject's reproduction (Delay Condition). Poor and normal readers performed comparably in the No-Delay Condition but disparately in the Delay Condition. The deflated performance of poor readers in only the Delay Condition might suggest that poor readers can detect ordered relations but fail in remembering them. Corkin also reported that poor readers performed less accurately than normals in a task requiring that they remember the order of aurally presented digits.

Singer, Allen, and Lappin (1976) corroborated Corkin's (1974) finding with visual and auditory stimuli. In the auditory tasks, good and poor readers judged the similarity between two temporal sequences. In one condition, the number of tones in the two sequences was varied and subjects determined whether the two sequences contained the same number of tones. In that condition poor and good readers performed comparably. Another condition, however, manipulated the relationship between the pauses and tones within a sequence. Poor readers could not *detect* differences in these relationships between the two sequences.

That is, they failed to distinguish between a sequence of two successive tones, a pause, and two more successive tones and a sequence containing a tone, a pause, and three successive tones. Good readers, however, accurately made this discrimination (See also, Singer, 1976).

On a visual task, poor readers in the Singer et al. study also displayed an inability to discriminate various ordering of the same elements. In that task, subjects determined whether two successive displays were identical. Each display contained three elements and only the order of the elements within the display was varied. Poor readers were significantly less accurate at comparing these various orderings than were poor readers. It should be noted that on several other simultaneous and successive discrimination judgments that did not involve order, poor and good readers performed comparably.

The hypothesis that the ability to discriminate ordered information correlates with reading ability receives additional support from analyses of standard achievement and IQ measures (Fildes, 1921; Guthrie & Goldberg, 1972; McLeod, 1965). Fildes (1921) reported that reading ability differences between her "congenitally word-blind" group and normal reading group correlated strongly with the ability to remember the presentation order of a series of digits. She reported that "word-blind" children failed this task when the digits were presented visually or aurally. This task resembles the Digit Span subtest of the Wechsler Intelligence Scale for Children (WISC) and, importantly, McLeod (1965) found that the Digit Span and Coding subtests correlated with reading ability. McLeod reported that neither the Digit Span nor Coding subtests correlated with overall IQ for either group. He also claimed that with a given Verbal IQ, poor readers performed lower than good readers on the Digit Span and Coding subtest and that these differences predicted differences in reading ability.

Guthrie and Goldberg's (1972) study of other standard measures supports McLeod's (1965) analysis. They reported that performance on the Knox Cube Test and the sequential memory subtest of the Illinois Test of Psycholinguistic Abilities (ITPA) predicted reading ability. The Knox Cube Test actually was the first condition in Corkin's (1974) experiment. The task requires children to remember the order in which several blocks are tapped. The ITPA sequential memory subtest requires children to recall the order in which various items are presented. Both tasks tap the ability to discriminate or remember ordered information.

## RELATED STUDIES ON INTERSENSORY INTEGRATION

A group of experiments on matching information between different sense modalities also suggests that the ability to detect or remember ordered relations correlates with poor reading ability. These experiments attempt to relate reading failure to a deficit in integrating intersensory information, but clearly confound sequencing ability with **intersensory integration** (see Corkin, 1974, for a discussion of this problem).

An experiment done by Birch and Belmont (1964) provides an example of the confounding of sensory integration and sequencing skills. In that study Birch and Belmont required children between kindergarten and fourth grade to match visual and auditory patterns. The auditory patterns were presented by tapping a pencil on a table top. The visual patterns were **spatial distributions** of dots. The subject had to determine which of three visual patterns matched the auditory pattern. Birch and Belmont reported that accuracy in this task improved with age and reading ability. For the youngest subjects performance on this task correlated positively with reading readiness measures (.70) and accounted for approximately a third of the variance in predicting reading performance.

Birch and Belmont concluded from this result that an inability to integrate information across sensory modalities underlies early reading failure. Their conclusion may be accurate but does not follow clearly from their data. First, Birch and Belmont provided no control for general memory capabilities. That is, their sample of poor readers simply may have failed in remembering several items. Second, their task required the remembering of ordered information. An inability to detect or remember such information also could account for their data. One obvious control condition would be a within-modality comparison task: a task requiring that subjects match sequences within a particular modality. Third, the task involved a comparison of spatially (the visual pattern) and temporally (the auditory pattern) ordered information. This adds a third factor, one that might influence poor readers more than good readers.

Rudnick, Sterritt, and Flax (1967) and Muehl and Kremenak (1966) provided some of the control conditions absent in the Birch and Belmont (1964) study. Interestingly, both of the studies implicated an order-related deficit among poor readers. Muehl and Kremenak (1966) required retarded and normal readers to match sequences in a variety of circumstances. Subjects compared visual and auditory **temporal sequences** to a visual spatial pattern (printed dots) and two auditory sequences. Muehl and Kremenak reported that only the visual-to-auditory or auditory-to-visual matches predicted reading ability ($r = .52$). That is, retarded and normal readers performed comparably on intramodal comparison tasks but disparately on cross-modal comparisons. Their experiment, however, compares poor readers and normals only on tasks involving order. One knows only that poor readers can discriminate ordered information in one situation but not in another. The data suggests that the ability to remember ordered information interacts with the ability to integrate information across different modalities. The cross-modal comparison, for example, required that subjects compare a spatial sequence (visual) with a temporal sequence (auditory).

Rudnick, Sterritt, and Flax (1967) offer empirical support for this ordering deficit interpretation of the intersensory integration studies. They reported that the ability to match a visual temporal sequence (blinking lights) with a visual spatial sequence were significant and independent predictors of reading ability. These data implicate an inability to compare temporally ordered information with spatially ordered information as a correlate to reading failure. Their data further suggests that the ability to compare different types of sequences correlates with reading ability independently of the ability to integrate intersensory information.

## Summary

Two types of evidence support the hypothesis that order-related skills correlate with reading ability. First, poor readers have been reported to fail in tasks that require the discrimination or memory of ordered items. This performance deficit extends to visual and auditory stimuli (Corkin, 1974; Singer, 1976; Singer, Allen, & Lappin, 1976). The correlation of Digit Span and Sequential Memory subtests to reading ability corroborates these experimental findings (Guthrie & Goldberg, 1972; McLeod, 1965).

Second, experiments examining the relation between reading and intersensory abilities have implicated an order-related deficit in reading failure. These experiments suggest that poor readers fail in comparing temporal and spatial sequences within and across sensory modalities (Muehl & Kremenak, 1966; Rudnick, Sterritt, & Flax, 1967). Although these experiments offer no rationale for this failure, an inadequate memory for ordered information or a poor discrimination of the ordered relations could contribute to the poor readers' inadequate performance on these tasks.

The evidence that order-related skill correlates with reading ability is compatible with the information about competent reading. That is, the first section of the review presented evidence that competent readers rely on ordered information (orthography) in processing words (Massaro, 1975). Also, poor readers differed from good readers in their knowledge of orthographic rules (Schwartz & Doehring, 1977) and their ability to profit from orthographic information (Mason, 1975). An inability to detect, remember, or compare ordered information would explain, in some ways, the poor readers' lack of orthographic knowledge. Because orthographic knowledge includes sequential dependencies between letters as well as positional frequency information (spatial position within a sequence), order-related skills would be essential in abstracting that information. Interestingly, Rozin, Poritsky, and Sotsky (1971) reported that poor readers learned to read Chinese without difficulty. Chinese letters, they pointed out, circumvent any need to remember ordered information. Each character, rather than a string of letters, represents a word.[2]

---

[2]Yamadori (1975) reported a related finding. A Japanese **alexic** (a person who loses reading ability subsequent to some brain trauma) could read kanji script—where words are represented by single figures (ideograms), but not kana script—where words are composed with ordered phonograms (i.e., letters that correspond to specific sounds). One implication is that the alexic lost an order-related ability, not a general reading ability.

Order-related skills also would be implicated in other errors attributed to poor readers (e.g., transpositions). Singer (1976) has argued that an order-related deficit might account for the often reported confusion between letters such as *b* and *d*. One could consider these letters as combinations of a vertical line and a circle. If one failed to detect or remember the order in which these components occurred, one would confuse the two letters.

It should be added that an order-related deficit need not suggest that a poor reader would fail in remembering the order of words in a spoken sentence. The deficit might, for instance, interfere only with the detection or remembering of *arbitrary sequences*: orders lacking a context. The order of words in a sentence is not an arbitrary sequence; the words are meaningfully arranged. Strings of letters, however, for the beginning reader are an arbitrary ordering. Until the reader can successfully impose a phonetic or semantic organization on letter strings, remembering the order of the component letters requires an adequate memory for arbitrary sequences.

The remainder of this chapter discusses the possible origins (**etiological claims**) of an order-related deficit. Specifically, the review examines: (1) evidence supporting Vellutino's (1977) verbal deficit explanation; (2) the visual processing lag hypothesis and; (3) a directional confusion interpretation.

## EXPLANATIONS OF AN ORDER-RELATED SKILL DEFICIT

### The verbal deficit interpretation

Vellutino (1977) argues that we might best understand the poor reader's inability to retain ordered information as a verbal deficit. He argues that remembering sequences involves verbal labeling: One remembers a sequence by verbally coding the ordered information. Vellutino cites other evidence as directly or indirectly supporting a "verbal deficit" hypothesis and concludes that sequencing deficits are compatible with this hypothesis (Denckla & Rudel, 1976a, 1976b; Lyle & Goyen, 1968; Rabinovitch, 1968).

First, Vellutino never clearly explains why a verbal deficit interferes with memory for ordered information but not with memory for other types of information. This criticism raises several crucial questions for Vellutino's verbal deficit explanation of an inability to discriminate ordered information. In several studies (Corkin, 1974; Rudnick, Sterritt, & Flax, 1967; Singer et al., 1976), poor readers remember and detect certain types of information. Poor readers, for example, appear to remember the number of items in auditory and visual sequences and succeed at comparing some visual spatial sequences. Moreover, they remember the particular items in a Digit Span test but not the order. One wonders how a verbal deficit interferes with memory for ordered information but leaves other memorial capacities unsullied. If a verbal deficit plagues the poor reader then one must account for the interaction of this deficit with different memory tasks. One could maintain that the verbal deficit exists but its effect varies with the difficulty of the memory task. This position, however, avoids the real issue. If one explains that a verbal deficit interferes with memory for order because remembering order is more difficult than remembering other information, one still can reasonably wonder why the poor reader finds remembering order particularly difficult.

A second problem is that the data that support the verbal deficit hypothesis preclude clear interpretation. As an example, Vellutino cites studies by Denckla and Rudel (1976a, 1976b) as supporting the verbal deficit hypothesis. In those studies poor readers took longer and were less accurate in naming various items (i.e., objects, colors, letters, words, and numerals). They suggest on the basis of these data that poor readers may experience difficulty in retrieving words. One must hasten to note, however, that in one study (1976a) five items appeared within a single display. One might reasonably suppose that poor readers lack efficient scanning strategies or have less focused attention than poor readers. Poor scanning strategies or less focused attention could easily explain the poor reader's difficulty with a single, multi-element display. Also, repeated failure on other tasks may have altered their criterion for taking responses (which would account for their slowness). Finally, as discussed later, Stanley and Hall (1973b) have reported that poor readers may process visual stimuli more slowly than good readers. Thus, a rapid naming task may have strained the poor reader's ability to process quickly the five items within the display.

Other evidence cited by Vellutino (1977) also admits a variety of explanations. He notes studies that demonstrate that dyslexics lack various syntactic skills (Vogel, 1974). This represents, according to Vellutino, a verbal deficit and evidence that a verbal deficit causes reading failure. Clearly, low performance on syntactic skill measures might be understood as an effect rather than as a cause of poor reading. The same criticism can be leveled against Vellutino's argument that a low Verbal IQ relative to Performance IQ (Huelsman, 1970) indicates a verbal deficit. Also, as noted earlier, McLeod (1965) held Verbal IQ constant across various reading abilities and still found that performance on the Digit Span subtest correlated with reading achievement. According to this study, reading ability can be statistically related to memory for order independent of Verbal IQ.

## Summary

A verbal deficit may account for some instances of poor reading. It seems very reasonable that a general language deficit would interfere with the acquisition of reading skills. None of the evidence cited by Vellutino, however, explains how a verbal deficit could account for a specific failure to discriminate ordered information. He never proves that verbal labeling necessarily improves serial recall and never demonstrates why a verbal deficit would interfere selectively with order-related tasks. Also, some of the evidence cited by Vellutino is experimentally unsound.

## THE VISUAL PROCESSING LAG EXPLANATION

One could fail in detecting differences between various orderings of the same elements if one slowly processed individual items. For instance, temporally distinct and differently colored light pulses will appear to be a single pulse of colored light, at very brief **interstimulus intervals** (Efron, 1967). Also, any two temporally distinct events will become indistinguishable at certain brief interstimulus intervals (Kristofferson, 1967; Poltrock, 1977). Ordered items could also lose their relative order if the visual elements were scanned over time and if the processing of the individual elements proceeded slowly, not allowing the processor to appreciate the ordered relations between the various elements.

Studies reported by Stanley (1976), Stanley and Hall (1973a, 1973b) and O'Neill and Stanley (1976) all suggest that poor readers require more time than good readers to process visual stimuli. Stanley and Hall (1973b) presented two successive visual stimuli to good and poor readers. The two stimuli, if shown temporally close, were seen as a composite by both groups. It took significantly longer interstimulus intervals, however, before poor readers reported separate elements rather than a composite stimulus. For example, a vertical and horizontal line were seen as a "plus sign" unless sufficient time separated the two presentations. It took a longer separation before poor readers saw the two stimuli as separate lines. Stanley and Hall (1973b) also reported that at brief exposure durations poor readers failed to process as many digits (the dependent variable was the number of digits recalled) as normal readers.

O'Neill and Stanley (1976) corroborated the Stanley and Hall experiments. In that study poor and normal readers were required to determine whether one or two lines had been tachistoscopically presented. Their stimuli included vertical, diagonal, and horizontal lines. In all stimulus cases poor readers required longer separations between the stimuli than normals before reporting two discrete lines. They also reported that these differences persisted under a variety of masking conditions. Bakker (1970) supports these findings. He reported that the ability to distinguish temporally distinct light flashes decreased with decreasing reading ability.

Because there has been no strict attempt to correlate performance on order-related tasks and visual processing lags among poor readers one cannot demonstrate a connection between the two separate observations. There is, however, a logical relationship between speed of visual processing or auditory processing and the ability to discrminate and remember ordered information. This logical relationship warrants further experimental investigation.

## THE DIRECTIONAL KNOWLEDGE INTERPRETATION

An inability to remember or detect ordered relations may implicate an inadequate understanding of direction. For example, directional concepts such as left and right might be important in the memorial representation of letter strings. That is, "the" differs from "hte" in the relative orderings of the "h" and the "t." Stated differently, the two letter strings vary in terms of which letter occurs first or to the left. As "th" represents a common letter sequence, whereas "ht" is irregular, the question of which letter occurs to the left describes the distinction between a regular and an irregular bigram. Thus, in order to acquire the orthographic knowledge that "th" represents a common rather than an uncommon sequence one might need to remember the "leftness" or "firstness" of the "t."

One might predict, given the foregoing reasoning, that individuals who lack directional concepts would experience difficulty in acquiring or learning ordered relations. My review of the literature failed to find an experiment that attempted to link poor directional knowledge with an inability to learn sequences of items. There are, however, several researchers who note that poor readers experience difficulty in distinguishing left and right on themselves, on objects, and on others (Critchley, 1970; Johnson & Myklebust, 1967; Orton, 1966). Other researchers report that poor readers fail to develop clear manual preference and often display crossed dominance (Bryden, 1970; Orton, 1966; Zangwill, 1960, 1968; Zurif & Carson, 1970). This failure to develop dominance may result in inadequate directional sense as children may learn left and right through self-reference (Piaget & Inhelder, 1956). For example, if knowing which arm best throws a ball helps one to effectively learn left and right, then those lacking clear dominance may not learn direction easily. Moreover, this difficulty may relate, later, to a difficulty in learning ordered arrangements of letters. In this way the evidence suggesting that poor readers lack clear dominance may be compatible with the observations that poor readers lack order-related skills (Singer, 1976). This issue, the correlation of dominance to reading failure, will be discussed in Staller's chapter on neurological correlates to reading failure.

## CONCLUSIONS

Orthographic rules specify ordered relations among letters as well as the order of letters within a word. Experiments reviewed indicated that good but not poor readers utilized this ordered information. Although a lack of familiarity with text could explain the poor reader's insensitivity to orthographic regularity, other studies suggest that poor readers fail in many tasks involving ordered information. Possible explanations of this order-related deficit were discussed—a verbal deficit, a processing lag, and an absence of directional knowledge. Critical experiments, which might test these hypotheses, have yet to be implemented.

## GLOSSARY

**Alexia.**   A sudden loss of reading ability that can be attributed to some brain trauma.

**Etiological Claims.**   Statements concerning origin or cause.

**Intersensory Integration.**   The process of relating information from two (or more) distinct senses. An example would be appreciating the similarity between three dots separated by two equal intervals and three auditory bursts (e.g., a "beep") separated by two equally long intervals.

**Interstimulus Interval.**   In experimental procedures this refers to the time separating the presentation of two stimuli.

**Ordered Information.**   Any series of items that occurs over time (a temporal sequence) or across space (a spatial sequence). Strings of letters satisfy both of these definitions as they are distributed across some space (i.e., a page) and we apprehend them over time (i.e., one does not see all the letters on a page in a flash).

**Spatial Sequence** (Distributions).   A series of items that occurs across space. For example, a string of visually presented letters represents a spatial sequence.

**Temporal Sequence.**   A series of items that occurs over time. Music represents one example of a temporal sequence.

## REFERENCES

Bakker, D. J. Temporal order perception and reading retardation. In D. Bakker & P. Satz (Eds.), *Specific reading disability*. Rotterdam: Rotterdam University Press, 1970.

Birch, H. G., & Belmont, L. Auditory–visual integration in normal and retarded readers. *American Journal of Orthopsychiatry*, 1964, *34*, 852–861.

Bryden, M. Laterality effects in dichotic listening: Relations with handedness and reading ability in children. *Neuropsychologia*, 1970, *8*, 443–447.

Corkin, S. Serial-ordering deficits in inferior readers. *Neuropsychologia*, 1974, *12*, 347–354.

Critchley, M. *The dyslexic child*. London: Heinemann Medical Books, Ltd., 1970.

Denckla, M., & Rudel, R. Naming of object drawings by dyslexic and other learning disabled children. *Brain & Language*, 1976, *3*, 1–16a. (a)

Denckla, M., & Rudel, R. Rapid "automatized" naming (R.A.N.): Dyslexia differentiated from other learning disabilities. *Neuropsychologia*, 1976, *14*, 471–479. (b)

Efron, R. The duration of the present. *Annals of the New York Academy of Science*, 1967, *138*, 713–729.

Fildes, L. G. A psychological inquiry into the nature of the condition known as congenital word-blindness. *Brain*, 1921, *44*, 286–307.

Guthrie, J. T., & Goldberg, H. K. Visual sequential memory in reading disability. *Journal of Learning Disabilities*, 1972, *5*, 41–50.

Guttentag, R. *Word processing by good and poor readers*. Unpublished doctoral dissertation, University of Denver, 1978.

Huelsman, C. B. The WISC subtest syndrome for disabled readers. *Perceptual and Motor Skills*, 1970, *30*, 535–550.

Johnson, D., & Myklebust, B. *Learning disabilities*. New York: Grune & Stratton, 1967.

Kristofferson, A. B. Attention and psychophysical time. *Acta Psychologica*, 1967, *27*, 93–100.

Lyle, J. G., & Goyen, J. Performance of retarded readers on the WISC and educational tests. *Journal of Abnormal Psychology*, 1968, *73*, 25–29.

Mason, M. Reading ability and letter search time: Effects of orthographic structure defined by single-letter positional frequency. *Journal of Experimental Psychology: General*, 1975, *104*, 146–166.

Mason, M., & Katz, L. Visual processing of nonlinguistic strings: Redundancy effects and reading ability. *Journal of Experimental Psychology: General*, 1976, *105*, 338–348.

Massaro, D. W. *Understanding language*, New York: Academic Press, 1975.

McLeod, J. A comparison of WISC sub-test scores of preadolescent successful and unsuccessful readers. *Australian Journal of Psychology*, 1965, *17*, 220–228.

Muehl, S., & Kremenak, S. Ability to match information within and between auditory and visual sense modalities and subsequent reading achievement. *Journal of Educational Psychology*, 1966, *57*, 230–239.

O'Neill, G., & Stanley, G. U. Visual processing of straight lines in dyslexic and normal children. *British Journal of Educational Research*, 1976, *46*, 323–327.

Orton, S. *Word-blindness in school children and other papers on strephosymbolia*. Pomfret, Conn.: The Orton Society, Inc., 1966.

Piaget, J., & Inhelder, B. *The child's conception of space*. London: Routon and Kegan Paul, 1956.

Poltrock, S. *Models of temporal order discrimination*. Unpublished doctoral dissertation. University of Washington, 1977.

Rabinovitch, R. D. Reading problems in children: Definitions and classification. In A. Keeney & V. Keeney (Eds.), *Dyslexia: Diagnosis and treatment of reading disorders*. St. Louis: C. V. Mosby, 1968.

Reber, A. S. Implicit Learning of artificial grammars. *Journal of Verbal Learning and Verbal Behavior*, 1967, *6*(6), 855–863.

Reber, A. S. Implicit learning of synthetic languages: The role of instructional set. *Journal of Experimental Psychology: Human Learning and Memory*, 1976, *2*, 88–94.

Rozin, P., Poritsky, S., & Sotsky, R. American children with reading problems can easily learn to read English represented by Chinese characters. *Science*, 1971, *171*, 1264–1267.

Rudnick, M., Sterritt, G. M., & Flax, M. Auditory and visual rhythm perception and reading ability. *Child Development*, 1967, *38*, 581–587.

Schwartz, S., & Doehring, D. G. A developmental study of children's ability to acquire knowledge of spelling patterns. *Developmental Psychology*, 1977, *13*(4), 419–420.

Singer, M. H. The ability to sequence as an essential reading skill. In W. Engel (Ed.), *Child language—1975*. Milford, Conn.: International Linguistics Association, 1976.

Singer, M. H., Allen, T. W., & Lappin, J. S. *The ability of good and poor readers to discriminate ordered information*. Unpublished manuscript, 1976. (Also, paper presented at Southeastern Conference on Linguistics [SECOL], March 1975.)

Stanley, G. The processing of digits by children with specific reading disability (dyslexia). *British Journal of Educational Psychology*, 1976 (Feb.), *46*(11), 81–84.

Stanley, G., & Hall, R. A comparison of dyslexics and normals in recalling letter arrays after brief presentation. *The British Journal of Educational Psychology*, 1973, *43*, 301–304. (a)

Stanley, G., & Hall, R. Short-term visual information processing in dyslexics. *Child development*, 1973, *44*, 841–844. (b)

Vellutino, F. R. Alternative conceptualizations of dyslexia: Evidence in support of a verbal-deficit hypothesis. *Harvard Educational Review*, 1977, *47*, 334–355.

Vogel, S. A. Syntactic abilities in normal and dyslexic children. *Journal of Learning Disability*, 1974, *7*, 103–109.

Yamadori, A. Ideogram reading in alexia. *Brain*, 1975, *98*, 231–238.

Zangwill, O. *Cerebral dominance and its relation to psychological function*. Springfield, Ill.: Charles C. Thomas, 1960.

Zangwill, O. Dyslexia in relation to cerebral dominance. In J. Money (Ed.), *Reading disability*. Baltimore: Johns Hopkins Press, 1968.

Zurif, E., & Carson, G. Dyslexia in relation to cerebral dominance and temporal analysis. *Neuropsychologia*, 1970, *8*, 351–361.

# 5 Word Recognition Skill and Reading Ability

Keith E. Stanovich
*Oakland University*

## INTRODUCTION

Word recognition is a component of the total reading process, and it is therefore natural to attempt to determine the importance of word recognition as a component of reading. A related question concerns whether the ability to recognize words rapidly and accurately determines individual differences in reading fluency. Finally, if a relation were found between word recognition ability and reading fluency, interest would then center on the psychological processes responsible for the relationship (phonetic recoding, orthographic knowledge, etc.). This chapter focuses on these questions.

Our discussion requires some comment regarding terminology. The term *decoding* has been much used and abused in the reading literature. The use of the term has been so inconsistent that many researchers in the experimental psychology of reading prefer to avoid it completely (clear, *operational* definitions being a necessary component of good science). Some have used the term to mean translation to a speech-based code. For example, Carroll (1977) refers to: "the so-called 'decoding' aspects of reading—the translation of print into a representation parallel to that of spoken language [p. 1]." Others have used the term to mean accessing meaning in the mental lexicon. For example, Dechant and Smith (1977) state that decoding: "is more than a matching of phoneme to grapheme. This is *recoding*, but it is not *decoding*. Decoding occurs only when meaning is associated with the written symbol [p. 10]."

The Dechant and Smith (1977) definition of decoding is employed in this chapter. When the terms *word recognition* or *decoding* occur they refer to processes essential to *lexical access* (See Chapter 1 for a discussion of lexical access). It should also be noted that the term word recognition does not indicate whether the lexicon was accessed via a visual or a phonological process. Indeed, which process predominates in early reading and whether there are individual differences in the use of the visual or phonological codes are questions that are addressed in the present chapter.


## THE IMPORTANCE OF RAPID WORD RECOGNITION

### What Theories Have to Say

Theories of reading differ in the extent to which they view the pickup of visual information as being directed by contextual expectancies (refer to the ''plodder/explorer'' terminology of Rozin & Gleitman, 1977, that was introduced earlier). Models that emphasize the importance of higher-level contextual hypotheses in directing visual information pickup have been termed *top-down models* (see Goodman, 1976, and Smith, 1978, for examples of this type of model). Models that assume that the sequence of processing operations proceeds from the visual information to higher-level encodings have been termed *bottom-up models* (Gough, 1972; LaBerge & Samuels, 1974). Rumelhart (1977) has described a *hybrid* class of theory, known as interactive models, and Stanovich (1980) has discussed how this class of theory might explain individual differences in reading fluency. These hybrid models allow both ''bottom-up'' and ''top-down'' processing.

Despite differences among these models, they *all* agree that words must be rapidly processed for fluent reading to occur. Indeed, this may be the *only* point on which there is agreement among these three types of theory. Smith (1978, Smith & Holmes, 1971) has repeatedly emphasized that reading must be rapid so that several words can be integrated as a meaningful sequence (e.g., a sentence) in long-term memory. Slow reading strains *short-term memory* and leads to words being read as isolated units. Bottom-up models also stress the need for rapid reading of words; LaBerge and Samuels (1974) have argued that word-meaning codes: ''can be organized to make sense only if he can manage to shift his attention activation quickly among these meaning codes to keep them simultaneously active. We are assuming that the process of organizing is promoted by fast scanning at the semantic level in much the same way that fast scanning of feature detectors promotes unitizing of features into new letter patterns [p. 313].''

Perfetti and Lesgold (1977; Lesgold & Perfetti, 1978) have developed a type of limited-capacity model that is compatible with LaBerge and Samuels' (1974) claims (as well as Smith's [1978]). They argue that comprehension breakdowns will occur if words are not verbally coded into short-term memory at a fast enough rate. Stanovich (1980) has discussed how models that assume interactive processing at the word level also predict a relationship between context-free word-recognition speed and reading fluency. In these models, deficiencies in a low-level processing operation (e.g., feature analysis, letter or word recognition) may lead a reader to rely more on higher-level knowledge sources (e.g., prior contextual constraints). However, if the use of this higher-level knowledge source requires attention, then fewer cognitive resources will be available for comprehension. Thus, a reader who has no deficiencies in lower-level processing operations (i.e., recognizes words rapidly) will exhaust little attention developing higher-level contextual expectancies. Consequently that reader will have more capacity to allocate to comprehension processes. This relates to the earlier discussion of Bryan and Harter (1899), cited in Chapter 1. In addition to the theoretical arguments favoring a relationship between word recognition speed and reading ability, there are other logical arguments drawn from the literature on eye movements that would lead one to expect such a relationship. First, contrary to common belief, even fluent adult readers fixate virtually every content word in the text (Just & Carpenter, 1980). Readers do not sample words from text, but instead extract information from nearly every content word. Second, variables (e.g., word frequency) that are known to affect the recognition of words in isolation also have been shown to affect the length of eye fixations during ongoing reading (Rayner, 1977)

## Empirical Relationships Between Word Recognition Skill and Reading Ability.

When one turns from theory to the empirical research on the relation between word recognition skill and reading ability, it is heartening to note agreement among researchers. There is a strong relationship between word recognition speed and reading ability, particularly in early grades. Indeed, the relationship holds even for fluent adult readers, although less strongly (Butler & Hains, 1979; Mason, 1978; see Stanovich, 1980, for a review). Paragraph reading fluency can be predicted with high accuracy from the speed with which a subject names isolated words. Children defined as skilled readers on the basis of *comprehension* measures are markedly superior to below-average comprehenders in their ability to name words rapidly and accurately. Some representative studies that demonstrate this relationship are discussed later.

As already stated, Shankweiler and Liberman (1972) observed correlations in the range of .5 to .8 when word-naming speed and accuracy were correlated with paragraph-reading fluency. These high correlations were observed for second-, third-, and fourth-grade readers. Employing second-grade subjects, McCormick and Samuels (1979) found correlations of approximately −.55 between word recognition latency and comprehension ability, and approximately .60 between word recognition accuracy and comprehension ability. Groff (1978) reports correlations averaging over .80 between word reading and several standardized measures of paragraph reading. Biemiller (1977–1978) tested children in the second through sixth grades and observed that, on the average, 68% of the variance in text reading time was accounted for by letter and word-naming time. The variance accounted for was as high as 89% in the third grade.

In a different type of study, where vocalization latency was carefully measured, Perfetti and Hogaboam (1975) found that less-skilled third- and fifth-grade readers named even high-frequency words approximately 150 msec slower than skilled readers. (The procedure used by Perfetti and his colleagues is discussed in Chapter 3). Low-frequency words were named approximately 1 second slower by the poorer readers. In further experiments, Perfetti, Finger, and Hogaboam (1978) found that less skilled third-graders named colors, digits, and pictures just as fast as good readers of the same age. However, the skilled readers named words approximately 465 msec faster than the less skilled readers (see also, Stanovich, 1981b).

In summary, the relationship between word recognition skill and reading ability is well established. The relationship is very strong in the early grades, but declines somewhat as the reader develops fluency, probably because when a certain threshold of reading speed is passed (i.e., word recognition speed approaches *asymptote*), increases in fluency are more dependent on the development of more sophisticated language comprehension strategies that operate relatively independently of speed (Jackson & McClelland, 1979; Sticht, 1972). We now attempt to interpret the relationship between word recognition skill and reading ability.

### Interpretation of the Relationship: Spurious Correlations Revisited.

It is tempting to conclude from the empirical evidence and theoretical arguments just reviewed that word recognition ability is an important determinant of progress in reading, and that rapid word recognition should be taught as a subskill in order to improve reading ability. This temptation should, however, be resisted and the conclusion held in abeyance until some of the complexities of the inference are considered. The evidence linking word recognition skill and reading ability is correlational and, to reiterate a point stressed in previous chapters, a correlation by itself does not permit a causal inference. Although it seems logical, as words are the building blocks of text, to assume that increases in word recognition skill would lead to increases in general reading ability, the correlation could result from a causal chain running in the opposite direction. Namely, good readers may read more, receive more exposure to words (see Biemiller, 1977–1978, for empirical evidence of differential exposure as early as January of the first-grade year), and thus develop superior word recognition skills. Word recognition skill could be a consequence of superior reading rather than a cause.

Ehri (1979) has provided a useful discussion of the various possibilities that exist when it is found that a processing capability relates to the ease of reading acquisition. If a particular subskill relates to reading ability, four possibilities exist. First, the subskill might be a *prerequisite* to successful reading, in which case an improvement in the subskill would be a direct cause of an increase in reading ability. Furthermore, in the case of a *prerequisite subskill*, reading progress is simply not possible unless the subskill is mastered. Second, a subskill might be a *facilitator* of successful reading. Here, as in the prerequisite case, improvement in the subskill would be a direct cause of an increase in reading ability. However, failure to master a facilitator skill does not completely preclude the acquisition of reading. The development of a facilitator skill speeds reading acquisition but does not constitute a *necessary condition* for acquisition. Third, proficiency at a subskill may correlate with reading ability because the subskill is a *consequence* of the development of reading fluency. In this case, experience at reading causes increases in the proficiency of the subskill. Finally, a subskill may be an *incidental correlate* of reading ability. That is, both may develop independently but appear to be related due to a common relationship with a third variable (i.e., a spurious relation). All but the last possibility appear to be viable candidates as explanations for the empirical relationship between word recognition skill and reading ability.

Of course, there are strong a priori grounds for believing that the development of word recognition skill causes increased reading proficiency. Words are visually separated in text. Nearly all models of reading contain a processing substage that involves the recognition of words (Just & Carpenter, 1980). More specifically, several models explicitly predict a direct relation between word recognition speed and reading proficiency. This is especially true of the models of LaBerge and Samuels (1974), Perfetti and Lesgold (1977; Lesgold and Perfetti, 1978), and Stanovich (1980). Shankweiler and Liberman (1972) state flatly that: "poor reading of text with little comprehension among beginning readers is usually a consequence of reading words poorly [p. 294]." Still, we need to investigate *empirically* whether word recognition skills are determinants of reading comprehension. Biemiller (1970) reported a study that helps to untangle the relationship between word recognition skill and success in reading. He studied the oral reading errors of a group of first-grade children from October to May and argued for the existence of three stages of reading acquisition during this period. In the first stage, contextual information dominated reading and few of the children's errors were visual. That is, the children guessed from context and made errors related to their interpretation of the context. In the second stage, children made many more errors that were visual or "graphically constrained." Biemiller (1970) interpreted this stage as a transition period during which the children were moving from a context-using phase where they were attempting to avoid using graphic information to a stage where they focused attention on graphic information. In the third stage, the children's oral reading errors were both contextually and graphically constrained. Biemiller (1970) also reported that the students who by the end of the year had made the most progress in reading acquisition had moved into the second stage much faster than less successful children. This indicates that reading progress was, in part, determined by how early the child shifted attention to decoding words. Biemiller (1970) concluded that: "Data presented in this study indicate that the child's first task in learning to read is mastery of the use of graphic information. . . . The longer he stays in the early, context-emphasizing phase without showing an increase in the use of graphic information the poorer a reader he is at the end of the year [p. 95]."

Guthrie and Tyler (1976) conducted a study from which they also concluded that incomplete decoding was the cause of poor comprehension in a sample of disabled readers. Guthrie and Tyler (1976) used a design recommended by Bradley and Bryant (1978, 1979), in which poor readers are matched with a group of younger average readers who are at the same achievement level. This design makes it much less likely that any observed processing difference between the two groups will be the result of differential reading experience.[1] In the Guthrie and Tyler (1976) experiment, two matched groups of subjects who were at the fourth-grade level on the Gates–MacGinitie comprehension test listened to and read word strings of words that were either meaningful, anomalous (syntactic structure but not meaning was preserved), or random. Subjects recalled the word strings immediately after presentation.

Guthrie and Tyler (1976) reported that the two groups performed similarly when they listened to the stimuli, but that the poor readers recalled significantly less when the stimuli were read. Also, both groups recalled meaningful strings bettern than anomalous strings, and anomalous strings strings better than random strings. The similarity in average and poor readers' abilities to remember meaningful material, and their similarity in the listening conditions led Guthrie and Tyler to search for a processing difference between average and poor readers that was independent of general language ability. Of several hypotheses that were tested by detailed post hoc *error analyses*, only one received support, that "The frequency with which poor readers, during silent reading, decode words into forms that can be easily processed in STM (*Short-Term Memory*) and entered into language processors appears to be lower than the frequency for good readers. Consequently, reading comprehension deficiency is at least partially attributable to a failure to fully identify a sufficient number of words during the course of reading [p. 424–425]."

Lesgold, Resnick, Roth, and Hammond (1981) have recently reported on a longitudinal study where a group of children were repeatedly tested on their word recognition speed and reading progress. The pattern of correlations over time suggested that increased word recognition speed led to improved reading comprehension, rather than vice versa.

In summary, the bulk of the research evidence suggests that word recognition ability represents a causal factor in the development of reading skill. Although

---

[1]The rationale is that if poor readers have less experience reading than good readers at the same age, one can minimize this experience difference by matching poor readers with younger readers who have less experience.

there may be an occasional poor reader with good recognition skills, most children with reading difficulties have problems decoding words. Although word recognition may be causally related to reading development, it is more difficult to determine whether recognition skill is a facilitator or a prerequisite. The present state of the evidence appears to warrant the conclusion that word recognition skill is most certainly a facilitator, and quite likely a prerequisite of fluent reading, but the latter conclusion should be held tentatively, as we await further evidence.

## PSYCHOLOGICAL MECHANISMS THAT MEDIATE WORD RECOGNITION SKILL

Having established the relation between word recognition skill and reading ability, it is necessary to determine the psychological mechanisms that mediate word recognition. Psychologists have used the term *mental lexicon* to refer to a structured storage space in memory where information about words is represented (Barron, 1981). For each word there exists a location where various sources of information about the word (e.g., semantic, syntactic, phonological, and visual–orthographic) are interconnected. When this location is activated, information about the word (e.g., its meaning) becomes available to consciousness. A printed word has two access codes by which it can activate the mental lexicon. One is based on the visual–orthographic features of the word. These features can be coded by the visual system into a form that matches the visual–orthographic representation of that word that is stored in the lexicon. A match between the coded visual–orthographic features of the stimulus and the stored visual–orthographic representation activates the meaning of the word.

The other mechanism by which the lexicon can be accessed involves phonological processing. This process begins by transforming the visual representation of the word into a phonological representation, that is, a representation related to the sound of the word. Just how this translation is accomplished is a subject of much controversy (Baron, 1977; Barron, 1981, Glushko, 1979). Some of this controversy is reviewed in Chapter 1. The phonological representation of the stimulus word is then used to match the phonological representation of the word that is permanently stored in the lexicon. A match between these two representations activates the meaning of the word. It is generally believed (Meyer, Schvaneveldt, & Ruddy, 1974; Stanovich & Bauer, 1978) that upon presentation of a word, both the visual–orthographic and the phonological access processes can execute simultaneously (i.e., *in parallel*).

If two separate processes operate to achieve lexical access, then a deficiency in either could cause poor word recognition. Moreover, these two types of deficiencies (e.g., visual or phonological) may lead to different patterns of word recognition failure. The following section reviews evidence that links the *phonological process* with poor word recognition. The relationship between visual processes (e.g., sensitivity to ordered visual information) has already been discussed in the previous chapter by Singer.

## Lexical Access Based on a Phonological Code

In Boder's (1973) clinical sample of dyslexic children, dysphonic readers (children who had difficulty in deriving the phonological code of a written word) were six times as numerous as dyseidetic readers (children who could recode but could not deal with visual configurations). This clinical data supports experimental evidence indicating that the ability to use a phonological code to access the lexicon relates to reading fluency. We have already reviewed studies that demonstrate that less skilled readers verbally name words more slowly than skilled readers. Poor readers are even worse at processing *pseudo*words. As discussed in Chapter 1, a pseudoword is a pronounceable letter string that conforms to the orthographic and phonological structure of English. This letter string, however, is not a word. It is a string of letters that *could* be a word but just happens *not* to be. The nonword string "glurt" is a pseudoword, whereas "tlgru" is not. Pseudowords can be pronounced only by transforming the letter string into some type of phonological form. Thus, the ability to pronounce pseudowords in part reflects the ability to transform a sequence of letters into a phonological code.

The speed of naming pseudowords is one of the tasks that most clearly differentiates good from poor readers (Barron, 1978a, 1978b; Hogaboam & Perfetti, 1978; Perfetti & Hogaboam, 1975; Seymour & Porpodas, 1980). It is also interesting to note that skilled readers, because of their well-functioning phonological access mechanisms, can be "fooled" by pseudowords. In a study that required fifth- and sixth-grade children to determine that "rane" was not a word, skilled readers had more difficulty than less skilled readers (Barron, 1978b).

Other experimental results also indicate that skilled readers, but not unskilled readers, exploit a phonological code. This evidence concerns the speed with which skilled and unskilled readers can recognize regular and irregular words. *Regular words* (e.g., "cave") conform to spelling-to-sound correspondence rules. *Irregular words* do not follow these rules (e.g., "sword," "one"). Irregular, or exception words cannot be processed phonologically because the letter-to-sound translation rules simply do not work for them. Thus, these words are processed visually. Regular words, however, can be phonologically accessed.

Barron (1980, 1981) reported that skilled readers were slightly faster in recognizing irregular words (where phonological coding cannot take place). However, the difference between the two groups was much greater on regular words. Presumably, this reflects the skilled reader's ability to take advantage of phonological coding. Barron's experiments suggest that skilled readers are better able to employ a phonological code.

## Memory and Phonological Codes: Another Advantage for Skilled Readers.

Phonological coding can confer another processing advantage in addition to providing a lexical access code. During reading, sequences of words must be held in short-term memory while comprehension processes operate on the words to integrate them into sentences, paragraphs, and ideas. There is evidence (Baddeley, 1966; Conrad, 1964) that, for this purpose, the most stable short-term memory code is a phonetic code. It has been shown (Kleiman, 1975) that phonological coding is important even for the comprehension of adult readers who access words primarily via a visual–orthographic code. Thus, the ability to form a stable phonological code rapidly in short-term memory may be related to comprehension proficiency (see Perfetti & Lesgold, 1977). This section explores the differences between skilled and unskilled readers in their ability to exploit a phonological code for storing words in short-term memory.

Shankweiler, Liberman, Mark, Fowler, and Fischer (1979) tested the ability to second-grade children to recall random letter strings. Skilled readers recalled many more letters than did less skilled readers. However, when the letters were rhyming consonants, the performance of skilled readers deteriorated more than that of the less skilled readers. This deterioration probably indicates that skilled readers form a stable phonological code for maintaining letters in short-term memory. Manipulations designed to create confusions among phonological codes (e.g., rhyming strings of letters) are therefore more prone to disrupt the performance of the skilled readers. Shankweiler et al. (1979) showed that the same pattern of results obtained with auditory presentations, suggesting that it is the use of a phonological code in short-term memory, independent of the type of stimulus (e.g., letters versus sounds), that differentiates the two reader groups.

Other experiments support this view. Byrne and Shea (1979) presented second-grade children with lists of words and gave them a recognition test. Some of the *foils* in the recognition test were semantically related to words actually presented and some rhymed with words actually presented. Skilled readers made more *false positives* to rhyming words than to semantically related words. In contrast, less skilled readers made many semantically based false positives, but very few rhyme-based false positives. These results support the hypothesis that skilled readers are more likely to store words in short-term memory in a phonological form.

Importantly, Mann, Liberman, and Shankweiler (1980) established that the results of Shankweiler et al. (1979) and Byrne and Shea (1979) extend to stimulus materials that more closely resemble actual text. They required second-grade children to recall meaningful sentences. The sentences contained either phonetically nonconfusable words (e.g., Poor Jim stayed inside when the snow covered up the back yard) or phonetically confusable words (e.g., Lou knew that the blue shoe in the new canoe belonged to you). Skilled readers were superior to the less skilled readers in recalling the nonconfusable sentences. However, the two groups did not differ significantly when recalling the confusable sentences. Thus, phonetic confusability hurt the performance of skilled readers more than that of less skilled readers. The results demonstrate, again, a greater use of phonological coding by skilled readers.

## Phonologically Related Skills that Contribute to Early Reading Success

In the previous two sections we have discussed aspects of phonological processing that could be related to reading success at all levels of reading fluency. That is, the ability to access the lexicon rapidly via a phonological code, and to form a more lasting short-term memory code, could distinguish skilled and less skilled readers at all experience levels. In the present section we ask the question whether there are phonologically related skills that may determine, in part, the ease of reading *acquisition*.

Gough and Hillinger (1980) have conceptualized one of the early stages of learning to read as a problem in *cryptanalysis*. That is, the child must pass through a stage where he or she realizes that written language is a coded form (actually a *cipher*) of spoken language, and that breaking the code will allow him or her to transform written words into speech-related representations, which he or she is already proficient at using, to access meaning in the mental lexicon. Much has been written about the complex nature of the spelling-to-sound correspondence rules of English. This complexity has been used to support the argument that it is impossible to solve the cryptanalysis problem and that this is not a stage that early readers go through. However, Gough and Hillinger (1980) present convincing arguments against this view. They argue that the irregularity of English spelling has been overemphasized, pointing to the relative success of an effort to build a reading machine for the blind that is based on spelling-to-sound correspondence rules. Secondly, they point out that even when the irregularity of English spelling yields an incorrect pronunciation, the result is often close to the correct form, usually close enough so that a very small amount of context would result in a correct identification. Finally, it appears that in order to get *started*, to *begin* to attain levels of practice that make fluent reading possible, the child must engage in an effort to break the spelling-to-sound code. Otherwise, it is hard to see how the child is to acquire the reading independence, the ability to read on his or her own, that is necessary if he or she is to acquire enough exposure to words to enable him or her to develop the strategies (e.g., visual–orthographic access) and automaticities (see Chapter 1) characteristic of the fluent reader.

If the child is to discover spelling-to-sound correspondences, however, he or she must possess certain prerequisite skills. He or she must be able to recognize the units of both visual and phonological codes, letters, and phonemes. Visually segmenting and identifying letter units appears no to be a problem in the early reader (Fischer, Liberman, & Shankweiler, 1978; Fisher & Frankfurter, 1977; Gibson & Levin, 1975). *Phonemes*, however, are another matter. Evidence indicates that early readers and prereaders have difficulty in becoming explicitly aware of the phoneme as the basic unit of the spoken word, and that phonemic awareness is related to early reading success. Young children display difficulty in *segmenting* a word into separate phonemes and synthesizing a word from separate phonemes. Note before we begin our discussion that to say that a child can *discriminate* two phonemes is different from saying that he or she is explicitly *aware* of the phoneme as a speech unit. Gough and Hillinger (1980) have cautioned that: "to say that the child can tell one word from another, or produce one word from another, on the basis of a single phonemic contrast, is not to say that he realizes that each word is composed of a sequence of phonemes [p. 190]." Thus, the discussion that follows concerns the ability to analyze phonemes and become aware of them as units, not the ability to discriminate phonemes.

Young children have great difficulty with tasks that require phonemic segmentation skills. Such skills also are related to early reading success (see Ehri, 1979, and Golinkoff, 1978, for reviews). Calfee, Chapman, and Venezky (1972) found that the performance of kindergarten children was at chance on tasks where they had to decide whether or not two words "sound the same at the end" and whether or not two words "start with the same sound." Liberman, Shankweiler, Fischer, and Carter (1974) had children tap a table to indicate how many sounds were in a one-syllable word (phonemic segmentation) or tap to indicate how many syllables were in a multisyllable word (syllable segmentation). Syllable segmentation was much easier than phomene segmentation. Very few preschoolers and kindergarten children were successful at phoneme segmentation. Liberman (1973) reported that the reading progress of beginning second-graders was strongly related to their performance on the phoneme segmentation task when tested as first-graders. Helfgott (1976) found that the ability to segment one-syllable words in kindergarten was stongly predictive of reading progress in first grade. Savin (1972) observed that poor readers were deficient at rhyming and pig-Latin games. Calfee, Lindamood, and Lindamood (1973) found that skill at matching discrete phonetic segments with colored blocks was related to reading ability. Fox and Routh (1980a) tested a group of first-graders on a relatively simple phoneme segmentation task. The experimenter simply asked the child to "say a little piece of" a one-syllable word. The performance of the first-graders who were average readers was at ceiling on the task, whereas a group of children with severe reading disabilities could segment hardly any of the words. Fox and Routh (1980b) followed up these children 3 years later and found that the children who could not segment in first grade showed marked deficiencies in reading achievement and displayed a pattern of reading disability similar to Bodor's (1973) dysphonetic dyslexics.

Given that phoneme segmentation ability in kindergarten (prior to exposure to a significant amount of written language) predicts later reading success, it seems unlikely that segmentation skills are merely correlates or consequences of reading experience. Indeed, other evidence suggests that phoneme segmentation skill is a prerequisite or facilitator of reading ability. Bradley and Bryant (1978) employed a unique design that was mentioned earlier in this chapter. They tested a group of children whose mean age was 6 years 10 months and who were progressing normally in reading (note that reading instruction generally begins earlier in England, the home country of these subjects, than in the United States). These subjects were matched to a group of children whose mean age was 10 years 4 months and who were reading at the same level. Thus, the 10-year-old group was delayed in their reading progress. Again, the advantage of this design is that it is much less likely that any processing difference that is uncovered between the two groups will be due to greater experience with text on the part of the normal readers. Bradley and Bryant (1978) gave the children an oddity task where four words were spoken to them and they had to say which was the odd word out. Three of the four words had a sound in common that the fourth did not share (e.g., weed, need, peel, deed). On a series of trials, only 27% of the normally progressing readers made more than one error, whereas 85% of the reading-delayed sample made more than one error. The delayed readers were also inferior on a rhyming task.

Training studies also help to determine the nature (i.e., causal or correlational) of the connection between phonemic segmentation skill and progress at reading. Fox and Routh (1976) studied a group of 4-year-old children who could segment syllables and a group that could not. One-half of each group received *phonic blend training*. All children were then taught to associate sounds with letterlike forms. They were then tested in their ability to read pairs of letterlike forms. Children who could segment syllables performed better than children who could not. Phonic blend training improved the performance only of those children who could segment. The latter finding suggests that the ability to segment phonemes facilitates the acquisition of the skills necessary to recognize words during early reading.

Other studies yield similar conclusions (see Goldstein, 1976). Williams (1980) conducted a large-scale field study that examined the efficacy of a supplemental reading program that emphasized phoneme analysis and blending. The experimental subjects were learning-disabled students in the early grades. After the training, experimental subjects were significantly better at reading words that had not been presented to them during training than were control subjects who had not received the supplemental program. Litcher and Roberge (1979) trained beginning first-grade children who were "at risk" for reading failure. The experimental children received a program that emphasized the structured teaching of phonetic units, whereas the control children were taught by the standard methods used in their respective schools. At the end of the academic year the reading levels of the experimental children were significantly higher.

In summary, there appears to be a reasonable amount of evidence that phonemic segmentation ability is causally related to success in the initial acquisition of reading and word recognition skills. This ability appears to be a strong facilitator of early reading success. Whether it is a prerequisite to reading acquisition, that is, whether it must be mastered before reading progress can occur is, as Ehri (1979) has emphasized, an inference that requires stronger evidence than is presently available.

## Coordination of the Phonological and Visual–Orthographic Codes

The research reviewed in the foregoing has established the existence of two processes that operate in parallel during word recognition. Breakdowns or deficiencies in either of the two processes can result in deficiencies in word recognition performance. Most of the research, however, has focused on one or the other of the processes. That is, researchers have tended to concentrate on tracing how breakdowns in the use of a phonological or a visual–orthographic code result in quantitative and qualitative changes in word recognition ability. Little research has been carried out on how the two processes are used together during recognition, individual differences in the use of phonological and visual–orthographic codes, and developmental changes in the relative reliance on the two codes. What little research exists, however, is extremely interesting and deserves mention.

Baron (1979) had children in the early grades read lists of pseudowords (e.g., *tave*), words that follow regular spelling-to-sound correspondence rules (e.g., *dive*), and words that violate such rules (e.g., *sugar*). The latter two classes were termed regular and exception words, respectively. Pseudowords are presumably read by phonologically recoding the letter strings. Exception words are probably recognized via a visual–orthographic code, as no easy rules exist for transforming their letter sequences into a phonological code. Regular words can be accessed by either code and thus it is of interest to see which code dominates when regular words are presented. Baron's (1979) paper contains evidence relevant to this issue, because he found that the ability to read pseudowords correlated more highly with the ability to read regular words than did the ability to read exception words (i.e., pseudoword reading is a better predictor of regular word reading than is exception word reading). This finding indicates that phonological coding is the predominant mechanism by which regular words are accessed. However, there was evidence that the visual–orthographic mechanism was contributing also to regular word reading, although to a lesser extent than the phonological mechanism. Specifically, the correlation between exception word reading and regular word reading was higher than the correlation between exception word reading and pseudoword reading. In short, both phonological and visual–orthographic mechanisms were operative in the recognition of regular words, but the phonological mechanism appeared to be dominant. Baron (1979) speculated that the visual–orthographic mechanism might become more important at later stages of learning, a hypothesis that Doctor and Coltheart (1980) tested in a developmental study.

Doctor and Coltheart (1980) had children from ages 6 to 10 read sentences and decide whether they made sense. Half of the sentences were meaningful and half were meaningless. The meaningless sentences were of four types: meaningless all-word sentences that sounded correct (e.g., I have know time); meaningless all-word sentences that sounded wrong (e.g., I have blue time); meaningless sentences containing nonwords that sounded correct (e.g., I have noe time); and meaningless sentences containing nonwords that sounded wrong (e.g., I have bloo time).

If the words of the sentence are being coded phonologically, then incorrect "yes" responses may occur when the meaningless sentences sound correct. This is exactly what happens when 6-year-old children respond to the sentences. They give incorrect "yes" responses 70.8% of the time to meaningless all-word sentences that sound correct. This is in contrast to an error rate of only 8.3% to meaningless all-word sentences that sound wrong. A similar pattern is apparent in the responses to meaningless sentences containing nonwords. When the sentence sounds correct, 6-year-olds respond incorrectly 56.3% of the time, in contrast to an error rate of just 10.4% when the sentence sounds wrong. These findings indicate a great deal of phonological coding on the part of 6-year-old children. These phonologically based errors diminish fairly rapidly, however, decreasing from 70.8% for 6-year-olds on all-word sentences to 43.7%, 31.2%, 18.7%, and 20.8%, across ages 7, 8, 9, and 10 years respectively. A similar decrease occurs for nonword sentences that sound correct. Error rates decline from 56.3% to 27.1%, 25.0%, 4.2%, and 4.2% across the groups. There is only a slight decline in the error rates for meaningless sentences that sound wrong, due to ceiling effects. After conducting several other experiments to test alternative explanations, Doctor and Coltheart (1980) concluded that a great deal of phonological coding takes place when 6-year-old children read sentences, but the prevalence of phonological coding decreases as the child progresses through the early grades (see also Ehri & Wilce, 1979). It should be noted, however, that even the 6-year-olds were using a visual–orthographic code to some extent. This is indicated by the improved performance on meaningless sentences that sounded correct when a nonword was present, even though the nonword sounded like a real word.

Bradley and Bryant (1979), using the same two groups of children that they examined in their 1978 paper, tested the ability to read and to spell a set of words. They found a degree of disassociation between reading and spelling. That is, most children could read some words they could not spell, and could spell some words they could not read. This disassociation was greater for the poor readers. Spelling was more dependent on phonological cues than reading, although errors in both reading and spelling tended to be phonologically based. Reading presumably depended more on visual–orthographic information than did spelling. Poor readers spelled almost as well as good readers. If spelling is indeed a phonologically based skill, then the latter finding is especially interesting, because these were the same poor readers who displayed deficient phonological processes in the 1978 study conducted by Bradley and Bryant. In the 1979 paper, they speculated that it is easier to apply a phonological code to spelling than to reading because phonological production is easier than phonological recognition. Thus, they argued that the phonological skills of both the normal and the poor readers were sufficient to support spelling, but that the poor readers were unable to make the transfer to the full use of such a code for reading. As a result, they do not show normal progress in reading.

Finally, it should be emphasized that the phonological and visual–orthographic processes, in addition to being independent mechanisms for lexical access may, in some cases, function in a mutually supportive manner. For example, Barron (1981) has suggested that use of the phonological access strategy may encourage the child to attend to the sequential constraints of the letters within words. This would in turn facilitate the development of the visual–orthographic access strategy. Singer (Chapter 4) also suggests an interdependence between phonological and visual–orthographic processes when he hypothesizes that remembering the order of component letters is facilitated when a phonetic organization is imposed on the letter strings.

## Word Recognition in Context

Smith (1978) has hypothesized that due to sensitivity to the semantic and syntactic cues (i.e., redundancy) afforded by sentences, the reader develops hypotheses about upcoming words and is then able to confirm their identities by sampling only a few features from their visual representations. Thus, words in context require the extraction of fewer features than do words in isolation, and as a result are recognized faster. There is nothing in this idea that contradicts any of the data or models of word recognition that were discussed previously. The contextual mechanisms proposed by Smith (1978) can simply be added to what we know about the recognition of isolated words to form a more encompassing model of reading performance.

Smith (1978), however, has proposed also that the fluent reading of the good reader is due primarily to his superior ability to utilize contextual redundancy. Because good readers make better use of redundancy they process words faster; their use of redundancy lightens the load on their stimulus-analysis mechanisms. Poor readers, on the other hand, are less facile in their use of contextual redundancy, make incorrect or few hypotheses, are forced to process more visual information in order to recognize a word, and thus read slowly. According to this view, poor readers tend to depend excessively on graphic and phonetic information. This "context-use" hypothesis was reviewed earlier (Singer, Chapter 3) and it was concluded that, despite its popularity, there is little evidence supporting Smith's proposal. Much evidence suggests that poor readers are not less likely to use context to facilitate word recognition. (Allington, 1978; Allington & Fleming, 1978; Allington & Strange, 1977; Biemiller, 1977–1978; Doehring, 1976; Juel, 1980; Marsh, Desberg, & Carpenter, 1979; Perfetti, Goldman, & Hogoboam, 1979; Perfetti & Roth, 1981; Schvaneveldt, Ackerman,

& Semlear, 1977; Stanovich, 1980; Stanovich, 1981a; Stanovich, West, & Feeman, 1981; West & Stanovich, 1978).

Before leaving this topic, a word should be said about a potential source of
confusion. The term *context effect* is bandied about with some regularity in the
reading literature. Often its users fail to appreciate that there can be many
different *types* of context effects. For example, context can act to speed ongoing
word recognition. This was the effect discussed previously. Alternatively, context
can act to facilitate the memory and comprehension of subsequent text (Bransford
& Johnson, 1973). This is a very different type of context-use skill and its
relation to reading ability may be quite different from that discussed previously.
Bransford, Stein, and Vye discuss other context-use skills in Chapter 9.

## Applying Research Findings

Educators *should* be encouraged to draw implications from research and to allow
these implications to influence teaching techniques and materials. Generalizations
from research, however, can be made only after careful thought. The history of
reading instruction demonstrates the danger of basing instructional techniques
on hastily drawn conclusions. Two famous examples illustrate this point. Cattell's
(1886) classic finding, that tachistoscopically presented words are perceived
better than random letters, was long used as a justification for "whole-word"
and "look–say" reading curricula. In fact, Cattell's result probably indicated
that competent readers exploit relations among the letters of regularly spelled
words. This process would involve the recognition of individual letters and *not*
a "whole-word" perception.

The second classic example of misinterpretation of research concerns eye
movements in reading. Early research indicated that the eye-movement patterns
of poor readers were different from those of good readers. This finding led to
many misguided attempts at "eye-movement training." It is now generally
thought that eye-movement patterns do *not* "cause" good reading; instead, poor
reading results in eye-movement patterns that are different from eye-movement
patterns in good reading. Examples such as these are common in the reading
field. Recent efforts to suppress subvocalization in children (see Groff, 1977)
and to train "perceptual-motor" processes (Coles, 1978; Hammill & Larsen,
1978; Larsen & Hammill, 1975; Mann, 1970; Seaton, 1977) would appear to
fall in the same category.

These examples should caution us in deriving educational implications from
the foregoing discussion of word recognition. I have argued that skill at recognizing words relates to reading ability and that recognition speed facilitates
reading comprehension. Assuming that practice would increase speed of word
recognition, should we conclude that poor readers should practice word recognition? The answer is yes. On the other hand, should poor readers practice at
recognizing isolated words? Not necessarily! Not a single study reviewed previously recommends a specific *kind* of practice (isolated word or otherwise) for

poor readers. A variety of techniques might be effective and the literature indicates *only* that word recognition skills must be taught. In deciding what kind of practice would be most appropriate, one should consider the literature on the effects of various types of practice (See Ehri & Roberts, 1979; Perfetti & Lesgold, 1979; Samuels, 1979).

## GLOSSARY

**A Priori.**  Not based on prior study or empirical examination.

**Asymptote.**  Approaching a limit.

**Bottom-up Models.**  Models of reading that assume that the sequence of processing begins with the pickup of visual information and only later proceeds to higher-level encodings.

**Converging Evidence.**  Evidence that comes from a variety of different sources but leads to the same conclusion.

**Cryptanalysis.**  The procedures involved in interpreting the meaning of a code.

**Empirical.**  Based on experiment or observation.

**Facilitator Subskill.**  A subskill that, if developed, will improve reading. However, failure to master the subskill does not preclude reading acquisition.

**False Positive.**  A response in a recognition test where the subject incorrectly indicates that he or she has seen a stimulus before.

**Foils.**  The alternatives in a recognition test that are incorrect.

**Graphically Constrained Errors.**  Errors that are visually similar to the word that was actually presented.

**In Parallel.**  At the same time, simultaneously.

**Incidental Correlate.**  A subskill that is related to reading that is not a direct cause of increases in reading ability.

**Irregular Word.**  A word that does not follow the spelling-to-sound correspondence rules of English.

**Lexical Access.**  The process by which visually stored information makes contact with information about a word's meaning.

**Necessary Condition.**  A condition that is essential if a desired outcome is to occur.

**Operational Definition.**  A definition of a concept in terms of a specific experimental measurement.

**Phoneme.**  The smallest unit of speech that will distinguish one utterance from another.

**Phonetic Blend Training.**  Training at merging separate phonemes into a whole word.

**Phonetic Segmentation.**  The analysis of a word into phonemic units.

**Phonological Code.**  An access code based on the (highly encoded) sound characteristics of a word.

**Post hoc Error Analysis.**  An analysis of errors that is not planned, but is undertaken because of suggestive trends apparent after the data were collected.

**Prerequisite Subskill.** A subskill that must be mastered before reading can occur.

**Pseudoword.** A string of letters that does not violate the orthographic or phonological rules of English, but that happens not to be a word.

**Regular Word.** A word that follows the spelling-to-sound correspondence rules of English.

**Short-Term Memory.** A memory storage system of limited capacity (approximately six items) where conscious mental operations are carried out.

**Top-Down Models.** Models of reading that assume that the pickup of visual information is directed by higher-level contextual processes.

**Visual Code.** An access code based on the visual features of a word.

**Visual Segmentation.** The analysis of a word into letters.

## REFERENCES

Allington, R. L. Effects of contextual constraints upon rate and accuracy. *Perceptual and Motor Skills*, 1978, *46*, 1318.

Allington, R. L., & Fleming, J. T. The misreading of high-frequency words. *Journal of Special Education*, 1978, *12*, 417–421.

Allington, R. L., & Strange, M. Effects of grapheme substitutions in connected text upon reading behaviors. *Visible Language*, 1977, *11*, 285–297.

Baddeley, A. D. Short-term memory for word sequences as a function of acoustic, semantic, and formal similarity. *Quarterly Journal of Experimental Psychology*, 1966, *18*, 362–365.

Baron, J. Mechanisms for pronouncing printed words: Use and acquisition. In D. LaBerge & S. Samuels (Eds.), *Basic processes in reading: Perception and comprehension*, Hillsdale, N.J.: Lawrence Erlbaum Associates, 1977.

Baron, J. Orthographic and word-specific mechanisms in children's reading of words. *Child Development*, 1979, *50*, 60–72.

Barron, R. W. Access to the meanings of printed words: Some implications for reading and learning to read. In F. Murray (Ed.), *The recognition of words: IRA series on the development of the reading process*. Newark, Del.: International Reading Association, 1978. (a)

Barron, R. W. Reading skill and phonological coding in lexical access. In M. Gruneberg, R. Sykes, & P. Morris (Eds.), *Practical aspects of memory*. London: Academic Press, 1978. (b)

Barron, R. W. Visual–orthographic and phonological strategies in reading and spelling. In U. Frith (Ed.), *Cognitive processes in spelling*. London: Academic Press, 1980.

Barron, R. W. Reading skill and reading strategies. In A. Lesgold & C. Perfetti (Eds.), *Interactive processes in reading*. Hillsdale, N.J.: Lawrence Erlbaum Associates, 1981.

Biemiller, A. The development of the use of graphic and contextual information as children learn to read. *Reading Research Quarterly*, 1970, *6*, 75–96.

Biemiller, A. Relationship between oral reading rates for letters, words, and simple text in the development of reading achievement. *Reading Research Quarterly*, 1977–1978, *13*, 223–253.

Boder, E. Developmental dyslexia: A diagnostic approach based on three atypical reading–spelling patterns. *Developmental Medicine and Child Neurology*, 1973, *15*, 663–687.

Bradley, L., & Bryant, P. E. Difficulties in auditory organization as a possible cause of reading backwardness. *Nature*, 1978, *271*, 746–747.

Bradley, L., & Bryant, P. E. Independence of reading and spelling in backward and normal readers. *Developmental Medicine and Child Neurology*, 1979, *21*, 504–514.

Bransford, J. D., & Johnson, M. K. Consideration of some problems in comprehension. In W. G. Chase (Ed.), *Visual information processing*. New York: Academic Press, 1973.

Bryan, W. L., & Harter, N. Studies on the telegraphic language: The acquisition of a hierarchy of habits. *Psychological Review*, 1899, *6*, 345–375.

Butler, B., & Hains, S. Individual differences in word recognition latency. *Memory & Cognition*, 1979, *7*, 68–76.

Byrne, B., & Shea, P. Semantic and phonetic memory codes in beginning readers. *Memory & Cognition*, 1979, *7*, 333–338.

Calfee, R. C., Chapman, R., & Venezky, R. L. How a child needs to think to learn to read. In L. W. Gregg (Ed.), *Cognition and learning in memory*. New York: Wiley, 1972.

Calfee, R. C., Lindamood, P., & Lindamood, C. Acoustic–phonetic skills and reading—kindergarten through twelfth grade. *Journal of Educational Psychology*, 1973, *64*, 293–298.

Carroll, J. B. Developmental parameters of reading comprehension. In J. T. Guthrie (Ed.), *Cognition, curriculum and comprehension*, Newark, Del.: International Reading Association, 1977.

Cattell, J. M. The time it takes to see and name objects, *Mind*, 1886, *11*, 63–65.

Coles, G. S. The learning disabilities test battery: Empirical and social issues. *Harvard Educational Review*, 1978, *48*, 313–340.

Conrad, R. Acoustic confusions in immediate memory. *British Journal of Psychology*, 1964, *55*, 75–84.

Dechant, E. V., & Smith, H. P. *Psychology in teaching reading*. Englewood Cliffs, N.J.: Prentice–Hall, 1977.

Doctor, E. A., & Coltheart, M. Children's use of phonological encoding when reading for meaning. *Memory & Cognition*, 1980, *8*, 195–209.

Doehring, D. G. Acquisition of rapid reading responses. *Monographs of the Society for Research in Child Development*, 1976, *41*(2, Serial No. 165).

Ehri, L. C. Linguistic insight: Threshold of reading acquisition. In T. G. Waller & G. E. MacKinnon (Eds.), *Reading research: Advances in theory and practice* (Vol. 1). New York: Academic Press, 1979.

Ehri, L. C., & Roberts, K. T. Do beginners learn printed words better in context or in isolation? *Child Development*, 1979, *50*, 675–685.

Ehri, L. C., & Wilce, L. S. The mnemonic value of orthography among beginning readers. *Journal of Educational Psychology*, 1979, *71*, 26–40.

Fischer, F. W., Liberman, I. Y., & Shankweiler, D. Reading reversals and developmental dyslexia: A further study. *Cortex*, 1978, *14*, 496–510.

Fisher, D. F., & Frankfurter, A. Normal and disabled readers can locate and identify letters: Where's the perceptual deficit? *Journal of Reading Behavior*, 1977, *9*, 31–43.

Fox, B., & Routh, D. K. Phonemic analysis and synthesis as word-attack skills. *Journal of Educational Psychology*, 1976, *68*, 70–74.

Fox, B., & Routh, D. K. Phonemic analysis and severe reading disability. *Journal of Psycholinguistic Research*, 1980, *9*, 115–119. (a)

Fox, B., & Routh, D. K. *Reading disability, phonemic analysis, and dysphonetic spelling: A follow-up study*. Paper presented at the annual meeting of the Midwestern Psychological Association, St. Louis, May 1980. (b)

Gibson, E. J., & Levin, H. *The psychology of reading*. Cambridge: MIT Press, 1975.

Glushko, R. The organization and activation of orthographic knowledge in reading aloud. *Journal of Experimental Psychology: Human Perception and Performance*, 1979, *5*, 674–691.

Goldstein, D. M. Cognitive–linguistic functioning and learning to read in preschoolers. *Journal of Educational Psychology*, 1976, *68*, 680–688.

Golinkoff, R. M. Phonemic awareness skills and reading achievement. In F. Murray & J. Pikulski (Eds.), *The acquisition of reading*. Baltimore, Md.: University Park Press, 1978.

Goodman, K. S. Reading: A psycholinguistic guessing game. In H. Singer & R Ruddell (Eds.), *Theoretical models and processes of reading* (2nd ed.). Newark, Del.: International Reading Association, 1976.

Gough, P. B. One second of reading. In J. F. Kavanagh & I. G. Mattingly (Eds.), *Language by ear and eye*. Cambridge: MIT Press, 1972.

Gough, P. B., & Hillinger, M. L. Learning to read: An unnatural act. *Bulletin of the Orton Society*, 1980, *30*, 1980, *15*, 179–196.

Groff, P. Subvocalization and silent reading. *Reading World*, 1977, *16*, 231–237.

Groff, P. Should children learn to read words? *Reading World*, 1978, *17*, 256–264.

Guthrie, J. T., & Tyler, S. J. Psycholinguistic processing in reading and listening among good and poor readers. *Journal of Reading Behavior*, 1976, *8*, 415–426.

Hammill, D. C., & Larsen, S. C. The effectiveness of psycholinguistic training: A reaffirmation of position. *Exceptional Children*, 1978, *44*, 402–417.

Helfgott, J. A. Phonemic segmentation and blending skills of kindergarten children: Implications for beginning reading acquisition. *Contemporary Educational Psychology*, 1976, *1*, 157–169.

Hogaboam, T. W., & Perfetti, C. A. Reading skill and the role of verbal experience in decoding. *Journal of Educational Psychology*, 1978, *70*, 717–729.

Jackson, M., & McClelland, J. L. Processing determinants of reading speed. *Journal of Experimental Psychology: General*, 1979, *108*, 151–181.

Juel, C. Comparison of word identification strategies with varying context, word type, and reader skill. *Reading Research Quarterly*, 1980, *15*, 358–376.

Just, M. A., & Carpenter, P. A. A theory of reading: From eye fixations to comprehension. *Psychological Review*, 1980, *87*, 329–354.

Kleiman, G. M. Speech recoding in reading. *Journal of Verbal Learning and Verbal Behavior*, 1975, *14*, 323–339.

LaBerge, D., & Samuels, S. J. Toward a theory of automatic information processing in reading. *Cognitive Psychology*, 1974, *6*, 293–323.

Larsen, S. C., & Hammill, D. C. Relationship of selected visual perception abilities to school learning. *Journal of Special Education*, 1975, *9*, 281–291.

Lesgold, A. M., & Perfetti, C. A. Interactive processes in reading comprehension. *Discourse Processes*, 1978, *1*, 323–336.

Lesgold, A. M., Resnick, L. B., Roth, S. F., & Hammond, K. L. *Patterns of learning to read: A longitudinal study.* Paper presented at the meeting of the Society for Research in Child Development, Boston, April 1981.

Liberman, I. Y. Segmentation of the spoken word and reading acquisition. *Bulletin of the Orton Society*, 1973, *23*, 65–77.

Liberman, I. Y., Shankweiler, D., Fischer, F. W., & Carter, B. Explicit syllable and phoneme segmentation in the young child. *Journal of Experimental Child Psychology*, 1974, *18*, 201–212.

Litcher, J. H., & Roberge, L. P. First-grade intervention for reading achievement of high risk children. *Bulletin of the Orton Society*, 1979, *29*, 238–244.

Mann, L. Perceptual training: Misdirections and redirections. *American Journal of Orthopsychiatry*, 1970, *40*, 30–38.

Mann, V. A., Liberman, I. Y., & Schankweiler, D. Children's memory for sentences and word strings in relation to reading ability. *Memory & Cognition*, 1980, *8*, 329–335.

Marsh, G., Desberg, P., & Carpenter, P. *Developmental changes in strategies in proofreading.* Paper presented at the annual meeting of Psychonomic Society, Phoenix, November 1979.

Mason, M. From print to sound in mature readers as a function of reader ability and two forms of orthographic regularity. *Memory & Cognition*, 1978, *6*, 568–581.

McCormick, C., & Samuels, S. J. Word recognition by second graders: The unit of perception and interrelationships among accuracy, latency, and comprehension. *Journal of Reading Behavior*, 1979, *11*, 107–118.

Meyer, D., Schvaneveldt, R., & Ruddy, M. Functions of graphemic and phonemic codes in visual word recognition, *Memory & Cognition*, 1974, *2*, 309–321.

Perfetti, C. A., Finger, E., & Hogaboam, T. Sources of vocalization latency differences between skilled and less skilled young readers. *Journal of Educational Psychology*, 1978, *70*, 730–739.

Perfetti, C. A., Goldman, S. R., & Hogaboam, T. W. Reading skill and identification of words in discourse context. *Memory & Cognition*, 1979, *7*, 273–282.

Perfetti, C. A., & Hogaboam, T. Relationship between single word decoding and reading comprehension skill. *Journal of Educational Psychology*, 1975, *67*, 461–469.

Perfetti, C. A., & Lesgold, A. M. Discourse comprehension and sources of individual differences. In M. Just & P. Carpenter (Eds.), *Cognitive process in comprehension*. Hillsdale, N.J.: Lawrence Erlbaum Associates, 1977.

Perfetti, C. A., & Lesgold, A. M. Coding and comprehension in skilled reading and implications for reading instruction. In L. B. Resnick & P. Weaver (Eds.), *Theory and practice of early reading*. Hillsdale, N.J.: Lawrence Erlbaum Associates, 1979.

Perfetti, C. A., & Roth, S. Some of the interactive processes in reading and their role in reading skill. In A. Lesgold & C. Perfetti (Eds.), *Interactive processes in reading*. Hillsdale, N.J.: Lawrence Erlbaum Associates, 1981.

Rayner, K. Visual attention in reading: Eye movements reflect cognitive processes. *Memory & Cognition*, 1977, *5*, 443–448.

Rozin, P., & Gleitman, L. R. The structure and acquisition of reading II: The reading process and the acquisition of the alphabetic principle. In A. Reber & D. Scarborough (Eds.), *Toward a psychology of reading*. Hillsdale, N.J.: Lawrence Erlbaum Associates, 1977.

Rumelhart, D. E. Toward an interactive model of reading. In S. Dornic (Ed.), *Attention and performance VI*. Hillsdale, N.J.: Lawrence Erlbaum Associates, 1977.

Samuels, S. J. The method of repeated readings. *The Reading Teacher*, 1979, *32*, 403–408.

Savin, H. B. What the child knows about speech when he starts to learn to read. In J. F. Kavanagh & I. G. Mattingtly (Eds.), *Language by ear and by eye: The relationship between speech and reading*. Cambridge: MIT Press, 1972.

Schvaneveldt, R., Ackerman, B. P., & Semlear, T. The effect of semantic context on children's word recognition. *Child Development*, 1977, *48*, 612–616.

Seaton, H. W. The effects of a visual perception training program on reading achievement. *Journal of Reading Behavior*, 1977, *9*, 188–192.

Seymour, P. H. K., & Porpodas, C. D. Lexical and nonlexical processing in developmental dyslexia. In U. Frith (Ed.), *Cognitive processes in spelling*. London: Academic Press, 1980.

Shankweiler, D., & Liberman, I. Y. Misreading: A search for causes. In J. F. Kavanagh & I. G. Mattingly (Eds.), *Language by ear and by eye*. Cambridge: MIT Press, 1972.

Shankweiler, D., Liberman, I. Y., Mark, L. S., Fowler, D. A., & Fischer, F. W. The speech code and learning to read. *Journal of Experimental Psychology: Human Learning and Memory*, 1979, *5*, 531–545.

Smith, F. *Understanding reading*. New York: Holt, Rinehart, & Winston, 1978.

Smith, F., & Holmes, D. L. The independence of letter, word, and meaning identification in reading. *Reading Research Quarterly*, 1971, *6*, 394–415.

Stanovich, K. E. Toward an interactive compensatory model of individual differences in the development of reading fluency. *Reading Research Quarterly*, 1980, *16*, 32–71.

Stanovich, K. E. Attentional and automatic context effects in reading. In A. Lesgold & C. Perfetti (Eds.), *Interactive processes in reading*. Hillsdale, N.J.: Lawrence Erlbaum Associates, 1981. (a)

Stanovich, K. E. Relationships between word decoding speed, general name-retrieval ability, and reading progress in first-grade children. *Journal of Educational Psychology*, 1981, in press. (b)

Stanovich, K. E., & Bauer, D. W. Experiments on the spelling-to-sound regularity effect in word recognition. *Memory & Cognition*, 1978, *6*, 410–415.

Stanovich, K. E., West, R. F., & Feeman, D. J. A longitudinal study of sentence context effects in second-grade children: Tests of an interactive-compensatory model. *Journal of Experimental Child Psychology*, 1981, *32*, 185–199.

Sticht, T. G. Learning by listening. In R. O. Freedle & J. B. Carroll (Eds.), *Language comprehension and the acquisition of knowledge*. Washington, D.C.: Winston, 1972.

West, R. F., & Stanovich, K. E. Automatic contextual facilitation in readers of three ages. *Child Development*, 1978, *49*, 717–727.

Williams, J. P. Teaching decoding with an emphasis on phoneme analysis and phoneme blending. *Journal of Educational Psychology*, 1980, *72*, 1–15.

# 6 Neurological Correlates of Reading Failure

Joshua Staller
*SUNY at Oswego*

Why might a child with normal intelligence and adequate instruction fail to learn to read? There are no simple answers to "unexpected reading failure" (Symmes & Rapoport, 1972), but current knowledge suggests that some of the variability in reading ability can be traced to individual differences in brain structure and function. For example, a child's difficulty in decoding printed words may be the result of faulty connections between visual and auditory language centers in the brain. Similarly, individual differences in verbal sequencing may be related to maldevelopment of brain areas that control planfulness and temporal ordering. The hope is that systematic research on brain activity during competent and incompetent reading may ultimately permit etiological claims about the causes and origins of reading failure. In the best of all worlds, the study of brain activity during reading might facilitate more accurate diagnosis and treatment of reading problems.

As emphasized throughout this book, there are several different patterns of reading impairment. These patterns arise due to the variety of behavioral skills that are required in competent reading. Words, for example, contain graphic, orthographic, phonologic, syntactic, and semantic information. A child who lacks the psychological resources to process any or all of these attributes of text may fail to learn to read. For instance, it appears that a small subset of dyslexics (Mattis, French, & Rapin, 1975; Chapter 4, this volume) have visuo–spatial deficits that preclude accurate processing of graphic information such as letter orientation and letter order. A larger group of individuals have difficulty understanding the auditory–linguistic attributes of words; they fail to learn the rules that relate orthographic patterns to phonological ones (See Stanovich, Chapter

5). Other reading-disabled individuals are unable to master the syntactic rules that govern language (Vogel, 1974). Finally, some children may succeed at decoding but cannot comprehend the semantic import of the text (Huttenlocher & Huttenlocher, 1973).

The present chapter considers current evidence on the neurological correlates of reading failure. In other words, this chapter analyzes reading at a different level from that in previous chapters. Whereas cognitive models of reading emphasize the component psychological skills that contribute to performance, neurological models attempt to identify areas of the brain that sustain particular cognitive skills.

In developing a neurological model of reading, data from both adults and children are evaluated. Children who have been unable to learn to read despite an otherwise adequate intellect, personality, and environment are referred to as **dyslexic**. Adults who have lost their ability to read due to brain injury are referred to as **alexic**. There are important differences between dyslexics and alexics, as well as some striking similarities. Before considering them, however, it is imperative to understand several fundamental characteristics of the human brain.

## THE BRAIN AND BRAIN RESEARCH

### Basic Principles of the Brain

The human brain contains three main subdivisions: the hindbrain, midbrain, and forebrain. Figure 6.1 illustrates these subdivisions. The hindbrain, the most primitive of these structures, regulates vital bodily functions such as heart rate and respiration. It also sustains balance and coordination. The midbrain mediates a variety of functions concerned with levels of arousal, such as sleep, wakeful-

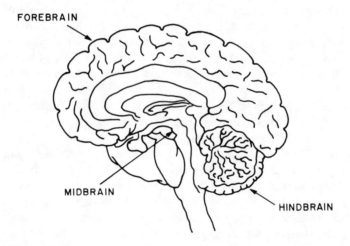

FIG. 6.1. Three main subdivisions of the brain. The front of the brain is at the left of the figure.

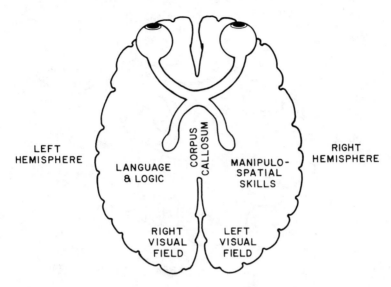

FIG. 6.2.   A cutaway view of the cerebral hemispheres from above.

ness, and attention. Our motivations and emotions also are controlled to a large extent by the midbrain. The forebrain, and in particular the cerebral cortex, innervates higher mental functions such as perception, memory, and language. This chapter focuses on the cerebral cortex, for it is there that the neural pathways in reading are found.

Several general principles of the cerebral cortex are important to the present discussion:

1. *Hemispheric Specialization.*   The cerebral cortex, as shown from above in Fig. 6.2, is subdivided into two hemispheres. Although the hemispheres share basic motor and sensory capabilities, they are also specialized to support quite different higher functions. For example, the left hemisphere is specialized to produce and comprehend spoken and written language. In contrast, the right hemisphere is best at spatial activities such as facial recognition and the localization of objects in the environment. The two hemispheres communicate via the **corpus callosum**; a connecting bundle of nerve fibers.

2. *Localized Function.*   Specific areas of the cortex control basic functions. For instance, a portion of the cortex underneath the back of the head mediates visual perception (Fig. 6.3). Motor commands originate from an area beneath the top of the head, whereas another area (just behind the motor cortex) receives touch and **kinesthetic** information. Similarly, auditory perception is governed by an area near the temples. Although Fig. 6.3 illustrates only the left hemisphere, the basic sensorimotor functions described here are represented **bilaterally** (in both hemispheres). Additional cortical subdivisions relevant to reading are discussed shortly.

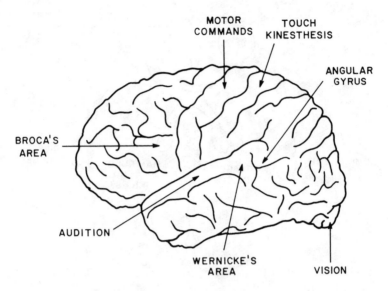

FIG. 6.3. Areas of specialization in the brain. The front of the brain is at the left of the figure.

3. *Contralateral Control.* The cerebral cortex receives stimuli from the senses and sends motor commands to the body in a nonintuitive way. The left hemisphere receives sensory information from the right side of the environment, whereas the right hemisphere monitors the left side of the environment. Motor commands also follow this **contralateral** arrangement. When you wave your right hand the neural commands originate in the left hemisphere.

## Methods of Brain Research.

How do scientists gather knowledge about the relationship between brain structure and behavior? Two types of research dominate the study of neurological correlates of reading ability. First, researchers depend on *clinical* case studies of individuals who have had a disease or injury. Secondly, *experimental* studies compare the performance of normal and disabled groups.

Clinical studies have focused on adults who have lost specific abilities due to a stroke, tumor, gunshot wound, or blow to the head. For instance, a tumor in the left hemisphere can lead to language impairment (hemispheric specialization). Similarly, gunshot wounds to the back of the cortex may cause blindness, whereas wounds to the side of the head may cause deafness (localized function). Finally, a stroke in the right hemisphere is likely to lead to paralysis on the left side of the body (contralateral control). Until recently, clinical efforts to study brain structure were hampered by the need for postmortem examination to determine the exact location and extent of damage, and many patients were understandably reluctant to donate their brains for this purpose. But the development of the Nobel Prize winning (sometimes the Nobel Prize syndrome pays off) brain scan technique known as **computerized tomography** now enables precise assessment of the damage while the patient is still alive. The obvious advantages of this technique have already led to rapid advances in the clinical study of brain and language.

A converging source of evidence about the brain is experimental research on normal and disabled readers. For instance, a number of experimental procedures have been developed to measure hemispheric specialization (Witelson, 1977). Typically, these techniques involve simultaneous presentation of information to both hemispheres, and the hemisphere that "performs" better is presumed to be specialized for the task under investigation. Research of this type suggests that hemispheric specialization is different in dyslexic than in normal readers. A second experimental approach has been to record electrical activity in the brain during perceptual and cognitive activities. Measures like the **electroencephalogram (EEG)** and **evoked potential (EP)** reveal patterns of hemispheric specialization, localized function, and contralateral control. Furthermore, these techniques can discriminate between dyslexic and normal readers (Duffy, Denckla, Bartels, Sandini, & Kiessling, 1980). A third promising experimental approach involves the measurement of patterns of blood flow in the brain during reading (Lassen, Ingvar, & Skinhoj, 1978). The amount of blood flow to a particular brain area is an indicator of the amount of energy required to perform a particular task. To date, blood flow research has helped to pinpoint areas of the brain that are active during skilled reading.

## Clinical Research on Adults

Consider the case of a 51-year-old man who was in good physical and psychological health until the day his car collided with a truck and his forehead struck the windshield (Staller, Buchanan, Singer, Lappin, & Webb, 1978). When he awoke from a coma 20 days later he experienced difficulty naming people and objects, as well as in writing and reading. He was also partially blind in the right visual field. Although his naming and writing abilities recovered quickly, his reading difficulty and blindness persisted. Even though he scored within normal limits on an intelligence test, his reading stabilized at a second-grade level. When he did read (something he rarely chose to do), he proceeded in a letter-by-letter fashion, sounding out letters to himself and trying to blend them into words. This painstaking process indicated that he could no longer visually recognize words as wholes. A computerized tomogram revealed that this man had permanent damage to the left hemisphere of the brain. Thus, chance events had conspired to conduct an "experiment" that no scientist would ever contemplate—the effects of selective destruction of the brain on human behavior.

The tradition of studying the effects of accidental brain damage on human language began over a century ago in France and Germany. Early pioneers like Paul Broca (1861), Carl Wernicke (1874), and Joseph Dejerine (1892) discovered that damage to the left hemisphere almost always resulted in language deficits, whereas damage to the right hemisphere rarely did so (hemispheric specialization). Furthermore, lesions at different sites in the left hemisphere resulted in different patterns of impairment (localized function). Paul Broca, for instance, discovered that damage to the front portion of the left hemisphere (Fig. 6.3) resulted in a loss of verbal fluency, although speech comprehension remained relatively unimpaired. In contrast, Carl Wernicke reported cases in which damage to the central portion of the left hemisphere (Fig. 6.3) impaired speech comprehension, although verbal fluency remained relatively intact. Finally, Joseph Dejerine is famous for his observation that lesions to the posterior part of the left hemisphere can result in a pure reading disability.

In recent years, there has been a rapid refinement of clinical techniques and increasing collaboration between clinical and experimental disciplines. A striking example is the so-called ''split-brain'' research of Roger Sperry and Michael Gazzaniga (Gazzaniga & Sperry, 1967). The term *split brain* refers to patients who were treated by experimental surgery to reduce the occurrence of chronic, debilitating epileptic seizures. The surgical procedure was relatively straightforward—simply cut the fibers in the cortex, including the corpus callosum, that connect the left and right hemispheres. This intervention resulted in a significant decline in seizure activity, with no obvious behavioral side effects. Only careful laboratory testing revealed a profound separation between the activities of the two hemispheres.

As an illustration of the split-brain phenomenon, imagine that you were blindfolded and a familiar object, such as a key, were placed in your left hand. It would be a trivial task to name the object, even though you were unable to see it. A split-brain patient, however, could not perform this task, although that same patient would succeed if the object were placed in the right hand. Let us try a second example. Imagine, again blindfolded, that an object were placed in your right hand and you had to find its match among a group of objects with your left hand. Simple enough, but a split-brain patient would fail this simple task, for the left hemisphere literally does not know what the right hemisphere is doing.

How can this be? The mysteries of this behavior can be easily explained by the principles of hemispheric specialization and contralateral control. When the key is placed in your left hand, its sensory image travels to the right hemisphere. This information then crosses the corpus callosum to the left hemisphere, which accesses and produces the name of the object. In the split-brain individual, the key cannot be named because the callosum has been cut; the sensory image of the object is trapped in the right hemisphere, which does not have expressive language. Similarly, although sensory images transmitted directly to the left hemisphere (e.g., right hand, left hemisphere) can be named, they cannot be matched with sensory input to the right hemisphere (e.g., left hand, right hemisphere).

Why don't these confusions occur in everyday life? In the normal environment, exploration is unlimited, and sensory information can travel to both hemispheres.

Therefore, split-brain patients rarely experience behavioral difficulties outside the laboratory. But in the laboratory, where sensory input can be restricted, the hemispheres clearly function as two separate, autonomous systems.

## Acquired Reading Disability: The Alexias

The split-brain patient also has a mild reading disability. When carefully tested, printed text that is briefly presented to the left visual field cannot be read, although reading is intact in the right visual field (the principles of hemispheric specialization and contralateral control explain why this is the case). More extensive brain damage can lead to more profound reading difficulties. Three major patterns of reading disability have been associated with **brain trauma: Alexia without agraphia; alexia with agraphia;** and **frontal alexia**.

*Alexia Without Agraphia.* As noted previously, the Frenchman Joseph Dejerine was the first to offer a comprehensive case report of pure alexia, an acquired *specific* reading disability. Dejerine's patient, "Monsieur C," was a stroke victim who could speak, listen, and write with relative ease, but was unable to read. A postmortem examination of Monsieur C's brain revealed damage to the visual cortex of the left hemisphere, as well as the corpus callosum. The clinical name for Monsieur C's malady is **alexia without agraphia**.

A schematic view of the damage to Monsieur C's brain is shown in Fig. 6.4. Because of the lesion to the left visual cortex (Site 1) Monsieur C was blind in

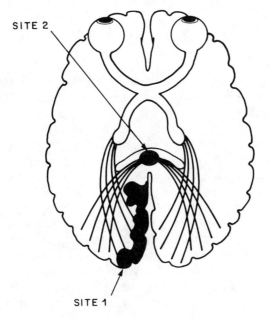

FIG. 6.4. Cerebral lesions that can induce alexia without agraphia. Site 1 indicates a lesion to the left visual cortex and Site 2 a lesion to the corpus callosum.

the right visual field. This alone could not prevent reading, however, because the right visual cortex was intact. But the sensory information transmitted from the left visual field to the right hemisphere was trapped there due to the lesion of the corpus callosum (Site 2). The net effect of these lesions, then, was to disconnect the language areas of the left hemisphere from the visual receiving area of the intact right hemisphere.

*Alexia With Agraphia.* Dejerine also delineated a second disorder known as alexia *with* agraphia. In this syndrome both reading and writing are impaired, as are spelling, language comprehension, and spatial abilities. The alexic with agraphia may sometimes comprehend the meaning of a word without explicitly decoding it, as if printed text could map directly onto meaning. Striking confirmation of a direct pathway to meaning can be found in cross-cultural studies of Japanese alexics (Yamadori, 1975). Japanese text is unique because it is both **syllabic** and **logographic**. In the syllabic portion of the language each printed symbol is consistently related to a spoken sound (much like English). But in the logography each printed character represents a whole word or concept. Remarkably, Japanese alexics with agraphia are more impaired in their ability to read the syllabary than the logography, whereas the opposite is true for alexics without agraphia. Thus it seems that the alexic with agraphia has a decoding deficit, whereas the alexic without agraphia cannot recognize visual word forms.

Anatomically, alexia with agraphia usually involves damage to the central portion of the left hemisphere, including a region known as the angular gyrus (Fig. 6.3). The angular gyrus is an association area that lies between the visual and auditory cortex. The integrity of this region seems essential for relating visual to auditory language (as in reading) and auditory to visual language (as in writing).

*Frontal Alexia.* A third pattern of **acquired reading disability**, frontal alexia, has only recently been recognized as a separate syndrome (Benson, 1977). In frontal alexia both reading and writing, as well as spelling, are impaired. In contrast with alexia with agraphia, the frontal alexic has difficulty with expressive language, syntax, and verbal sequencing. In reading, the frontal alexic can comprehend words better than single letters, and content words (e.g., *Bee*) are easier to comprehend than function words (e.g., *Be*). Anatomically, this disorder involves damage to the front portion of the left hemisphere.

*Summary.* In summary, the pure alexic (alexia without agraphia) can not recognize visual word forms, the alexic with agraphia can not relate visual to auditory language, and the frontal alexic can not organize the components of language into meaningful sequences. It is probably more than a coincidence that *dyslexics* share many of these symptoms. Dyslexics often have difficulty writing and spelling; they sometimes have spatial disorders; they seem to confuse the serial order of linguistic events; and they may be deficient in cross-modal associations.

## THEORIES OF DYSLEXIA

It must be strongly emphasized, however, that the adult syndromes are qualitatively different from childhood syndromes. Adult alexics have lost a skill, whereas dyslexic children have failed to acquire one. Furthermore, adult symptoms rarely completely match those of the child. For instance, dyslexic children simply do not have the characteristic right visual field blindness found in alexics without agraphia, nor are they markedly impaired in speaking (frontal alexia) or in comprehending the spoken word (alexia with agraphia). Finally, and most important, there is no conclusive evidence that dyslexics in general have *any* brain damage.

Despite these differences between children and adults, the data from adults have provided much of the impetus for theorizing about children. Thus, neurological theories of dyslexia tend to speculate about the development of hemispheric specialization and the localization of cortical function.

A seminal theory of hemispheric specialization and its application to reading was developed by Samuel Orton (1937). Orton was aware of the classic 19th-century studies of acquired deficits in adults, and the characteristic pattern of left hemisphere specialization for language. He proposed that in dyslexia the usual pattern of cerebral specialization is delayed or fails to emerge. As a result, the dyslexic child does not develop consistent language pathways in the brain.

Orton was particularly intrigued that the two hemispheres of the brain are virtual mirror images in structure, and he theorized that this structure might contribute to left–right confusions in reading and writing. Orton believed that confusions between mirror-image letters (e.g., *b* and *d, p* and *q*) and words (e.g., *saw* and *was*) were a central symptom of dyslexia, and he coined the term **strephosymbolia** (literally, twisted symbols) to characterize this disorder. Because of the symmetry of the hemispheres, Orton thought that information stored in the left hemisphere would have a mirror–image counterpart in the right hemisphere (and vice versa). This dual representation of information would presumably pose no difficulties (it might even be advantageous) as long as information was stored and retrieved consistently from the same hemisphere. In normal children, it was believed that hemispheric specialization ensured that this took place. But in dyslexic children, in whom specialization failed to develop, information would be stored and retrieved inconsistently and errors would result. In other words Orton claimed that in "strephosymbolic," or dyslexic children, the two hemispheres competed with each other in processing verbal information.

A more recent theory of dyslexia has proposed that a particular portion of the brain—the parietal lobes—may be maldeveloped (Geschwind, 1965). Part of the rationale for this theory is based on the observation that damage to the left parietal lobe in adults can lead to alexia with agraphia, a syndrome that is similar in some respects to dyslexia. In both syndromes, reading, writing, spelling, and spatial abilities may be impaired. Furthermore, a salient characteristic of the alexic with agraphia as well as some dyslexics is their inability to decode printed language. Thus, damage or maldevelopment of the parietal lobes may disrupt decoding, and deficiencies in this skill may preclude competent reading.

*Clinical Research on Children.* With these theoretical approaches in mind, let us consider the sparse clinical evidence on dyslexia. At this time there are only two postmortem case studies of dyslexics. One study reported bilateral maldevelopment of the parietal lobes (Drake, 1968), whereas a second found structural abnormalities in the left hemisphere (Galaburda & Kemper, 1979). On a more general level, computerized tomography has revealed that although normal brains tend to be larger in the left hemisphere, a relatively high proportion of dyslexics' brains are larger in the right hemisphere (Hier, LeMay, Rosenberger, & Perlo, 1978).

Although hardly conclusive, these studies pose difficulties for both theories of dyslexia. Geschwind's theory is at risk because structural abnormalities are not restricted to the parietal lobes. Orton's theory does not seem entirely correct because the dyslexic brain is not just "younger"; it is different. Furthermore, some of the observed abnormalities are localized in traditionally nonlanguage areas of the brain.

We are left with the unsettling conclusion that both theories are wrong, or that they are both correct in some cases. Given the heterogeneity of reading failure, the latter conclusion seems closer to the truth.

*Experimental Research on Children.* Current experimental research, which compares groups of individuals, suggests that Orton's emphasis on left–right reversals was misplaced. Such reversal errors are a relatively minor source of difficulty for most readers, and dyslexics don't seem to make any more of these errors than nondyslexic poor readers (Fischer, Liberman, & Shankweiler, 1977). In addition, it is unlikely that reversals in reading are due to inadequate hemispheric specialization. Normal readers make reversals when they first enter school, even though their hemispheres are specialized by that time. Also, Staller and Sekuler (1976) have shown that children's concepts of "same" and "different" play an important role in their judgment of stimuli like "b" and "d" or "p" and "q." When children are allowed to classify such stimuli as "same," they make relatively few errors on them. Special difficulty with these forms in school probably reflects the fact that, in the three-dimensional world, objects are the same despite changes in their orientation (i.e., object permanence). This pervasive rule is violated, however, when the child steps into the classroom and is asked to treat mirror-image letters as "different."

Although Orton's theory is incorrect in some details, it still has contemporary heuristic value, particularly with respect to the role of hemispheric specialization in reading. In recent years, special behavioral techniques have been developed to measure hemispheric specialization. For instance, in dichotic listening, auditory information is presented simultaneously to both ears via headphones. Each ear receives a different message, and input to the left ear travels primarily to the right hemisphere, while input to the right ear impacts primarily on the left hemisphere. Because of these contralateral connections, a left ear advantage is typically found for nonlinguistic sounds (such as music), whereas a right ear advantage is obtained for linguistic stimuli.

How might dyslexic children perform on tasks of this type? One investigator (Witelson, 1977) has tested performance in the auditory, haptic, and visual modalities in both normal and dyslexic boys. The results were as follows: Both dyslexic and normal children were specialized for linguistic information in the left hemisphere; normal children were specialized for nonlinguistic information in the right hemisphere; and dyslexic children were good at processing nonlinguistic information in both hemispheres. Simply put, normal boys had the usual pattern of specialization, but dyslexics seemed to have extra nonlinguistic abilities in the left hemisphere. Witelson proposed that, in essence, dyslexic boys had "two right hemispheres and none left," with the implication that extra nonlinguistic abilities in the left hemisphere might interfere with reading. This intriguing result, however, has not been replicated in other laboratories (Rourke, 1978), and it now seems that hemispheric specialization may vary complexly with age, sex, and reading ability.

Another experimental approach that shows promise involves the measurement of electrical activity in the brain during reading and other tasks. One recent study (Duffy, Denckla, Bartels, & Sandini, 1980) recorded electroencephalograms and evoked potentials in normal and dyslexic children as they read, learned, and listened. Abnormal patterns of activity were observed in dyslexics in *all* the traditional language areas of the brain; the frontal, central, and posterior regions of the left hemisphere. Moreover, systematic differences between groups were also found in the right hemisphere. Specifically, tasks that required cross-modal associations and phonetic discriminations produced the greatest differences between groups. In general, dyslexic language centers seemed to be underactivated: less active during language and language-related activities. These data strongly suggest that the deficit in dyslexia is global; that is, not localized in a particular area of the brain. As such, the data seem more in accord with theories of hemispheric specialization (e.g., Orton) than theories of focal maldevelopment (e.g., Geschwind).

## SUMMARY

### Heterogeneity Revisited

Reading is a multifaceted cognitive skill that is mediated by multiple areas of the brain. It should be clear at this point that both behavioral and neurological data support the conclusion that there are different patterns of reading impairment in both adults and children. In adults, the pattern of neurological impairment is strongly related to the pattern of reading disability. Thus, when the corpus callosum is severed, text cannot be read in the left visual field. Additional damage to the left visual cortex leads to a complete and pure reading disorder (alexia without agraphia). Similarly, damage that is limited to the central portion of the left hemisphere can lead to alexia with agraphia, whereas frontal lesions lead to frontal alexia.

Although it is not yet possible to relate dyslexic behavior to specific neurological correlates, there are some striking behavioral similarities between dyslexics and alexics. Both groups may sometimes experience difficulties in writing, spelling, cross-modal association, sequencing, visual pattern analysis, spatial activities, and general language skills. Current clinical and experimental evidence indicates that there are global differences between the normal and dyslexic child in terms of the activation of the brain during reading. In the years ahead, with the development of better research techniques (e.g., blood flow, EEG, computerized tomography), it may be possible to differentiate reliably the subtypes of dyslexia.

## GLOSSARY

**Acquired Reading Disability** (alexia).   Refers to skilled readers who have lost their reading ability due to brain trauma.

**Alexia.**   The clinical term for an acquired reading disability.

**Alexia with Agraphia.**   An acquired reading and writing disability that is often accompanied by other language disturbances as well as the loss of spatial skills.

**Alexia Without Agraphia.**   A pure reading disability that is often accompanied by blindness in the right visual field.

**Bilateral.**   On both sides; in both hemispheres.

**Brain Trauma.**   Injury to the brain that may result from a stroke, tumor, blow to the head, gunshot wound, etc.

**Clinical Research.**   In this context, clinical research refers to the careful documentation of individual cases of developmental or acquired language disabilities.

**Computerized Tomogram.**   An advanced, computer-controlled X-ray technique that enables precise localization of tissue damage in living individuals.

**Contralateral Control.** Each hemisphere of the brain receives sensory information from and sends motor commands to the opposite (contralateral) side of the body. Thus the right hemisphere mediates functions on the left side of the body, whereas the left hemisphere mediates functions on the right side.

**Corpus Callosum.**   A bundle of nerve fibers that connects the left and right hemispheres of the brain.

**Dyslexia.**   A developmental reading disability in children who have otherwise adequate intelligence, personality, and educational opportunities.

**Electroencephalogram (EEG).** A record of electrical activity in the brain during global behavioral activities such as reading.

**Evoked Potential (EP).** A record of electrical activity in specific areas of the brain after the presentation of specific stimuli.

**Frontal Alexia.** An acquired reading disability that is often accompanied by disturbances of expressive language and verbal sequencing.

**Hemispheric Specialization.** The two hemispheres of the brain are specialized to perform different functions. In most individuals the left hemisphere is best at language and logic, whereas the right hemisphere is best at manipulo–spatial skills.

**Kinesthesis.** The sense of body position and movement.

**Localized Function.** Particular areas of the brain are specialized to perform particular functions.

**Logographic.** A language in which each printed character is unique in pronounciation and interpretation. Each character represents a whole word or concept.

**Strephosymbolia** (twisted symbols). Orton's term for developmental reading disability. It reflects his belief that mirror-image reversals are the fundamental problem in this disorder.

**Syllabic.** A language in which printed characters consistently match spoken syllables. Syllables can be interchanged to form different words.

## REFERENCES

Benson, D. F. The third alexia. *Archives of Neurology*, 1977, *34*, 327–331.

Broca, P. Remarques sur le siège de la faculté du langage articulé. *Bulletin de la Société d'anthropologia*, 1861, *6*, 330–357.

Dejerine, J. Contribution à l'étude anatomo–pathologique et clinique des différentes variétés de cécité verbale. *Comptes Rendus Des Séances de la Société de Biologie et de Ses Filiales*, 1892, *4*, 61–90.

Drake, W. E. Clinical and pathological findings in a child with a developmental learning disability. *Journal of Learning Disabilities*, 1968, *1*, 486–502.

Duffy, F. H., Denckla, M. B., Bartels, P. H., & Sandini, G. S. Dyslexia: Regional differences in brain electrical activity by topographic mapping. *Annals of Neurology*, 1980, *7*, 412–420.

Duffy, F. H., Denckla, M. B., Bartels, P. H., Sandini, G. S., & Kiessling, L. S. Dyslexia: Automated diagnosis by computerized classification of brain electrical activity. *Annals of Neurology*, 1980, *7*, 421–428.

Fischer, F. W., Liberman, I. Y., & Shankweiler, D. *Reading reversals and developmental dyslexia: A further study.* Haskins Laboratories: Status report on speech research SR–51/52, 1977.

Galaburda, A. M., & Kemper, T. L. Cytoarchitectonic abnormalities in developmental dyslexia: A case study. *Annals of Neurology*, 1979, *6*, 94–100.

Gazzaniga, M. S., & Sperry, R. W. Language after section of the cerebral commisures. *Brain*, 1967, *90*, 131–148.

Geschwind, N. Disconnexion syndromes in animals and man. *Brain*, 1965, *88*, 237–294.

Hier, D. B., LeMay, M., Rosenberger, P. B., & Perlo, V. P. Developmental Dyslexia: Evidence for a subgroup with a reversal of cerebral asymmetry. *Archives of Neurology*, 1978, *35*, 90–92.

Huttenlocher, P. R., & Huttenlocher, J. A. A study of children with hyperlexia. *Neurology*, 1973, *23*, 1107–1116.

Lassen, N. A., Ingvar, D. H., & Skinhoj, E. Brain function and blood flow. *Scientific American*, 1978, *239*, 62–71 (October).

Mattis, S., French, J. H., & Rapin, I. Dyslexia in children and young adults: Three independent neuropsychological syndromes. *Developmental Medicine and Child Neurology*, 1975, *17*, 150–163.

Orton, S. T. *Reading, writing and speech problems in children.* London: Chapman and Hall, 1937.

Rourke, B. P. Neuropsychological research in reading retardation: A review. In A. L. Benton & D. Pearl (Eds.), *Dyslexia: An appraisal of current knowledge.* New York: Oxford University Press, 1978.

Staller, J., Buchanan, D., Singer, M., Lappin, J., & Webb, W. Alexia without agraphia: An experimental case study. *Brain and Language*, 1978, *5*, 378–387.

Staller, J., & Sekuler, R. Mirror image confusions in adults and children: A non-perceptual explanation. *American Journal of Psychology*, 1976, *89*, 253–268.

Symmes, J. S., & Rapoport, J. L. Unexpected reading failure. *American Journal of Orthopsychiatry*, 1972, *42*, 82–91.

Vogel, S. A. Syntactic abilities in normal and dyslexic children. *Journal of Learning Disabilities*, 1974, *7*, 103–109.

Wernicke, C. *Der aphasische Symptomenkomplex.* Breslau: Cohn and Weigart, 1874.

Witelson, S. Developmental dyslexia: Two right hemispheres and none left. *Science*, 1977, *195*, 309–311.

Yamadori, A. Ideogram reading in alexia. *Brain*, 1975, *98*, 231–238.

# III APPLICATIONS:
Introduction

Martin H. Singer

The discussions in Sections I and II provided descriptions of the skills essential to competent reading and the sources of difficulty for poor or disabled readers. These reviews have stressed the heterogeneity of disabled readers, the importance of lower-level skills to the successful operation of higher-level skills, and the variety of skills that competent readers must master.

Section III attempts to describe applications of the preceding information. First, Thomas Carr reviews the utility of a **model** of reading in selecting curricula and in diagnosis. The model discussed by Carr is based on the descriptions of competent and incompetent reading provided in earlier chapters of this volume (Carr stresses the hierarchical organization of the component skills in his reading model). Second, John Bransford, Barry Stein, and Nancy Vye describe an **engineering** approach to improving comprehension skills. Although Bransford et al. do not claim that poor comprehension predicts poor reading, they point out that skilled and less skilled readers (or learners) apply different strategies when attempting to understand text. Finally, I describe a technique, already available in programmed form, that focuses on lower-level skills important to successful reading. Specifically, I describe a procedure that improves visual discrimination and knowledge of orthographic structure (spelling), and that may be useful in eliminating reversal errors.

117

# 7 What's in a Model: Reading Theory and Reading Instruction

Thomas H. Carr
*Michigan State University*

Reading teachers and diagnosticians often get upset when they seek expert consultation. They discover that reading researchers lack a collective voice that offers established wisdom. Each speaks from an individual perspective with little but critical regard for other viewpoints. The result of this Babel among researchers is frustration and dismay among teachers and diagnosticians.

For example, Goodman (1969, 1973) tells us that poor readers lack two crucial characteristics possessed by good readers: a facile working knowledge of the overall structure of language and a propensity to attend to the "big picture" of what the text is really trying to say. Goodman warns that instruction in phonics and word recognition distracts young readers from understanding the text as a whole. Rozin and Gleitman (1977), on the other hand, tell us precisely the opposite. They argue that reading skill depends on adequate word recognition skill and that word recognition, especially phonetic decoding, should be the focus of intensive instruction.

Despite disagreements such as this, teachers and diagnosticians *can* obtain useful information from research on competent and incompetent reading. To do that, however, requires evaluating the research and deciding which findings are important and meaningful. A **model** provides guidance for this type of evaluation. A model is a description of how some task such as reading is learned and carried out. To be maximally helpful, the description must be derived from a systematic **theory** of the task. Two types of models follow from the available information on reading and learning. One model describes the steps that a novice has to take in order to become an expert (at reading or at any other skilled performance). This model would include the mechanisms by which a reader establishes **au-**

**tomaticity** (see Chapter 1). The second model is a description of the process of reading itself—the particular skilled performance in which we are interested. This model would describe **component reading skills and mechanisms** (such as the utilization of orthographic structure, visual-to-phonetic translation, context use, and so on).

The reviews in the previous sections of this book suggest that the outline of a model of the reading process already exists. The outline of a model that captures the most important characteristics of skill acquisition also exists. Though the details of both of these models are still being debated, their basic principles are ready for use. The present chapter summarizes the major components of the two models and demonstrates how they can be applied to reading research, instruction, and remediation. The goal of the chapter is to illustrate the power that having and using accurate and empirically defensible models can give to teachers, diagnosticians, and researchers.

## ACQUIRING SKILL: THE FIRST MODEL

A remarkable consensus is being reached on the nature of skill acquisition. This theory has been applied successfully to a variety of intellectual and physical accomplishments, including infant motor development (Case, 1977; Connally & Bruner, 1974), language acquisition and speech production (Bates, 1976; Bock, 1982, in press), the development of reasoning ability (Carey, 1974; Case, 1977; Siegler, 1977), the acquisition of chess-playing competence (Chase & Simon, 1973), and improvement in tasks that require rapid decision making or sequences of precisely timed movements (Carr, 1979; Keele, 1968; Keele & Summers, 1976). The broad applicability of this theory suggests that it may also help in understanding the acquisition of reading skill.

The theory can be summarized as follows: Any complex task is composed of a number of simpler component tasks. In order to learn a complex task, people break the task down into components that they already can perform with reasonable facility. They practice these parts in small combinations, gradually building up larger and larger chunks of the complex task that they are capable of performing competently. Parts are added together until finally the whole task can be carried out at once. After that point is reached, practice can alternate between the whole task—improving its overall coordination—and particular subunits that remain especially troublesome. Novice pianists, for example, first learn to play the individual notes and note sequences of simple melodies, then to combine notes into chords, then to combine chords with note sequences to form complex phrases, and finally to combine phrases into complex songs. Embedded in this progression is development of the ability to coordinate the two hands. Left-hand chords and right-hand chords are practiced separately, and then in combination with one another to form chord sequences.

Another example applies more directly to reading. Football teams spend a part of each practice session at individual skills like blocking or catching the ball, another part at particular plays like a sweep to the right or a pass to the left end, and a third part at scrimmage. Scrimmage combines plays into coherent sequences intended to gain first downs. First downs are themselves the units that hopefully will be combined into touchdown drives, which are the primary goal of the game. Achieving this primary goal, however, depends on carefully executing and coordinating the component parts at all the lower levels. Early in the season, coaches devote the largest amount of practice to the lowest level skills; teams whose players cannot block or catch will rarely score touchdowns.

Novice readers also must spend time practicing the lower-level skills involved in reading, time practicing the coordination of several component skills, and time actually *reading* (carrying out the whole task under "game conditions"). Developmentally, the less experienced the reader, the greater the time that must be devoted to individual component skills and skill combinations. As the reader gains in competence, a progressively greater proportion of time can be spent actually reading, exercising the skill as a whole.

This model of skill development corresponds quite closely to the description of how individuals proceed from novice to expert telegraphers (Chapter 1) and to the description of reading skill development that has been presented throughout the previous chapters. This model, though, is insufficient by itself. In order to employ the model successfully one must identify all the components of the specific task under study (in the present case, reading). One must also specify how the components are combined and coordinated to accomplish the task. Thus a fairly sophisticated understanding of reading as a process must accompany the general model of skill development.

## READING AS A PROCESS: THE SECOND MODEL

### Advantages of a Process Model

Many people respond negatively to claims about the need for models or theories. When there is hardly enough time to prepare the next day's lesson plans, for example, theory-building can seem like a very expendable luxury. A cookbook full of recipes for successful classes would be much more useful than an abstract exercise in modeling the mind. Theories, though, facilitate the implementation of recipes. Suppose that you are making bread. You carefully measure out the flour, the shortening, the yeast, and add the proper amount of water. You mix the ingredients together, knead the dough for a certain amount of time, and put the dough in the oven at the proper temperature to permit it to rise. If the bread rises perfectly, you smile and put the loaf in to bake. But what do you do if the bread fails to rise (or doesn't rise enough) and sort of falls apart (not quite, but it's sort of coarse and chunky) when you punch it down? You did everything exactly according to the recipe yet something went wrong.

If you are starting to think along the lines of "Was it whole wheat flour, or perhaps a very, very dry day—should have added more water'' then you already know something about the limitations of a recipe. One can rely on recipes when: (1) conditions are perfect; (2) one has all the same ingredients mentioned in the recipe; and (3) the instructions are clear and complete. If you were able to formulate reasons why the recipe might fail, then you also know something about the usefulness of having a theory. General knowledge about bread making (that is, a model or a theory) allows you to make an intelligent response when the conditions are not perfect for using a recipe. Understanding the process allows one to recover from unfavorable conditions and from mistakes. Without understanding one can only pick a recipe and hope.

Often, people who understand bread making are able to behave as if they did not, following a recipe passively and mechanically from beginning to end. They can do this with confidence because they know that, if necessary, they can shift into an active, theoretical mode of behavior and rely on their model of bread making to overcome a special problem. Someone who can follow a recipe but lacks a model or theory cannot do this. That person is an unskilled laborer. Someone with a model, however, is a true craftsman.

## Reading Diagnosis With and Without a Model

In order to demonstrate the difference between unskilled laborers who lack models and craftsmen who have them, I will describe some research done by John Vinsonhaler and George Sherman of the Institute for Research on Teaching at Michigan State University.

Vinsonhaler and Sherman conducted a **simulation study**. In this study, they invented cases of reading disability. Each case included documents such as academic progress reports, interview data, relevant test scores, and general background information (family history, etc.). Several of the cases were thinly disguised duplications of each other.

Vinsonhaler and Sherman used these cases to obtain two types of information about reading specialists. First, they attempted to determine whether the *same* reading specialist would offer the same diagnosis for each of the thinly disguised duplications of a case. Second, they attempted to determine whether *different* reading specialists would agree in their diagnoses when all of them evaluated the same case independently of one another. In other words, Vinsonhaler and Sherman attempted to measure the **reliability** (or consistency) of a single diagnostician (i.e., **test–retest reliability**) and, also, the agreement *among* diagnosticians (**interrater reliability**). If reading diagnosis is based on sound principles and produces sound results then both kinds of reliability ought to be high. Similar cases should result in similar choices of diagnostic tests, similar decisions about what is wrong (the actual diagnosis), and similar recommendations for remedial instruction.

In fact, the only thing on which the specialists agreed, either with each other or with themselves, was the test battery that ought to be given. Interrater reliability was *zero* on both the diagnosis and the recommended remediation; test–retest reliability was nearly zero. As a standard for comparison, the reliabilities of commonly used IQ tests generally range from about .85 to .95 (where 1.00 is the highest reliability that is possible).

These results indicate that specialists who had a fairly well-set schedule of tests to administer (a testing recipe) failed to come up with principled and consistent diagnoses. Sherman probed into this situation via intensive interviews with the specialists and found that they lacked a systematic understanding of the reading process: They had no model. Without a model they found it hard to relate the test scores to one another and to identify a meaningful pattern. The specialists had great difficulty with questions such as how many different component processes must be carried out in order to read, how these processes interact with one another, which of them seem to be the most common stumbling blocks that cause reading to break down, and which tests provide information about which component processes. Consequently, the specialists treated their test results as a hodgepodge of independent pieces of information, focusing first on one and then on another and finally guessing about why a particular child could not read.

Disheartened by the lack of systematic understanding displayed by the majority of specialists, Sherman developed a model of reading and learning based on his own clinical experience and his knowledge of research findings. Sherman's model represented a description of four major components of the reading process. According to Sherman, each of these components *could* break down and cause reading failure. Sherman taught several reading specialists this model and encouraged them to use it as a heuristic in making sense of a set of test results.

The components of Sherman's model were straightforward. He identified: (1) visual processes related to sight vocabulary; (2) decoding operations; (3) knowledge of syntax, semantics, and ways that these relations among words can be used to make predictions; and (4) the ability to integrate information into a coherent understanding of the text. Accordingly, Sherman grouped poor readers into four broad categories: (1) poor readers who lacked sight vocabularies, even though the spoken versions of the words were part of the readers' listening vocabularies; (2) poor readers with inadequate decoding skills; (3) poor readers who could recognize and decode words but failed to grasp the semantic and syntactic relations between words; and (4) readers who could perform all the lower-level skills but who still failed to comprehend and remember what they were reading.

Sherman supplemented his model with suggested reading-related tests that could tap the skill level a child maintained for each of these four major components of the reading process. In other words, Sherman provided something of a recipe for the reading specialist to accompany his model or theory. Armed with a recipe *and* a theory, Sherman's retrained diagnosticians greatly improved their interrater and test–retest reliabilities.[1]

## The Sherlock Holmes Model of Reading Ability

The previous sections of this book laid the groundwork for a valid model of the reading process by describing the processes and the knowledge that are important to reading. As shown in Figure 7.1, the major components of this model can be expressed as four groups of skills that correspond to the four levels of reading failure identified by Sherman. These are sight-word recognition, decoding, syntactic and semantic context use, and comprehension. Each of these skill groups consists of a particular kind of knowledge and the corresponding **mental operations** or information-processing procedures that make use of that knowledge. In addition to the four skill groups, the model includes a fifth component that is responsible for the allocation of *attention* and *processing capacity* to the various component skills. This component has two functions, called **executive control** and **working** (or primary) **memory**. First, it coordinates the operation of the component skills, and second, it stores on a temporary basis the information that is being processed, holding the information until processing has been completed.

What good is this model? The ability to read has often been discussed as if it were a mystery. "Dyslexia," for example, has been called "unexplained and unexpected reading failure [HEW, 1969]." An adequate model can de-mystify reading ability—analyzing a person's competence at each of the component skills represented in the model of reading can suggest why that person succeeds or fails at reading. I therefore call this model *The Sherlock Holmes Model of Reading Ability*. My argument is that good readers read a text in much the same way as Sherlock Holmes solves a mystery, and that poor readers read a text in much the same way as Dr. Watson *fails* to solve a mystery.

The first thing to point out in this argument is that it is no mystery that Sherlock Holmes solves mysteries. Unlike Perry Mason, Holmes does not need magical **deus ex machina** interventions. Indeed, characters often comment after meeting Holmes that his reputation is greatly exaggerated; he does nothing that other people could not do. Yet other people do not do what he does. What is the special quality that Holmes possesses?

Holmes actually possesses several special qualities. The first is knowledge

---

[1]One should remember, however, that *reliability* is not the same as **validity**. People might agree on diagnostic categories but these categories might be meaningless. In order to determine validity, one must evaluate the *model* that defines the categories, as we are doing in this book. If the model seems reasonable and accurate given available research knowledge one must then evaluate the outcomes of remediation based on the diagnostic categories. If the categories lead to successful remediation, then the diagnostic package as a whole (model plus remediation technique) is *valid* and useful.

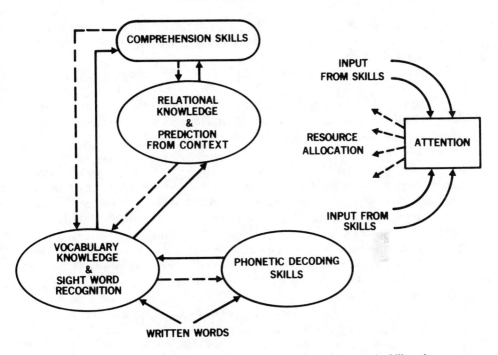

FIG. 7.1. The Sherlock Holmes Model of Reading includes four basic skills and a mechanism that allocates attention.

(or rather, knowledge, knowledge, and more knowledge). Holmes overflows with facts about everything under the sun, from train schedules to the hunting methods of South American Indians. He never encounters a situation without knowing something that will help him understand it. The second is his skill at observing detail. Holmes incessantly collects clues (data or information), finding in every quirk of habit, arrangement of schedule, and turn of phrase some piece of data. The third is his ability to perceive patterns. Holmes continually discovers relationships among the data that he has collected. Sometimes he struggles to see a pattern, rocking with his pipe in front of the fireplace for hours. More often, relations seem to leap out at him after little or no effort. Holmes' fourth outstanding quality concerns his memory. Putting elephants to shame, Holmes never fails to retrieve a long-buried bit of knowledge and he rarely forgets a recently discovered fact even in the heat of pursuing another. Finally, Holmes' fifth quality is that he can juggle a lot of things at once: He excels at simultaneously coordinating his existing knowledge, his clue collecting, and his pattern seeking. He derives the most out of each of his first four qualities by exploiting them all at once, using each to help the others. For Holmes, the whole is much greater than the sum of its parts.

And what about Watson? His failure is no more a mystery than Holmes' success: Poor Watson simply cannot do any of these things as well as Holmes.

Watson lacks knowledge, he misses clues, he cannot see relations for the details, he forgets critical information, and he cannot juggle different types of information or different mental operations.

The analogy that I propose is this: The good reader is to the poor reader what Holmes is to Watson. Accordingly, we can best begin to understand differences in reading ability by examining differences in the component skills of reading ability. Consider again the differences between Holmes and Watson as I describe the differences between good and poor readers.

First, like Holmes and Watson, good and poor readers differ in their general knowledge. The poor reader knows less about *language* than the good reader (most notably, orthography, phonology, and vocabulary). Second, just as Watson is not especially observant, the poor reader has inadequately developed visual recognition and decoding skills, the two main techniques of data collection during reading. Third, Watson's narrow focus on a few facts often interferes with his ability to see relations. He is stymied when events prove inconsistent with his current pet theory, and fails to notice other possible patterns ("By Jove, Holmes, why didn't *I* think of that?"). Poor readers, in comparison to good readers, may also maintain a narrow focus. Their poor decoding skills detract from the processing of relations and they cannot recover when their context-based predictions prove wrong (cf. Chapter 5, K. Stanovich).

Fourth, Watson's poor memory for detail parallels the poor reader's lack of skill in remembering essential information, such as the order in which a sequence of words occurred. Finally, just as Watson and Holmes differ in their ability to juggle different types of information and operations, good and poor readers differ in their ability to perform more than one mental operation at a time. The poor reader seems much more restricted than the good reader in exercising skills simultaneously. Hence the lament during oral reading practice that "I was too busy *reading* to understand." (See Biemiller, 1970; Weber, 1968, 1970).

This lament should remind us of a very important characteristic of reading skills that was first pointed out by Bryan and Harter (1899): reading skills are **hierarchically organized**, and the Sherlock Holmes Model must include that critical characteristic. In a hierarchically organized system, the component skills operate in a particular order, and the efficient operation of skills "late" in this order depends heavily on how well skills "early" in the order have done their jobs. Looking again at Fig. 7.1, you will see that solid arrows connect each individual component skill to other skills. These arrows represent the flow of information through the system, beginning with visual input from the printed page to the eye.

The visual input goes to sight word recognition and phonetic decoding processes, the two data collectors for reading. If neither of these components accomplishes its job, READING STOPS RIGHT THERE. If one or more words are recognized, then information can flow on to the **higher-order** (later-occurring) skills that identify relations among words, understand ideas conveyed by groups of words, and feed back information to the **lower-order** (earlier-occurring) skills.

This feedback, represented by dotted arrows in Fig. 7.1, helps the lower-order skills with their task of word recognition, primarily by narrowing the number of words that could possibly come next in the text. For example, if you have identified and understood the sequence "The little old lady lived in a ————," you can predict in advance that "house," "home," "shack," or even "shoe" could possibly come next. "Hammock," however, would be unlikely, and "hone," "have," or "shingle" would be impossible as long as the sentence consists of sensible English. *However, you still must be able to determine which of the many acceptable possibilities is in fact the next word.* If you perform the lower-order skills poorly, the higher-order skills will suffer no matter how well they might have done had they received good data from the lower-order skills. Bryan and Harter drew this conclusion from their research as Singer discussed in Chapter 1, Stanovich supported it in Chapter 5, and the Model includes it as a basic principle.

The Model's emphasis on lower-order skills might be taken to imply that word recognition is more important than any other component process in distinguishing between good and poor readers. So far, however, the Model has not made such a claim. It has described four different groups of skills plus a mechanism that allocates attention. As Sherman made clear, any or all of these components could create problems for any individual reader. Just as we were able to identify *several* reasons why Watson fails to keep pace with Holmes, the Model identifies several reasons why a child might fail to learn to read.

However, the Model would be more useful if it could tell us the relative importance of these skills by indicating how likely each one is to cause a problem and how severe the problem is likely to be. Thus, we want to find out how large a contribution each individual skill makes to overall reading ability. Stanovich has already argued in Chapter 5 that differences in word recognition skill contribute the most to individual differences in reading. The next section of this chapter examines a study that explicitly attempts to determine the relative importance of the component reading skills. The results of that study will help us to evaluate Stanovich's claim. Carrying out this evaluation will demonstrate the benefits of using the Sherlock Holmes Model of Reading Ability as a guide to the perplexing task of understanding the research literature on reading.

## USING THE MODEL TO EVALUATE RESEARCH

In a study conducted by Graesser, Hoffman, and Clark (1980), college students were required to read a series of passages. Each student controlled the rate at which material was presented by pushing a button after reading a sentence in order to see the next sentence on a television screen. Graesser et al. measured the amount of time required to read each sentence by timing the intervals between button pushes.

Six characteristics of the passages were manipulated in order to determine the extent to which each characteristic influenced reading time. These characteristics were: (1) the number of words in each sentence; (2) the **syntactic predictability** of the words (this was the proportion of words in each sentence whose part of speech could be accurately guessed, given the words that had already occurred in the sentence); (3) the number of meaningful **propositions** or separate ideas conveyed by each sentence; (4) the number of new nouns in each sentence that had not been used before in the passage; (5) the narrativity or "story-ness" of each passage, consisting of people's judgments about whether the passage told a story with characters and a plot (such as "Snow White") or presented facts as would a textbook or news article (such as "The eating habits of armadillos"); and (6) how much the readers already knew about the topic of the passage.

What can this study, with its long list of manipulated text characteristics, tell us about reading? Graesser, Hoffman, and Clark have collected a large number of reading times for sentences that differed from one another in six ways. Each of these differences among sentences might cause a difference in reading time or it might not. So what? Without a model the data of Graesser et al. are nothing but a few more facts. With a model, however, we may be able to relate each difference among sentences to a particular component skill that ought to be especially sensitive to that kind of text characteristic. If we can do this, then we can use the model to help decide what the reading time data mean in terms of how efficiently each component skill is being carried out by the readers.

## A Little Help From Statistics

The first step in such an analysis is to determine which component skill ought to be affected by each sentence characteristic. This is difficult because text characteristics are partially confounded with one another: A change in one sentence characteristic is often accompanied by changes in several other characteristics. For example, sentences with more words often convey more propositions. Furthermore, sentences with more propositions are likely to be more complex and therefore less syntactically predictable. Unless the influence of each text characteristic can be estimated independently of the effects of other characteristics, we will not be able to make a one-to-one match between the effects of text characteristics observed in the data and the operation of component skills in the heads of the readers.

Fortunately, a statistical technique exists that can accomplish this separation. *Multiple regression* allows the change in reading time that results from changes in one text characteristic to be separated from changes that result from other characteristics. Graesser et al. applied multiple regression to their data. This permitted them to obtain an independent estimate of each individual text characteristic's influence on sentence reading time. This is a help without which our analysis of the study could not proceed.

## Matching Text Characteristics to Component Skills

The next step in this analysis involves matching text characteristics to component skills. In the Sherlock Holmes Model, the number of words in a sentence determines the number of times that sight-word recognition and phonetic decoding will have to carry out their job of identifying a word. The more words, the more word recognition operations, and the more word recognition operations, the more total time will be devoted to word recognition in the course of reading a sentence. Thus a change in sentence reading time associated with a change in the number of words in a sentence ought to reflect the operation of the two word recognition components in the Model.

What about syntactic predictability? In order to be influenced by this text characteristic, a reader would first have to identify (consciously or unconsciously) the kinds of syntactic relationships that are present and use them in predicting (consciously or unconsciously) the type of word that should come next in the (You're expecting a noun, aren't you?) sentence. Because the Model includes a component that is specifically called Relational Knowledge and Prediction from Context, it is pretty clear what component skill would be involved in these activities. According to the Model, differences in reading time associated with differences in syntactic predictability ought to reflect the operation of this context-use component.

Next we need to consider the number of propositions. The comprehension component of the Model is responsible for integrating information obtained by the word recognition and context-use components into complete ideas representing the meaning of groups of related words (phrases, clauses, sentences, paragraphs). Therefore a change in sentence reading time associated with the number of propositions or ideas conveyed by the sentence ought to reflect the operation of the comprehension component.

Other variables in the Graesser et al. study relate to the model in more complex ways. For example, the mechanism that allocates attention seems to connect quite logically to the number of new nouns. New words might require more attention (greater allocation of resources) than words that had already been encountered in the text. This would mean that previously encountered words would reduce the load on the mechanism that allocates attention. However, other component skills could also benefit from a word's previous occurrence. For example, priming could facilitate word recognition (see Chapter 1). Similarly, making use of a word's meaning once in a text might facilitate comprehension of that word later on in the text. Thus, *new* words in a passage (which would not enjoy these benefits) could have effects on several components of the Model.

The remaining two text characteristics, narrativity and knowledge about the topic, could also cause multiple effects, simultaneously influencing several component skills. Therefore if good and poor readers were found to differ in the extent to which their reading times were influenced by the number of new nouns, the narrativity of the passage, or the reader's knowledge about the topic of the passage, it would be difficult to hold a single component skill responsible. It would be easier to identify the underlying cause of differences between good and poor readers if the readers differed on the variables that have simple connections to the Model (number of words, syntactic predictability, and number of propositions).

## The Results

Graesser et al. divided their subjects into fast and slow readers: The fastest 50% were in one group and the slowest 50% were in the other group. The effect of each of the six text characteristics on the reading times of the fast group was then compared to the effect of that characteristic on the reading times of the slow group. These comparisons revealed that fast and slow readers were very similar in their ability to process new nouns, in their sensitivity to distinctions between stories and narratives, and in their ability to deal with passages about unfamiliar topics. The two groups differed substantially, however, on the remaining three text characteristics. Fast readers recognized words 1.7 times more rapidly than slow readers, dealt with syntactically unpredicted parts of speech 6.4 times more rapidly, and understood propositions 2.2 times more rapidly.

Interpreting these data according to the Model, we can identify a difference between fast and slow readers in the efficiency of word recognition, of context use, and of comprehension. The size of the difference in efficiency for each of these component skills can be taken as one measure of the relative importance of that skill in distinguishing good from poor readers. This particular measure suggests that context-use skills are the most important, comprehension skills are next, and word recognition skills are the least important. This conclusion, however, requires a more careful analysis.

The efficiency of each component skill is not the only measure of that skill's importance. We can also ask how much time each of these skills consumes during reading, and whether the time consumed is different for good and poor readers. Using these times, we can then estimate the size of the skill's contribution to the difference in total reading time between fast and slow readers. By doing this for each skill, we can rank the skills according to their contribution to the overall reading process rather than their individual efficiencies. The results of this procedure, displayed in Table 7.1, show that context-use skill *does not* account for the largest portion of the total difference in reading times between fast and slow readers. Both groups of readers spent more of their time recognizing words than any other single component activity. Multiplying the number of words by the difference in efficiency between the two groups shows that word recognition accounts for the largest portion of the difference in total reading time between the groups. Therefore, equating fast and slow readers on word recognition time would do more to equate them on total sentence reading time than changing any other single component skill. If we could equate fast and slow readers on either context use or comprehension time, it would help the slow readers—but not as much as improving their word recognition.

## A Caveat

Keep in mind that the foregoing conclusion is drawn from a single study. The results of that study must be validated, replicated, and tested for generality. At

TABLE 7.1[a]

Differences Between Fast and Slow Readers in the Efficiency of Word Recognition, Syntactic
Context Use, and Comprehension (Taken from Graesser, Hoffman, & Clark, 1980).

|  | Efficiency | Total Time Spent Doing This Process | Difference in Total Sentence Reading Time Accounted for |
|---|---|---|---|
| Word Recognition |  |  |  |
| fast | 122 msec | 1454 msec |  |
| slow | 209 msec | 2491 msec | 1037 msec |
| Syntactic Context Use |  |  |  |
| fast | 21 msec | 148 msec |  |
| slow | 134 msec | 942 msec | 794 msec |
| Comprehension |  |  |  |
| fast | 93 msec | 458 msec |  |
| slow | 204 msec | 1006 msec | 548 msec |

[a]Efficiency is expressed as the number of milliseconds (msec) required to recognize one word,
identify one syntactically unpredictable part of speech, or understand one proposition after all of its
words have been recognized. Additional calculations show the total amount of time spent by fast
and slow readers in carrying out each of these processes while reading an average sentence. This
calculation was performed by multiplying the efficiency of the process by the number of times it
had to be carried out: the average sentence contained 11.92 words to be recognized, 7.03 of which
were syntactically unpredictable, and these 11.92 words conveyed 4.93 propositions. The last column
subtracts the total time spent by fast readers from the total time spent by slow readers to show the
difference in overall sentence reading between the two groups accounted for by each component
skill.

this point, the study provides a best guess about the cognitive determinants of
individual differences in reading ability. We still must confirm the accuracy of
the guess. To do so, we need to find other studies that examine the relative
contribution of word recognition skill to reading. We also need to make the
guess more specific. Our Model posits two groups of word recognition skills:
decoding and sight-word recognition. We therefore want to determine which
group of word recognition skills is more important in distinguishing fast from
slow readers.

Finally, the participants in the study by Graesser et al. were college students.
Therefore, that investigation might only highlight skill differences that produce
relatively fine-grained distinctions among fairly accomplished readers. Would
the same differences distinguish between success and failure among younger,
less experienced students during *early* stages of reading development? A focus
on word recognition might be the most efficient instructional approach with
Graesser's college students, but it remains to be seen whether word recognition
would be the best focus of instruction with first-graders just learning to read.

These last questions lead directly to issues related to reading instruction and
curricula. The final section of this chapter applies the Model to a comparison
of two classroom environments for teaching reading. The Model, with its em-

phasis on word recognition and other component skills, leads to the prediction that an advantage should occur for a certain type of curriculum. We can test the Model by asking whether this prediction proves to be right or wrong.

## USING THE MODEL TO EVALUATE CURRICULA

In 1979, Evans published a study of two first-grade curricula. One experimental curriculum implemented the British Infant School model of open-classroom or student-centered instruction; the other was a more traditional, teacher-directed, group-instruction program. Evans observed the operation of both curricula in 20 classrooms (10 classrooms devoted to each curriculum). She attempted to determine the learning activities associated with each curriculum and the time devoted to various activities during the school day.

Evans reported that students in the experimental, student-centered curriculum spent more than half the day in independent study or individual tutorial sessions with the teacher. The classroom permitted frequent peer interaction and language-based creative play. Reading was taught informally. Students composed their own stories, dictated them to the teacher, and then read the stories back to the teacher or to their peers. Students developed personalized banks of sight words as part of this process. The approach followed the philosophy that reading should be an enjoyable, self-selected activity, closely related to spoken language and personal experience.

In contrast, students in the traditional teacher-directed classrooms spent two-thirds of the day in closely supervised group instruction. They were drilled on various reading skills: phonics, guessing word meanings from context, and reading basal texts. During independent study, these students worked on paper-and-pencil elaborations of topics raised in group work. This approach followed the philosophy that reading ability depends on a number of component skills that require practice. Despite the radical differences between curricula, however, students in the two groups of classrooms spent about the same amount of time reading.

### Measuring Skills and Aptitudes

At the end of the year, Evans evaluated the 20 classrooms in several skill and aptitude areas. She measured three general information-processing capabilities (serial short-term memory, pattern analysis and predictive reasoning, and Piagetian class-inclusion operations). In addition, Evans measured linguistic capabilities displayed in conversations with an experimenter about a standardized set of topics. Specifically, she measured the mean length of utterances (roughly speaking, the number of morphemes in an average sentence), syntactic complexity (the Developmental Syntax Score described in 1971 by Lee and Cantor), and the sophistication or maturity of descriptions of games and made-up stories.

Finally, Evans also evaluated reading achievement. She used the multiple-choice cloze task that is used to estimate comprehension skill in the Stanford Achievement Test and another comprehension test in which children were asked fact, inference, and vocabulary questions about a series of reading passages. Both of these reading tests tapped all five components of the Model, but emphasized some components more than others. The Stanford cloze task placed special demands on relational knowledge and prediction from context, whereas the passage comprehension test focused on comprehension and memory.

The results can be examined in several ways. The first involves comparing the two curriculum groups on the cognitive measures. Their performance was equivalent on all three of the information-processing tests. The two groups were also equal on the three linguistic measures, which is surprising given the student-centered classrooms' emphasis on spoken language. Despite this equality of basic skills and abilities, however, the *traditional teacher-directed classrooms outscored the experimental, student-centered classrooms on both reading tests.*

It is instructive to examine the correlations between performance on the basic skills tests and the reading tests. Carr and Evans (1981a) report that the three information-processing measures all correlated positively with the reading tests in all classrooms. The correlations, though, were generally higher in the traditional, teacher-directed classrooms. This indicates that *the teacher-directed approach produced conditions in which the information-processing capabilities of the children were more often reflected in reading progress.*

A similar but more exaggerated pattern existed in the correlations between the linguistic test scores and the reading tests. In the traditional classrooms, four of the six possible correlations between language scores and reading scores were positive. Thus, in these teacher-directed classrooms, greater language competence appears to have helped reading achievement. In the student-centered group, however, *all four of these correlations were significantly negative.*

Our model can help to explain these results. We have already seen that the Model gives an especially important role to lower-order skills such as decoding and sight-word recognition. These skills are specific to reading. The perceptual process by which one recognizes a printed word is quite different from the recognition of spoken language. Our model indicates that higher-order skills, which are general to both reading and listening, can only function at their best when lower-order skills have been adequately learned. Thus, students in the experimental, student-centered classrooms may have failed to translate their linguistic skill into reading skills *because successful use of their linguistic skill depended on adequate decoding and recognition skills.* In the teacher-directed classroom, these lower-level, print-specific skills had been developed through carefully supervised practice. This enabled children in the teacher-directed classes to exploit higher-level linguistic skills to their fullest, resulting in positive correlations between linguistic capabilities and reading performance.

This argument is supported by the correlations between reading performance and the time spent practicing the various component skills of the reading process.

Carr and Evans (1981b) calculated these correlations and attempted to determine which classroom practice activities were the most helpful. Table 7.2 displays the correlations for all twenty classrooms, regardless of curriculum.

TABLE 7.2
Correlation Between Reading Performance and Amounts of Time Spent in Various Reading Activities During the School Day

| Decoding Practice | Sight-Word Practice | Context-Use Practice | Silent Reading | Oral Reading | ACTIVITY |
|---|---|---|---|---|---|
| + .30 | − .06 | + .16 | + .38 | − .06 | CORRELATION |

These data show that phonetic decoding, practice at relational knowledge and prediction from context, and silent reading were all positively related to reading scores. Importantly, the traditional teacher-directed classrooms spent more time at these activities than the student-centered classrooms. For example, the traditional, teacher-directed classrooms devoted nearly *four times* more practice to phonetic decoding than the student-centered classrooms. As expected from the model, then, an emphasis on systematic practice of component reading skills predicts better reading progress.

These results allow me to comment on the questions raised at the end of the previous section. First, it appears that lower-order component skills are very important to the young reader as well as to the older, more expert reader. Second, practice at the two word recognition skills is not equally valuable. At least among beginning readers, time spent practicing decoding seems to influence reading skill more than time spent practicing sight-word recognition.

## A Special Kind of Practice

What accounts for the reading achievement advantage of the teacher-directed classrooms? To me, the explanation seems straightforward. The teacher-directed classrooms required children to practice: (1) decoding; (2) predicting known words and guessing the meaning of unknown words from context; and (3) reading basal readers that contained stories written by someone else. This type of practice made the children's existing skills more general; they were not simply practicing restricted versions of the component reading skills that would work only on particular materials. They were required to deal with unfamiliar words and text, continually expanding their skills in new directions. Also, teachers provided immediate corrective feedback, telling students as soon as they made mistakes and helping students to correct their mistakes. We know that the combination of corrective feedback and practice with unfamiliar material seems to maximize transfer in learning (Campione & Brown, 1978; Gibson & Levin, 1975). When the time came to take the reading tests, which included unfamiliar material and required students to rely on general knowledge and skills, it is not very surprising that these students were well prepared.

The situation in the experimental, student-centered curriculum was quite different. Using stories written by the children themselves as the main source of reading practice decreased the demands placed on comprehension skills. Readers never encountered unfamiliar material, and as a consequence they were rarely required to exercise general skills such as context use and decoding. Building sight-word banks from these same stories also decreased demands place on the development of context use and decoding skills and on the expansion of vocabulary knowledge. The "look–say" techniques by which the sight banks were built placed a premium on recognizing particular words at the expense of generalizable decoding skills. These readers were poorly prepared for unfamiliar material. The reading tests constituted their first experience with material that did not reflect their own vocabularies and experiences. In terms of the Model, these students had practiced only very restricted and specialized versions of the various component skills.

Teachers in the experimental classrooms were unaware of their students' lack of reading progress. A closed system of instruction had been established and no one evaluated the strength and generality of component skills. As far as the teachers could tell, their students were progressing well. This illusion was reflected in estimations of classroom reading skill: Teachers of student-centered classrooms were significantly more likely to overestimate how well their students would do on the reading tests than teachers of the traditional teacher-directed classrooms.

Two conclusions can be drawn here to complete my discussion of the Model. First, the correlations between classroom activities and reading performance demonstrate that *children learn what is taught*. If emphasis is placed on general skills, then children will tend to acquire general skills; if emphasis is placed on restricted skills, then children will tend to acquire restricted skills. Second, the preceding description of the relation between classroom activities and the requirements of the reading tests demonstrates that having a model of the skills involved in reading can help in determining the activities to be included in a curriculum. The Model provides guidance in deciding what children need to learn. Curricular activities can be checked against the knowledge and skills represented in the model to ensure adequate training of component reading skills. In this way the Model can be as useful in making curricular decisions as it is in understanding the research literature and improving diagnosis.

## SUMMARY

This chapter has described a general model of skill acquisition and a more specific model of a particular skill, the process of reading. When these two models are used together, they provide a powerful and useful theoretical framework within which to organize one's thoughts about learning to read. The two models can help tremendously with four tasks that often prove difficult and frustrating without the kind of intellectual guidance that the models supply: (1) diagnosing reading ability and recommending remedial treatments; (2) evaluating basic research results in order to determine what reading-relevant skills they illuminate and what instructional approaches they suggest; (3) evaluating the goals and techniques of particular curricula; and (4) determining whether classroom testing procedures used to check student progress fit with the tests that will later be used to measure students' levels of proficiency after teaching is completed.

Some specific points made in this chapter are the following:

1. Models help you to decide what aspects of a complicated phenomenon such as reading are important and what aspects can safely be ignored. More importantly, models help you to *understand* the phenomenon so that you can tell when things are going well and make informed and intelligent adjustments when things are going poorly.

2. The general model of skill acquisition says that any complex skill is mastered by: (1) breaking down the complex skill into simpler components; (2) learning the components; and (3) learning how to put the components together into a well-coordinated and effective whole.

3. The Sherlock Holmes Model of Reading Ability says that five component skill groups are important to overall reading success. These are: (1) phonetic recoding; (2) sight-word recognition; (3) syntactic and semantic context use; (4) integrative comprehension; and (5) executive control of working memory. Each of these component skills consists of *knowledge* and *mental operations that use the knowledge* to carry out some part of the job of reading text.

4. Without a model of the reading process, diagnosticians are highly unreliable in attempting to decide why an individual has trouble learning to read and what remedial techniques are likely to help that individual.

5. Without a model, basic research on reading can be a confusing hodgepodge of unrelated facts. With a model, facts about reading performance can be interpreted and related to one another in a systematic and meaningful way.

6. A model can help in choosing activities to be included in a curriculum and in testing students as they go through the curriculum in order to ensure that the curriculum is doing its job. The model provides this help by identifying the components of the task that must be learned and explicating how the components work. Armed with this knowledge, teachers can make principled decisions as to whether each skill is being covered in an appropriate way by the curriculum.

7. The Sherlock Holmes Model has been used as a guide both to evaluate research and to evaluate curricula. These evaluations suggest that a critical goal in reading instruction should be to establish the automaticity of *print-specific* component skills (such as phonetic recoding and sight-word recognition) and integrate the print-specific skills into already existing language comprehension processes.

## GLOSSARY

**Attention.**    (a) The ability to focus on some information and ignore other information, such as listening to one voice while ignoring another in a crowded room or deciding that ''f'' and ''F'' are different because they have different *shapes* even though their *names* are the same. Similarly, the ability to focus on one task or one component skill of a task in order to carry it out more effectively. For example, a reader might attend much more to decoding than to other components of reading because without such concentrated attention the decoding process operates poorly. (b) The mental processes that underlie these abilities, by which one actually carries out the act of attending to a piece of information or a task component. These processes of attention require *processing capacity.*

**Component Reading Skills and Mechanisms.**    The particular mental processes that must be carried out efficiently and in coordination with one another in order to perform the overall task of reading. (See **skill**.) For more extended discussions, see Posner (1973), Chase, (1978), and Welford (1976).

**deus ex machina.**    A new and surprising fact, thing, person, or other kind of development that appears suddenly and inexplicably, without any forewarning, and is used to explain a mystery—an artificial or contrived solution to an apparently insoluble problem.

**Executive Control.**    Allocation of limited processing capacity to the component skills that need the most energy in order to operate at their best, and allocation of attention and short-term storage space in working memory to the information that is most critical to successful completion of the task being carried out. Thus executive control rations limited processing capacity on the basis of need. Processes that need the most get the most, until the supply runs out.

**Hierarchical.**    Organized or arranged in a sequence of layers or levels, as in a pyramid. Layers lower in the pyramid are subordinate to layers higher in the pyramid. For example, the chain of command in an army is hierarchical, with privates making up the lowest layer and generals making up the highest. In our hierarchical model of reading, phonological recoding and sight-word recognition are *lower-level* or *lower-order* skills at the bottom of the hierarchy, whereas comprehension is a *higher-level* or *higher-order* skill at the top of the hierarchy.

**Model.**    A description of the major working parts of a real-life entity or process. The description captures the *most important* characteristics of each part's operation, though it might leave out large amounts of detail. A model airplane, for example, has parts that represent all the most critical features of a real airplane—fuselage, cockpit, wings, engines—but many lesser details of the real plane are missing. Models can be constructions, as are model airplanes, or pictures, such as the flow chart on page 125 that constitutes the Sherlock Holmes Model of Reading Ability. (See **theory**.)

**Processing Capacity.**   Refers to two different but related things. (a) The mental energy needed to operate the processes of *attention* (automobile engines need gasoline to operate, calculators need batteries to operate, and attention needs processing capacity or mental energy to operate). Mental energy is a limited resource, like gasoline in the tank or electricity in the battery. There is only so much of it to go around, and as a result, attentional processes can run out of capacity and fail to operate or operate poorly. (b) The storage space in short-term memory where information to which one is attending is kept ready for use. One can think of this attended information as conscious (or nearly conscious) information, those things of which one is currently aware. Storage space in short-term memory is also limited, so that you can consciously think about (attend to) only a limited number of things (pieces of information) at a time.

**Proposition.**   A single thought or complete idea, independent of the words used to express it. For example, "John loves Mary" and "Mary is loved by John" express the same proposition or complete idea, despite the difference in wording. A proposition is a *simple* idea, a basic building block of more complex meanings, and a sentence often conveys several propositions rather than a single one. "The hungry ants ate the sweet jelly that was on the table," for example, conveys four propositions that could also be expressed in four separate sentences: "The ants were hungry," "The jelly was sweet," "The jelly was on the table," and "The ants ate the jelly."

**Reliability.**   Consistency in making a measurement or a decision based on a test or measurement. *Interrater reliability* is the extent to which different judges agree or come up with the same answer when judging the same case. *Test–retest reliability* is the extent to which a single judge comes up with the same answer when judging or rating the same case on two different occasions.

**Simulation Study.**   As used in this chapter, research in which the phenomenon or process under study is simulated, rather than studying the real thing. This is done under special circumstances in which the real phenomenon is so changeable from one moment to the next that a scientific study could not be carried out with confidence if the simulation were not done. The particular simulation study described in this chapter compiled standardized sets of information representing the characteristics of poor readers, in order to assess the reliability of diagnosticians' judgements about those "readers." If real children had been diagnosed rather than simulation cases, the results could have been distorted because the children changed from time to time, rather than the diagnosticians' judgment.

**Skill.**   A specific task that a person must learn to perform such as reading, doing arithmetic, riding a bicycle, serving at tennis, or playing chess. The performance of a skill involves carrying out a carefully timed sequence of task components. These components can be mental processes such as identifying letters, retrieving a word meaning, or comparing two ideas, or they can be physical actions such as raising the racquet over one's head, tossing the ball vertically into the air, or swinging the racquet forward. A person's proficiency at a skill is determined by a combination of: (1) the individual efficiencies of the various components; and (2) the degree to which the components are effectively coordinated.

**Syntactic Predictability.**   The ease or difficulty with which a reader can predict or guess the grammatical part of speech of a word in a sentence before actually seeing that word. Here is an example of high syntactic predictability: "John wrote to the president of the ————." You can be reasonably sure that the next word will be a noun, such as "United States" or "corporation," or else an adjective, such as "large (corporation)." A few other constructions are possible but *much* less likely ("John wrote to the president of the most southerly country in North America"), and many constructions are simply impossible, such as filling in the blank with a verb ("regulate," "is") or a preposition ("in," "on"). Here is an example of low syntactic predictability: "John wrote ————." The next word in this sentence could be a preposition ("to"), an adverb ("poorly"), an adjective ("long"), a noun ("Jane"), or any of several other parts of speech.

**Theory.**   A set of principles (assumptions and rules or laws) that together constitute a verbal or mathematical description of an interesting phenomenon, and an explanation of how or why the phenomenon happens. The theory of gravity, for example, is a set of assumptions and rules intended to describe and explain the phenomenon that when an object has no support, it falls in a particular direction until it comes to rest on something. A theory defines the important characteristics of a phenomenon that are then included in a *model* of the phenomenon.

**Validity.**   The accuracy, truth, and utility of a measurement, decision, or test. In order to be scientifically acceptable, a test must be more than just reliable (giving the same answer every time it is applied to the same case). It must tell something that is: (1) accurate or true; and (2) useful or worth knowing. (See Footnote 1 on page 124 of this chapter.)

**Working Memory.**   The part of the human information-processing system that *attends, allocates processing capacity*, and *stores information*. Thus working memory is an information-processing mechanism that does two jobs: executive control and short-term memory.

## REFERENCES

Bates, E. *Language and context: The acquisition of pragmatics*. New York: Academic Press, 1976.

Bryan, W. L., & Harter, N. Studies in the acquisition of a hierarchy of habits. *Psychological Review*, 1899, *6*, 345–375.

Biemiller, A. J. The development of the use of graphic and contextual information as children learn to read. *Reading Research Quarterly*, 1970, *6*, 75–96.

Bock, J. K. Toward a cognitive psychology of syntax: Information-processing contributions to sentence formulation. *Psychological Review*, 1982, in press.

Campione, J. L., & Brown, A. L. Toward a theory of intelligence. Contributions from research with retarded children. *Intelligence*, 1978, *2*, 279–304.

Carey, S. Cognitive competence. In K. Connally & J. Bruner (Eds.), *The growth of competence*. New York: Academic Press, 1974.

Carr, T. H. Consciousness in models of human processing: Primary memory, executive control, and input regulation. In G. Underwood & R. Stevens (Eds.), *Aspects of consciousness*. London: Academic Press, 1979.

Carr, T. H., & Evans, M. A. *Influence of learning conditions on patterns of cognitive skill in young children*. Paper presented to the Society for Research in Child Development, Boston, 1981 (a).

Carr, T. H., & Evans, M. A. Classroom organization and reading ability: Are motivation and skill antagonistic goals? In J. Edwards (Ed.), *Social psychology of reading*. Baltimore, Md.: Institute for Modern Languages, 1981 (b).

Case, R. Intellectual development from birth to adulthood: A neo-Piagetian interpretation. In R. Siegler (Ed.), *Children's thinking: What develops?* Hillsdale, N.J.: Lawrence Erlbaum Associates, 1977.

Chase, W. G. Elementary information processes. In W. K. Este's (Ed.), *Handbook of learning and cognitive processes. Vol. 5. Human information processing*, Hillsdale, N.J.: Lawrence Erlbaum Associates, 1978.

Chase, W. G., & Simon, H. A. The mind's eye in chess. In W. G. Chase (Ed.), *Visual information processing*. New York: Academic Press, 1973.

Connally, K., & Bruner, J. (Eds.). *The growth of cognitive competence*. New York: Academic Press, 1974.

Evans, M. A. A comparative study of young children's classroom activities and learning outcomes. *British Journal of Educational Psychology*, 1979, *49*, 15–26.

Gibson, E., & Levin, H. *The psychology of reading*. Cambridge, Mass.: MIT Press, 1975.

Goodman, K. Reading: A psycholinguistic guessing game. In K. Goodman & J. Fleming (Eds.), *Selected papers from the IRA Preconvention Institute*. Newark, Del.: International Reading Association, 1969.

Goodman, K. (Ed.). *Miscue analysis: Application to reading instruction*. Detroit: Wayne State University Press, 1973.

Graesser, A. C., Hoffman, N. L., & Clark, L. F. Structural components of reading time. *Journal of Verbal Learning and Verbal Behavior*, 1980, *19*, 135–151.

Health, Education & Welfare (HEW). *Report of the secretary's national advisory committee on dyslexia and related reading disorders*. Washington, D.C.: US Government Printing Office, 1969.

Keele, S. W. Movement control in skilled motor performance. *Psychological Bulletin*, 1968, *70*, 387–403.

Keele, S. W., & Summers, J. J. The structure of motor programs. In G. Stelmach (Ed.), *Motor control: Issues and trends*. New York: Academic Press, 1976.

Lee, L. L., & Cantor, S. H. Developmental sentence scoring: A clinical procedure for estimating syntactic development in children's spontaneous speech. *Journal of Speech and Hearing Disorders*, 1971, *40*, 315–340.

Posner, M. I. *Cognition*. Glenview, IL: Scott-Foresman, 1973.

Rozin, P., & Gleitman, L. R. The structure and acquisition of reading II: The reading process and the acquisition of the alphabetic principle. In A. S. Reber & D. L. Scarborough (Eds.), *Toward a psychology of reading*. Hillsdale, N.J.: Lawrence Erlbaum Associates, 1977.

Siegler, R. The origins of scientific reasoning. In R. Siegler (Ed.), *Children's thinking: What develops?* Hillsdale, N.J.: Lawrence Erlbaum Associates, 1977.

Weber, R. M. The study of oral reading errors: A survey of the literature. *Reading Research Quarterly*, 1968, *4*, 96–119.

Weber, R. M. First graders' use of grammatical context in reading. In H. Levin & J. P. Williams (Eds.), *Basic studies on reading*. New York: Basic Books, 1970.

Welford, A. T. *Skilled performance: Perceptual and motor skills*. Glenview, Ill.: Scott, Foresman, 1976.

# 8 Helping Students Learn How to Learn from Written Texts

John D. Bransford
*Vanderbilt University*

Barry S. Stein
*Tennessee Technological University*

Nancy J. Vye
*Vanderbilt University*

One of the major advantages of being able to read is that people have the potential to learn new information by consulting written documents. People who cannot decode written messages cannot hope to learn from them, of course, but the ability to decode does not guarantee effective learning. As emphasized throughout this book, several factors contribute to successful reading. In this chapter, we focus on some **cognitive activities** necessary to understand what one reads and to remember this information at later points in time. Our analysis pertains to the higher-order components of Carr's Sherlock Holmes Model of Reading (Chapter 7). Although we recognize that the automatization of lower-level skills is important to successful reading, there are other prerequisites to reading that also seem important. In particular, we argue that academically successful and less successful students adopt different approaches to the problem of learning new information by reading. Accordingly, we discuss some instructional procedures that may help students improve their abilities to comprehend and learn from written texts.

## ACTIVITIES NECESSARY FOR EFFECTIVE COMPREHENSION

Imagine overhearing the following portion of a conversation: "I'm sorry to be late for our meeting; my husband's bicycle had a flat tire so he would have been late for work." Most adults comprehend statements such as this with little difficulty. However, the activities necessary for comprehension involve much more than the ability to understand each of the words that the message contains.

Consider first your interpretation of the fact that the bicycle had a flat tire. You undoubtedly assumed that this made the bicycle difficult or impossible to ride, but nothing in the preceding sentence stated this explicitly. You had to make an assumption about the significance of having a flat tire, an assumption based on your general knowledge of the world.

An additional assumption is that the husband usually rides his bicycle to work and that the wife gave her husband a ride to work. She therefore prevented him from being late, but this caused her to be late. Still another assumption is that the husband's job is not within easy walking distance of his home. If it were, he would not have needed a ride.

The preceding example illustrates that comprehension involves much more than the ability to understand facts that are explicitly stated (e.g., that the husband's bicycle had a flat tire); one also has to activate general knowledge in order to understand the significance of these facts (that having a flat tire makes it difficult or impossible to ride a bicycle, that the bicycle was the husband's usual means of transportation to work, etc.). It would be extremely cumbersome if speakers and writers had to state explicitly all the information necessary to comprehend a message. Effective comprehenders must activate knowledge that fills in the gaps that messages contain (see Anderson, 1977; Bransford, 1979; Spiro, Bruce, & Brewer, 1980, for additional examples).

## ACTIVITIES NECESSARY TO LEARN NEW INFORMATION

The preceding example involves concepts that are relatively familiar; most of us are well acquainted with bicycles, for example. In cases such as these, the activation of knowledge necessary to fill in the gaps in messages seems almost effortless or automatic. When we are trying to learn unfamiliar material, however, we frequently have to make more of a conscious effort to activate knowledge that can clarify the significance of facts.

Imagine that someone who is a novice in biology is presented with a passage describing the similarities and differences between veins and arteries. The passage might state that arteries are thick, relatively elastic, and carry blood rich in oxygen from the heart. In contrast, veins are thin, less elastic, and carry blood rich in carbon dioxide to the heart. Even this simple set of facts can seem arbitrary and confusing: Was it the veins or arteries that are more elastic? Did the thick one carry blood from the heart or to the heart? Which one carries the freshly oxygenated blood?

Imagine that students who can decode each of the words in a passage about veins and arteries are asked to study it until they feel ready for a test. Imagine further that one group of students is able to understand and remember the information whereas the second group exhibits a much poorer level of performance. What might be responsible for the differences between the groups?

There are two major reasons why students who are motivated and are able to decode may fail to learn about a topic such as veins and arteries. One is that students lack the knowledge necessary to fill in the gaps in the passage. If students do not understand how elasticity is important for handling the spurts of blood from the heart, then they might be unable to make sense of the passage. Similarly, imagine attempting to understand a statement such as "Jane decided not to wear her matching silver belt, necklace, and bracelet because she was going to the airport." A person who had no knowledge of metal detectors in airports might not be expected to understand the significance of a statement such as this.

A second reason why students might not learn from a passage is that they fail to activate knowledge that is potentially available. For example, students may have knowledge of elasticity yet fail to ask themselves about the significance of this property; they may not ask how elasticity relates to the functions that arteries perform. In contrast, an effective learner may seek information that can clarify this relationship. For example, our imaginary passage states that arteries carry blood from the heart—blood that is pumped in spurts. This provides one clue about the significance of elasticity—arteries may need to expand and contract to accommodate the pumping of blood. Some learners might then ask why veins do *not* need to be elastic. Because veins carry blood back to the heart, perhaps they have less of a need to accommodate the large changes in pressure resulting from the heart pumping blood in spurts.

Some learners may carry this process a step further. Because arteries carry blood *from* the heart there is a problem of directionality. Why doesn't the blood flow back into the heart? This will not be perceived as a problem if one assumes that arterial blood always flows downhill, but let's assume that our passage mentions that there are arteries in the neck and shoulder regions. Arterial blood must therefore flow uphill as well. This information might provide an additional clue about the significance of elasticity. If arteries expand from a spurt of blood and then contract, this might help the blood move in a particular direction. In short, the learner's activities are similar to those employed by good detectives or researchers when they confront a new problem. Although their initial assumptions about the significance of various facts may ultimately be found to be incorrect, the act of seeking clarification is fundamental to the development of new expertise.

## COMPARISON OF SUCCESSFUL AND LESS
## SUCCESSFUL LEARNERS

The veins and arteries example illustrates the importance of activating knowledge that can clarify the significance of factual content (e.g., knowledge that can help one understand why arteries are elastic). Students who can decode and who have acquired the background knowledge necessary to understand a topic may still fail to learn if they do not perform these types of activities. Our work with academically successful and less successful fifth-graders (where degree of academic success is defined by teacher ratings and achievement test scores) suggests that less successful students do indeed frequently fail to activate knowledge that can help them understand and remember new information (see Baker & Brown, in press; Bransford, Stein, Shelton, & Owings, in press; Brown, 1977; Brown & DeLoache, 1978). As an illustration of this work we focus on a passage that is analogous to, but simpler than the veins and arteries passage discussed earlier. We use simpler passages in order to increase the probability that the less successful learners have the background knowledge necessary to understand the information they are asked to learn.

In one study, academically successful and less successful students received the following instructions: "We're going to give you a passage that describes two different kinds of robots. Each robot has a particular type of head, particular types of arms, body, feet, and so forth. We would like to you read this passage and study it as long as you wish. Try to *remember* the properties of each robot and to *understand why* each robot has the properties that it does." Here is the passage.

> Billy's father works for a company that makes robots. His company made robots for a business that washed outside windows. They needed two kinds of robots. One kind of robot was needed to wash the outside windows in two-story houses. These windows were small. The other kind of robot was needed to wash the outside windows of very tall, high-rise office buildings. These windows were big.
>
> Billy went to visit his father at work. He saw the new robots that his father had made. The robot used for houses was called an extendible robot. It could extend itself so it would be almost as tall as a two-story house. Billy saw that this robot had spikes instead of feet. It had legs that did not bend. Its stomach could extend in length to make it taller. The arms on the robot were short. Instead of hands, it had small sponges. In its head was a nozzle attached to a hose. Billy also saw that the extendible robot was made of heavy steel. It had an electric cord that could be plugged in. The robot also had a ladder on its back.
>
> Billy then saw another robot called a nonextendible robot. This robot could not extend in length. Billy saw that this robot had suction cups instead of feet. It had legs that could bend. Its stomach was padded. The arms on the robot were long. Instead of hands, it had large sponges. In its head was a bucket. Billy also saw that the nonextendible robot was made of light aluminum. There was a battery inside the robot. The robot also had a parachute on its back.
>
> Billy liked his visit and asked to come back again.

The academically successful students were able to remember most of the properties of each robot and to explain why each robot had particular properties. For example, they remembered that the nonextendible robot, the one designed to wash outside windows in high-rise buildings, had suction cup feet (to help it climb); that it ran on a battery rather than on electricity supplied through an extension cord (high-rise buildings would require too long a cord); that it was made of light aluminum (so it wouldn't be too heavy); that a parachute was attached to its back (in case it fell); and so forth. Similarly, the successful students remembered that the extendible robot, the one that washed outside windows in two-story houses, had spiked feet (to help it gain stability by sticking them into the ground); that it ran on electricity supplied through an extension cord (the cord need not be too long); that it was made of heavy steel (for stability); and so forth. Note that the preceding passage did not explicitly state why each robot had the properties that it did. The students had to activate knowledge that enabled them to understand how the properties of each robot permitted it to perform its particular function; this is analogous to asking how various properties of veins and arteries (e.g., the elasticity of arteries) relate to their particular functions. Another group of academically successful students received an explicit version of the robot passage in which the relevance of each property was explained in the text. The ability of these students to remember the properties and explain their significance was equivalent to the performance of the students in the first group, the implicit group.

The academically less successful students exhibited a different pattern of performance. Those who received the **implicit version** were quite poor at recalling properties and explaining their significance. Performance for those receiving the explicit version was considerably improved. It seemed clear that the less successful students who received the implicit version had the potential to understand the significance of the properties (or the vast majority of the properties, at least), but they failed to ask themselves how potentially available information (about the functions of each robot) might make each fact more relevant or significant. These students could decode quite effectively, but they failed to perform the types of cognitive activities necessary to understand and learn.

The data from the robot study are highly consistent with the results from other studies that we have conducted with academically successful and less successful fifth graders. In another study, for example, students received a passage about two different types of boomerangs. Each boomerang had particular properties and particular functions; the passage was therefore analogous to the robot and the veins and arteries passages described above. Once again, academically successful students spontaneously used information about the function of each type of boomerang to understand its structural features, and vice versa. The less successful students took a much more passive approach to the problem of learning the information. Their primary mode of study was simply to reread the passage. After rereading, they would invariably declare themselves ready for the test.

The most striking result from the studies we have conducted (see Bransford et al., in press, for additional studies) is that the less successful learners exhibited only a superficial knowledge of each topic (e.g., boomerangs, the robots) despite their apparent motivation to learn, and despite the fact that they seemed to feel ready to take the test. The less successful students therefore appeared to have difficulty assessing their current level of mastery; they had little idea of how to judge their readiness for a test and how to make information easier to understand and retain. From our perspective, the ability to assess one's current level of comprehension and mastery is extremely important. Without such assessments, one has no information about the need to reread, study selectively, ask questions, and so forth (see Bransford, 1979; Bransford et al., in press). Our approach to learning emphasizes the importance of helping students become aware of the factors that make information easier to understand and retain.

## Learning to Learn

In our attempts to help academically less successful fifth-graders learn to learn, we have found it useful to create special sets of materials that enable the students to experience the effects of their own learning activities. For example, imagine reading 10 sentences such as the following:

The kind man bought the milk.
The short man used the broom.
The funny man liked the ring.
The hungry man purchased the tie.
The bald man read the newspaper.
The tall man used the paintbrush.

People who simply read each of these sentences have a very difficult time remembering which man did what (e.g., which man liked the ring, which man read the newspaper, etc.). These sentences are difficult to remember because the relationships between the type of man (e.g., kind man) and the actions performed (buying milk) are **arbitrary**. These relationships become less arbitrary if one activates knowledge that clarifies why each type of man performs each activity. For example, the kind man might buy some milk *and give it to a hungry child*; the short man may use the broom *to reach the lightswitch*; and so forth. Note that the activation of knowledge that helps one understand why each man may perform a particular action is analogous to activating knowledge that can help one understand why a robot, artery, boomerang, and so forth has particular properties. For example, the nonextendible robot discussed earlier has suction cup feet *in order to help it climb*.

When academically less successful fifth-graders are asked to read and remember a list of 10 sentences such as the preceding, they usually remember only one or two of the sentences. (The memory test involves questions such as ''Which man did X?'') We want them to realize that these sentences are extremely difficult to remember because we eventually want to help them learn how to make the sentences easy to retain. However, the students undoubtedly would feel very badly about their performance if we simply gave them a memory test with no explanation. We therefore preface our training sessions by emphasizing that the goal is to understand why some things are harder to learn than others. The students are told that even college students have a difficult time remembering the sentences they will read (which is true, if college students simply read each sentence), and we remind the fifth-graders of this fact while they are taking the memory test. The purpose of this exercise is to set the stage for: (1) analyzing why the materials are so difficult to retain; (2) getting the children to activate relevant knowledge that can make the sentences less arbitrary and hence easier to retain (i.e., getting the children to precisely elaborate each sentence); and (3) allowing the children to experience the dramatic improvements in memory that occur when precise elaborations are produced.

After the memory test, we return to the sentences from the original list. Given a statement such as "The kind man bought the milk," for example, we first prompt students to ask themselves questions that will enable them to realize that the relationship is arbitrary. We might therefore ask, "Is there any more reason to mention that a kind man bought the milk than a tall man, or a mean man?" This sets the stage for the next step, which is to prompt students to activate knowledge that can make the relationship between "kindness" and "milk buying" less arbitrary (e.g., "Why might a kind man be buying milk?"). The third step in our intervention is to prompt students to evaluate their own continuations. For example, less successful students might say or write, "The kind man bought the milk because he was thirsty." We would then ask, "What does this have to do with being kind? Wouldn't a mean man be just as likely to do the same thing?" Given these explicit queries, the children are eventually able to write continuations that clarify the significance of kindness; for example, "The kind man bought the milk to give to the hungry child."

During the first few trials of the intervention the students frequently need to be reminded to ask themselves relevant questions. For example, they may eventually activate information that clarifies the significance of the first sentence (e.g., kind man) yet fail to do this spontaneously for the second sentence. After a few trials, however, most children begin to internalize the process of question asking and to evaluate whether their **elaborations** clarify the significance of the facts. For example, given the Base Sentence "The rich man walked to the store," one student said, "to buy some candy." She then remarked, "Wait, candy doesn't cost that much; I need something different," and after a brief pause said (smiling), "and bought the whole store." Many of the children's responses are quite creative, and they seem to enjoy the task thoroughly.

After the children have precisely elaborated the set of 10 sentences, we administer the same memory test that they had done so poorly on earlier. Nearly all of them do perfectly. The most interesting data involve their excitement and pleasure; a task that had initially been extremely difficult has become very easy to perform. We have also given these children new sets of arbitrary sentences and asked them to write phrases that make the facts nonarbitrary and hence easier to remember. The vast majority of their elaborations are precise (i.e., they clarify the significance of the factual content). The students' memory for the sentences is excellent as well.

It should be obvious that the training procedures we have described will not suddenly transform less successful learners into successful learners. The purpose of this initial training is simply to provide a basis for helping students continue to learn how to learn. We believe that the two most important aspects of these initial training exercises are: (1) that students begin to understand why some materials are harder to learn and remember than others; and (2) that they begin to realize that they have some control over their own comprehension and memory processes. For many students, these insights seem to be very important; this affects their attitudes toward subsequent learning tasks.

There are many directions that teachers can take following the initial phase of **precision training**. An important direction is to help students understand the relationship between elaborating individual sentences and elaborating texts. For example, consider once again the robot passage presented earlier. Students need to be helped to realize that, like the training sentences, the properties of each robot can seem arbitrary and hence difficult to remember unless one asks oneself why this particular robot might have this particular property (e.g., why the nonextendible robot that washes windows in high-rise buildings has a battery rather than an electric cord). It is especially important to help students realize that only certain types of elaborations will facilitate understanding and retention. Just as an elaboration such as "The kind man bought the milk *because he was thirsty*" doesn't clarify the significance of "kindness"; elaborations such as "Extendible robots have spiked feet *so they don't need to have shoes*," or "*so they can crush ice*" does not help one understand how spiked feet help the robot perform its particular job. Prior to training, we find that even when less successful students do activate previously acquired knowledge, they tend to produce imprecise elaborations rather than elaborations that are precise (see Bransford et al., in press).

Perhaps the most important aspect of "precision training" involves its emphasis on evaluation. Children seem to enjoy evaluating whether passages seem arbitrary; they also seem to enjoy activities that encourage them to revise passages in order to make them easier to understand and remember. (For example, one might ask students to revise the implicit version of the robot passage by explicitly providing elaborations that would enable third-graders to understand the passage.) This emphasis on evaluation and revision seems especially important because many of the passages that children are asked to read in school seem to be quite arbitrary. For example, one passage designed for elementary school students discussed the topic of "American Indian Houses." It consisted of statements such as "The Indians of the Northwest Coast lived in slant-roofed houses made of cedar plank. . . . Some California Indian tribes lived in simple, earth-covered or brush shelters. . . . The Plains Indians lived mainly in tepees," etc. The story provided no information about why certain Indians chose certain houses. For example, it said nothing about the relationship between the type of house and the climate of the geographical area, nor about the ease of finding raw materials to build houses depending on the geographical area. Furthermore, the story said nothing about how the style of house was related to the life-style of the Indians (e.g., tepees are relatively portable). If students either do not know, or fail to activate this extra information, the passage is essentially a list of seemingly arbitrary facts.

Lessons that involve passages such as the one we have described (we have found numerous passages that are quite arbitrary) may not facilitate the development of students' abilities to evaluate the degree to which they have understood and mastered information. For example, if students are instructed to "learn the information in the passage" they may assume that the passages are optimally written and hence may simply try to reread the information while studying. If they then do poorly on subsequent comprehension and memory tests, the invited inference is that "they can't learn." Our assumption is that *no one* can learn if the information seems arbitrary and is not precisely elaborated. In short, we assume that there are some universal principles that affect human comprehension and memory; our goal is to help students become aware of these universals. The "precision training" we have described is one approach to helping students understand some of these universal principles. If students are helped to use these principles to evaluate and revise passages (such as the one about Indians' Houses), they should learn something about their roles as learners and should develop the ability to learn on their own (also see Feuerstein, 1980; Nash & Torrance, 1974; Singer, 1978).

We find that students are very receptive to the general concept of "the need for precision." They seem to grasp the notion that precise elaborations affect understanding and memory, and that precise communication affects people's ability to perform various tasks. However, we believe that students need to *experience* the effects of precision; it is not sufficient simply to tell them about it. By helping students experience the effects of their own activities and then helping them evaluate why they were successful or unsuccessful, teachers can help students improve their approaches to a variety of tasks, including the comprehension of text.

## ACKNOWLEDGMENT

The research reported in this paper was supported, in part, by Grant NIE-G-79-0117.

## GLOSSARY

**Cognitive Activities.**   Hypothetical processes that people use in order to understand and remember information. Rehearsal and elaboration of information are examples of cognitive activities that people may employ.

**Elaboration.**   The act of using previously acquired knowledge to embellish or enrich one's encoding of information. For example, the statement "The woman bought the food" could be elaborated to assume that the woman was very kind and that she was buying it for a hungry child. Only some types of elaboration (precise elaboration) facilitate understanding and remembering.

**Implicit Version.**   A version of a story or passage that does not explicitly supply most of the information necessary for understanding. People who attempt to understand and remember implicit versions must supply this extra information on their own.

## REFERENCES

Anderson, R. C. The notion of schemata and the educational enterprise. In R. C. Anderson, R. J. Spiro, & W. E. Montague (Eds.), *Schooling and the acquisition of knowledge.* Hillsdale, N.J.: Lawrence Erlbaum Associates, 1977.

Baker, L., & Brown, A. L. Metacognitive skills of reading. In D. Pearson (Ed.), *Handbook of reading research.* New York: Longmans, in press.

Bransford, J. D. *Human cognition: Learning, understanding and remembering.* Belmont, Calif.: Wadsworth Publishing Co., 1979.

Bransford, J. D., Stein, B. S., Shelton, T. S., & Owings, R. A. Cognition and adaptation: The importance of learning to learn. In J. Harvey (Ed.), *Cognition, social behavior and the environment.* Hillsdale, N.J.: Lawrence Erlbaum Associates, in press.

Brown, A. L. Knowing when, where, and how to remember: A problem of metacognition. In R. Glaser (Ed.), *Advances in instructional psychology.* Hillsdale, N.J.: Lawrence Erlbaum Associates, 1977.

Brown, A. L., & DeLoache, J. S. Skills, plans, and self-regulation. In R. Siegler (Ed.), *Children's thinking: What develops?* Hillsdale, N.J.: Lawrence Erlbaum Associates, 1978.

Feuerstein, R. *Instrumental enrichment.* Baltimore, Md.: University Park Press, 1980.

Nash, W. A., & Torrance, E. P. Creative reading and the questioning abilities of young children. *Journal of Creative Behavior*, 1974, *8*, 15–19.

Singer, M. H. Active comprehension from answering to asking questions. *Reading Teacher*, 1978, *31*, 901–908.

Spiro, R. J., Bruce, B. C., & Brewer, W. F. *Theoretical issues in reading comprehension: Perspectives from cognitive psychology, linguistics, artificial intelligence, and education.* Hillsdale, N.J.: Lawrence Erlbaum Associates, 1980.

# 9 Perceptual Learning: Letter Discrimination And Orthographic Knowledge

Martin H. Singer
*Bell Laboratories*

Chapter 1 reviewed experimental results that suggested an important role for visual information in competent reading. First, competent readers exploit their visual knowledge of probable letter positions and letter sequences to guess a word's identity. Second, a complete mastery of low-level skills (e.g., letter discrimination) might be necessary before the reader can sample higher-order information (e.g., context). That is, a competent reader overcomes the difficulty of paying attention to both visual and contextual information by *automatizing* his or her processing of visual information: the less attention paid to visual features, the more attention available for the syntactic and semantic structure of a paragraph.

The evidence on disabled reading suggests that an absence of certain types of visual information plagues poor readers. Poor readers lack orthographic knowledge and are particularly bad at context-free word recognition. Although these deficits may underlie only a certain proportion of reading disorders, it is interesting that *some* poor readers lack the knowledge that competent readers exploit. This convergence makes it reasonable to devote some discussion to the improvement of visually based knowledge.

## PERCEPTUAL LEARNING

Several reading materials claim to improve letter discrimination skill. Some of these depend on rote memorization, some on the reinforcement of correct discriminations, and others on the process of **perceptual learning**. The following discussion focuses on programs that employ perceptual learning. The focus of this chapter on perceptual learning programs does not imply that such programs are the most effective; this discussion attempts only to outline the rationale for a particular technique and some specific applications of that technique.

*Perceptual learning*, an idea promoted by James and Eleanor Gibson (Gibson, E., 1965; also see Gibson, J., 1966, and Smith, 1976) means the *acquisition of progressively finer distinctions or contrasts*. Anyone who has ever taken a biology, physiology, or anatomy course that required the identification of structures on a slide, knows something about perceptual learning. At first, only the largest and darkest structures seem clearly distinct. Later, and with considerable practice, other structures become clearly defined—ones that the beginning student cannot see. It is important to note that the *slide has not changed*; rather, the experience or practice has enhanced the perceptual sensitivity of the student.

Perceptual learning also applies to less academic pursuits. Imagine, for example, that someone confronts you with the enviable task of learning the subtle differences among 10 different white wines. Initially, many of them would taste the same: you could only distinguish those that differed greatly along a dimension such as sweetness. In other words, you would appreciate only the *maximum contrast*. With practice (and *without* reinforcement), however, you would acquire the ability to distinguish less obvious or finer contrasts among the 10 wines. This example provides a perfect instance of the preceding definition of perceptual learning: *the acquisition of progressively finer distinctions* (among wines).

## PERCEPTUAL LEARNING AND LETTER DISCRIMINATION

Instead of confronting a poor reader with a random series of letters to learn, a creative teacher can exploit the principle of perceptual learning to facilitate successful letter discrimination. The procedure is simple: Initially require the student to discriminate **maximally contrastive** letters (i.e., *x* and *i*); later, require more demanding discriminations (i.e., *g* and *q*). Fortunately, this logic has already been incorporated into existing materials.

Figure 9.1 illustrates two pages from Visual Tracking (Geake & Smith, 1975). The task for the student is to "circle the letters of the alphabet in order." Thus, the student first finds an *a*, then a *b*, and so on. The alphabet above the paragraph of nonsense strings allows the student an easy reference should the student's alphabetic knowledge be incomplete. A proficient reader can finish the task in under 30 seconds.

Comparing the two paragraphs (which are actually separated by 44 pages of paragraphs in the manual) indicates the perceptual learning component of the program. In the large-typed paragraph, the letter *a* in the first line is flanked by a *z* and a *e*. Just below the *a* is *yx vop*; the task in this paragraph demands only an easy discrimination between highly contrastive letters. Now consider the

Neoz wtvx lky njt sjo uz aetr btc.
gohn wrmz kd eofr.  Jho vqr yx vop lm.
Apf. oon bcg.  Pph ooq wca.  Xzt ltoi.
Dojn Xzt kru w ol.  Sma bbqo.
doc bn wrar ogf tpu.  Dec bgh ih cf.  Ya
dfe kcq tw gff.  Bjf rb cff.  Djc tvd.
Pok sjdf kgect nja bu ceh.  Lwnv heg
rnwq kirx pf.  Njaf rrxe qeb yne ponaz.

Min___Sec___

Ifligger mort newqapto iblix morsn tspt flopi morcner.
Iglox ponur hloffdon strik hloffe ris zmo loox pliggirs.
Ragbaf mort bagc trakt.  Mort klappi horatis ignori.
Destxro rotatrs, obnojo mort dbra, rstv op oppa aklappa.
Grag ponur mortn dextr rexa zmo iffer sidwit ponur hied ibbi.
Jeggle ijjiffle abaced.  Jakkeg hiffle, haegda bced ieqb efrl.
Mini nowg klosspo.  Oattle, no jie fkag baed nokel iuntec ixv.
Fliwer reprixco ipyaz.

Min ___ Sec ___

FIG. 9.1.  This paragraph of nonsense strings was taken from Geake and Smith's
(1975) *Visual Tracking*. Reprinted with permission from Ulrich's Books.

other, smaller-typed paragraph. The first *a* is preceded by an *o* and flanked by
a *q* and a *p*. All these letters are similar to the *a* and demand finer discriminations
than the surrounding letters. The decrease in print size and the space between
letters and lines also increases the difficulty of the discrimination.

The Visual Tracking program does not accomplish perfectly the progression
from maximum to **minimum contrasts**. Sometimes the letter arrangement simply
conforms to the frequency with which the various letters occur in normal writing.
Thus, highly contrastive letters occasionally surround the target letter at advanced

levels in the program. Insofar as this happens, the program deviates from the principle of perceptual learning and does not increase the sensitivity of the student to differences among letters. Generally, however, the program does facilitate the acquisition of letter discrimination skill, placing greater demands on the learner as the program progresses.

## PERCEPTUAL LEARNING AND ORTHOGRAPHIC KNOWLEDGE

The same principle—that of proceeding from a maximum to a minimum contrast—applies to the instruction of orthography (or more simply, spelling patterns). Learning the order and position in which letters commonly occur implies an *ability to discriminate probable from improbable letter strings*. This ability results from experience with written words and can be improved with a perceptual learning training device. *Programmed Spelling* (Smith, Farrell, Wolter, & Smith, 1978) represents an attempt to use a progression from maximum to minimum contrasts to teach spelling and, correspondingly, orthographic knowledge. Figure 9.2 illustrates the basic procedure of the program.

This method of systematically teaching spelling leads a student to make more and more difficult distinctions. The first exercise requires the student to circle the target word on lines one, two, and three. The program attempts to make each discrimination more difficult than the preceding one. Visual similarity, word shape, and sound are all appropriate dimensions along which the program (or a creative teacher) can vary similarity. The second exercise represents a miniature version of the letter-tracking procedure. The target word is embedded in a string of letters. Again, the visual similarity of adjacent letters can increase from lines four to five.

Third, the program attempts to increase the student's sensitivity to the letter combinations that represent specific word parts. Lines seven, eight, and nine duplicate the first exercise but diminish the contrast between the target word and the **foils**. After the four exercises the student writes down the target word on the same page.

This program is particularly appealing for two reasons: (1) The student's sensitivity to orthographic structure can be increased during normal spelling instruction; and (2) children can (and do!) program words for each other. In other words, blank forms can be made and children can develop a perceptual learning program for a colleague.

## INCREASING SENSITIVITY TO VISUAL DIMENSIONS

Poor readers often confuse letters that differ only in orientation (e.g., *b* and *d*). Such errors have falsely led researchers, popular writers, television documen-

Look at the word in the box. Read the definition.

| catch | to capture or seize

Circle the correct word in each line.

1. latch        catch        batch
2. cat          hatch        catch
3. catch        match        couch

'Track' each letter in the word. That is, circle each letter in the word in order.

4.  o   c   e   a   f   k   l   t   p   c   k   n   h   m
5.  c   a   k   l   t   o   v   e   c   n   k   m   u   h

Fill in the missing letters.

6.  c a t c _        c a t _ h        c a _ ch
    c _ t c h        c a t c h

Circle the correct word in each line.

7.  cotch        catck        catch
8.  catch        ctach        hctac
9.  cath         catch        cateh

Write the word on the line. Try to write it without looking at the model.

_____

FIG. 9.2.   (Reprinted with permission from Ulrich's Books; Adapted from Smith, Farrell, Wolter, & Smith, 1980.)

taries, and others to conclude that "dyslexics" see backwards or have a "tendency to reverse." In fact, though, anyone unfamiliar with an alphabet will confuse letters that differ only in orientation. Figure 9.3 helps illustrate this

**ALPHABET I**

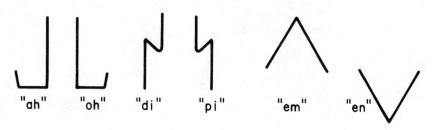

**ALPHABET II**

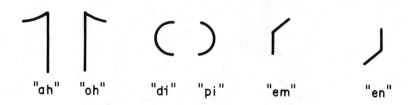

**ALPHABET III**

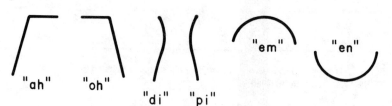

FIG. 9.3.  Attempt to learn and reproduce these letters. Do you make any reversals when reproducing? Does that mean you suffer from a "tendency to reverse"?

point. If you attempt to memorize and reproduce any of the short alphabets in Fig. 9.3, you will experience difficulty and, probably, reverse a few of the letters. Imagine if your task were to learn clusters of these novel letters: Without doubt, you would scramble many of these strings. (Clearly, any insensitivity to the dimension of direction would impede further the learning of letter orders and positions—orthographic knowledge as well as individual letters.)

Instead of suggesting vague ''reversal tendencies'' to explain a poor reader's errors, one can devise a perceptual learning procedure to increase a student's sensitivity to the dimension of direction. The *American Language Program* (Smith & Smith, 1980), for example, teaches children the difference between, and the meaning of vertical and horizontal lines. Later, vertical lines are employed as a frame of reference to discriminate among differently oriented letters. Figure 9.4 illustrates this general procedure. Clearly, one can increase the difficulty of this discrimination by increasing the distance of the letters from the vertical line, gradually fading the line, and eventually teaching students to employ the paper's margin or edge as the frame of reference. This procedure can be used also to teach students to discriminate among probable and improbable letter combinations.

FIG. 9.4.   The dark line serves as a frame of reference for discriminations between confusable letters.

## SUMMARY

*Perceptual learning*, or the acquisition of progressively finer contrasts, provides teachers with a system for developing programs to teach lower-level reading skills. Programs, such as Visual Tracking or the American Language Program, appear to conform to the basic system of proceeding from obvious to less obvious discriminations.

Perceptual learning programs that effectively teach letter discrimination and impart orthographic knowledge are important for reasons discussed in Chapters 1 and 3. *Automatization* of these discrimination skills *may permit readers to attend to higher-level, linguistic information.* Certain types of information must be well learned so that the reader need not devote conscious attention to that information. This automatization permits human beings to overcome their difficulty in attending to more than one source of information. Thus, the effective learning of discrimination skills allows readers to take advantage of contextual information. This implies an important point: *A basic skills program is compatible with a program to improve comprehension or context-use skills.*

## GLOSSARY

**Foils.**   Items that one must distinguish from a target stimulus.
**Maximally Contrastive.**   A difference that one detects easily.
**Minimally Contrastive.**   A difference that one detects with difficulty; similarity.
**Perceptual Learning.**   The acquisition of progressively finer distinctions or contrasts.

## REFERENCES

Geake, R. R., & Smith, D. E. P. *Visual tracking* (Rev. ed.). Ann Arbor: Ulrich's Books, Inc., 1975.

Gibson, E. J. Learning to read. *Science*, 1965, *148*, 1066–1072.

Gibson, J. J. *The senses considered as perceptual systems.* Boston: Houghton Mifflin Co., 1966.

Smith, D. E. P. *Learning to read and write: A task analysis.* New York: Academic Press, 1976.

Smith, D. E. P., & Smith, J. M. *The American language program.* Niles, Ill.: Argus Communications, 1980.

Smith, J. M., Farrell, C. A., Wolter, J. B., & Smith, D. E. P. *Programmed spelling.* Ann Arbor: Ulrich's Books, 1978.

# Author Index

# Subject Index